THE TOWER

AND

THE BRIDGE

THE TOWER AND THE BRIDGE

THE NEW ART OF
STRUCTURAL ENGINEERING

DAVID P. BILLINGTON

Basic Books, Inc., Publishers

NEW YORK

Library of Congress Cataloging in Publication Data

Billington, David P.
  The tower and the bridge

  Includes bibliographical references and index.
  1. Structural engineering.   2. Towers—Design
and construction.   3.   Bridges—Design.   I. Title.
TA636.B54 1983   624'.2   83–70758
ISBN 0–465–08677–2

CONTENTS

v

Contents

PART II
The New Age of Steel and Concrete

Contents

LIST OF ILLUSTRATIONS

Unless otherwise stated, photographs are by the author.

PREFACE

The Eiffel Tower and the Brooklyn Bridge became great symbols of their age because the general public recognized in their new forms a technological world of surprise and appeal. I have written this book to show how that tower and that bridge are only two of the numberless works of recent engineering that constitute a new art form, structural art, which is parallel to and fully independent of architecture.

The ideas upon which this study is based came originally from teaching structures to graduate students in architecture. Bored with typical engineering texts, they showed me their ideas of beautiful structures, such as the bridges of the Swiss engineer Robert Maillart and the buildings of the Catalan architect Antonio Gaudí. Gradually, beginning in 1962, I developed for the architecture students a series of slide lectures on engineering structures. In 1974, I put these lectures together to make up a new course at Princeton for engineers, architects, and liberal arts students. This book comes directly out of that course. But the central idea that engineering structures could be an art form also had another source, my research on the life and works of Robert Maillart.

With my colleague, Robert Mark, I organized a 1972 conference at Princeton commemorating the centennial of Maillart's birth. Particularly memorable were talks given by the Swiss bridge designer, Christian Menn; the Spanish thin-shell vault designer-builder, Felix Candela; and the Chicago skyscraper designer, Fazlur Khan. Each spoke about Maillart's influence on his own work and about the similarity between Maillart's ideas and his own. It was clear that all four designers held aesthetics to be a major aspect of engineering design, and that the audience was moved by the beauty of their constructed works. Here was, for me, the first demonstration of a tradition, the new art of structural engineering.

Following that conference, I began detailed research on the life and works of Robert Maillart. The first major result of this research, *Robert Maillart's Bridges: The Art of Engineering,* appeared in 1979. In writing that book, I came to realize that Maillart was really an artist in the same sense that, for example, Alberto Giacometti and Le Corbusier were artists. Maillart was surely neither sculptor nor architect; all of his works were rooted in the numerical, rational world of engineering structure. Yet, somehow, out of that austere discipline he was able to create objects of great beauty that reflect his personality. I was greatly aided in this Maillart study by Christian Menn; he not only put me in contact with all the right Swiss people, but he also showed me his own bridges and explained to me their designs. Slowly I began to see both in Maillart and in Menn how the structural artist thinks and works.

One more major event put this new art form in focus for me. In 1978, I attended a lecture by the Swiss thin-shell vault designer Heinz Isler who showed stunning examples of his completed structures. At the time, I was revising my book, *Thin Shell Concrete Structures;* Isler's designs caused me to rethink that book and eventually to add a new final chapter about roof design centered on his shells. Here was another structural artist of the same quality as Candela. Most importantly, Isler shows how the discipline of engineering goes together with the play of imagination to create new forms.

Meanwhile I was trying with difficulty to complete a biography of Maillart and to include within it all of these ideas about structural art. Then, by good luck, Martin Kessler of Basic Books came to see me in the spring of 1981 with the suggestion that I write a book about this new art form. My brother, James H. Billington, had described my work to him, and by the fall I was at work on this book. With its completion I have been able to return to the Maillart biography with a clearer focus, not having to develop in detail all the ideas that I discussed in this book.

Since this subject of structural art is somewhat new, it is perhaps well to explain the criteria upon which the book has been constructed.

First, I wanted to show the best works of structural engineering completed during the last two hundred years. This idea is related to my wish to create a course in structural art similar to courses in painting or literature in which the finest works are studied one after another, thereby suggesting the evolution of principles of form. It seemed to me crucial to write a history of the works of selected artists rather than a narrative that included all engineers who have made contributions to modern structures. I believe it essential to emphasize major works, both as an introduction for engineering students and as a survey for non-engineers, in the same way that it is essential to introduce students to the last two centuries of literature by selecting for study artists of great stature rather than every novelist of merit. The structural artists singled out have all done pioneering engineering work, were (except for a few) well trained in schools of engineering, and were deeply concerned with combining economy with elegance.

Second, I have chosen to start this narrative in the late eighteenth century with the beginning of the use of cast iron for complete structures. Before then, the principle building materials were stone and wood, materials in which it is difficult to separate structural from architectural design. Starting with Thomas Telford's iron bridges, however, new structural forms began to appear; these required special study and training, which led to the creation of the modern engineering profession. Therefore I have not discussed any designs prior to the 1779 Iron Bridge. Like that other Industrial Revolution art form, photography, the development of the new technology of industrialized iron brought forth a new means of artistic expression. Just as there are artists such as Charles Sheeler who have practiced both painting and photography, so there are artists like Felix Candela who have created works of structure and works of architecture. But the distinction between the two is, as I have tried to show in this book, just as clear as that between photography and painting. Indeed, both the more traditional art forms of painting and architecture suffered a special modern trauma because of the supposed competition of the new arts of photography and structure.

My third criterion for the shape of this book has been the independence of structural art from architecture. Repeatedly, people suggest that structural engineering and architecture are really one thing and have the same ideals for design. They go on to propose new educational programs to bring these two groups together. Such ideas have sound motives but questionable results. It is as crucial for engineers to learn about art and aesthetics as it is for architects to learn about structures and construction. But as this book will seek to demonstrate, the most beautiful works of structural art are primarily those created by engineers trained in engineering and not in architecture. Almost without exception it seems that the best works of structural art would have been compromised had there been architectural collaboration in the design of the forms. Yet, in spite of that fact, perceptive architects and writers on architecture have been quick to recognize structural artists and have often publicized their works before the engineering profession itself did. It was, therefore, my major goal to present a coherent picture of this new art form from the perspective of structural engineering and to show that the best designs in the strictest technical sense were often also the most beautiful ones.

Fourth and finally, I have come to believe that there is a set of ideals for structural art that separates it from architecture or sculpture. Central to these ideals is the belief held by all the major engineers discussed in this book that they had considerable freedom of aesthetic choice in design without compromising the discipline of engineering. In short, the simple-minded idea that a structure designed to be efficient will automatically be beautiful is just as false as the fashionable notion that a beautiful structure demands the assistance of a non-engineering consultant on aesthetics. I have tried to show throughout this book that the best engineers followed certain general principles of design to arrive at fine works, and that these general principles allowed for their own specific and personal vision of structure.

ACKNOWLEDGMENTS

Throughout the twenty years that I have been struggling with these ideas, no one has helped me more than Norman Sollenberger, who first encouraged me to join the Princeton faculty and then, as chairman of the department of Civil Engineering, continuously supported my studies in art and engineering between 1961 and 1971. Through him I met Robert Mark who has become my closest colleague. For over twenty years he and I have collaborated on research, and in 1968 we embarked on the program called Humanistic Studies in Engineering. He has counseled me continuously and read this complete manuscript, giving me considerable critical help. Both Robert Mark and I were aided by Joseph Elgin, then Dean of Princeton's School of Engineering and Applied Science; he gave me invaluable summer support. Whitney Oates, Chairman of Princeton's Council of the Humanities, and Robert Goheen, then President of Princeton, were also of great help, guiding us to the newly constituted National Endowment for the Humanities where we met Herbert McArthur, director of educational programs, whose early and steadfast sponsorship gained us both needed funding and personal encouragement. In 1970, John Abel, now at Cornell University, joined us at Princeton, working closely with us in our humanistic studies program. He too has been a close colleague ever since; chapter 12 was greatly improved thanks to his careful criticisms.

Ahmet Cakmak, Chairman of Civil Engineering at Princeton from 1971 to 1980, first suggested that I introduce the new course, "Structures and the Urban Environment," from which this book developed; he supported the course and taught in it with me for seven years. Robert Scanlan has also taught in the course and has given me great help in the sections on suspension bridges; he first acquainted me with Roebling's Cincinnati Bridge report, on which I drew heavily for chapter 5. Our present department chairman, George Pinder, has also encouraged this work and provided support.

The principal financial support for this book has come from the Division of Research Programs of the National Endowment for the Humanities headed by Harold Cannon and from the Program for the History and Philosophy of Science of the National Science Foundation headed by Ronald Overmann. Robert Mark and I have had grants from the National Endowment for the Humanities, from the Ford and Rockefeller Foundations, as well as from the Andrew W. Mellon and Alfred P. Sloan Foundations, all of which have helped the studies leading to this book. Of particular benefit to the thesis of this book were two grants from the National Endowment of the Arts and especially the encouragement of Thomas Cain. My Swiss studies have been aided by grants from the Federal Technical Institute, Zurich, thanks to Christian Menn, and from the Swiss Society of Cement, Gypsum, and Chalk Manufacturers whose director, Hans Eichenberger, has been of great help. In addition, the Ciba-Geigy Corporation and the Swiss Center Foundation, through Charles Ziegler, have provided help both for the exhibition, "Heinz Isler as Structural Artist," in the Princeton University Art Museum and for the Princeton Maillart archive. I am deeply grateful to the successive directors of the Princeton University Art Museum who have collaborated with me on a series of exhibitions portraying structure as art: David Steadman, Peter Bunnell, Fred Licht, and Alan Rosenbaum. I owe a debt of gratitude also to Marshall Claggett for enabling me to work at the Institute for Advanced Study in Princeton as a visitor in both 1974 and 1977.

In the fall of 1969, I came to know the late Donald Egbert, a professor of architectural history at Princeton, who read critically my first writings on structural engineering as an art form. His invaluable help was followed by continuing discussions with other historians, especially Carl Condit, George Collins, and Edwin Layton, whose insights have strongly influenced this book. Merritt Roe Smith kindly read major parts of the manuscript and gave me much guidance. Other historians who have been of considerable help are Tom Peters, Brooke Hindle, Ted Ruddock, Roland Paxton, Robert Vogel and Neal FitzSimons. Most of all, my brother, James H. Billington, has given me not only direct aid and encouragement but also a model for historical scholarship. Without his initial efforts this book would never have been started, and his careful reading of chapter 1 greatly improved the final version.

I owe a substantial debt to a large number of engineers whose thoughts on structural engineering have influenced my writing. While I cannot list them all, I am happy to single out Arthur Elliott, Jack Christiansen, Louis Pierce, Fred Law, Mario Salvadori, Boris Bresler, Stefan Medwadowski, Fred Lehman, Charles Seim, Mark Fintel, and also Fritz Leonhardt, who has freely shared his views on aesthetics with me in stimulating correspondence. Also over the past two decades Alexander Scordelis has strongly influenced my work by both his careful criticism and warm encouragement. Above all, Anton Tedesko has given me both a deeper insight into structural design and a clear reading of this entire manuscript.

All of this work would have been impossible without my long-term studies of Robert Maillart that began in 1969. For those studies, my principal colleague and supporter has been Marie-Claire Blumer-Maillart. Our close working relationship has been both professionally stimulating and personally joyful. From her came that illuminating focus on Maillart's personality and ideas that has shaped this book; her openness and critical commentary have been crucial to any success my work will have. Her late husband, Eduard Blumer, worked tirelessly on the Maillart archive and lent humor and order to this research.

Along with the Maillart studies, it was the direct personal contact with a few structural artists that gave me the courage to write this book. Christian Menn, Heinz Isler, Felix Candela, and Fazlur Khan have each lectured brilliantly at Princeton, talked at length about his own work, and shared with me his ideas about structural design. Many other fine designers have helped me to understand better the ideals of structural art. Especially important have been my many long discussions with Myron Goldsmith, who also kindly read several parts of the manuscript. Also, William F. Shellman of the School of Architecture at Princeton directed my early readings in architecture and in art. His deep understanding continually informs my attempts to think about structural art.

During the course of this work I have been aided by a dedicated

Acknowledgments

series of research assistants, especially Paul Gauvreau, who has worked with me throughout the writing of this book, as well as Brenda Robinson, Lisa Grebner, Jane Billington, and David P. Billington, Jr. Elizabeth Billington carefully edited the complete manuscript, prepared the index, and assisted in much of the research as well. I wish to thank the archivists at the Federal Technical Institute in Zurich, Alvin E. Jaeggli and Beat Glaus, for their ceaseless help, as well as the engineering librarian at Princeton, Dee Hoelle. I am grateful for the continual patience and competence of my secretary, Anne Chase, in keeping me organized and in typing part of the manuscript. I also thank Jeanne Carlucci for her fine typing of much of the manuscript. I want especially to thank J. Wayman Williams, a professional engineer and photographer who has worked closely with me in developing Art Museum exhibitions, course materials, and photographs for this book. In addition, I want to thank the staff of Basic Books, particularly the following: in addition to stimulating me to write this book, Martin Kessler provided both encouragement and a helpful critical review of the manuscript; Sheila Friedling greatly improved the entire work with her sympathetic and careful editing; and Vincent Torre has designed this book with great sensitivity and skill.

In the end, my wife, Phyllis, deserves the last and highest acknowledgment for keeping things together while all of the writing, traveling, and research goes on; and my three youngest children, Philip, Stephen, and Sarah, have all served at one time or another as assistants and scale factors in the photographic and visual search for structural art.

DAVID P. BILLINGTON
Princeton, New Jersey
April 29, 1983

THE TOWER

AND

THE BRIDGE

CHAPTER 1

A NEW TRADITION:
ART IN ENGINEERING

A New Art Form

While automation prospers, our roads, bridges, and urban civil works rot. Children control computers while adults weave between potholes. The higher that high technology sails the worse seem our earthbound services for water, transportation, and shelter. Yet civilization is civil works and insofar as these deteriorate so does society, our high technology notwithstanding. We forget that technology is as much structures as it is machines, and that these structures symbolize our common life as much as machines stand for our private freedoms. Technology is frequently equated only with machines, those objects that save labor, multiply power, and increase mobility. In reality, machines are only one half of technology, the dynamic half, and structures are the other, static, half—objects that create a water supply, permit transportation, and provide shelter.

This book is devoted to the idea that structures, the forgotten half of modern technology, provide a key to the revival of public life. The noted historian Raymond Sontag titled his book on the period between the two world wars *A Broken World,* and his pivotal chapter called "The Artist in a Broken World" characterized the persistent hopes of the time by "the vision of mending the broken world through a union of art and technology."[1] He had in mind groups like the ill-fated German Bauhaus, but he and all other historians missed the fact that such a union had for a long time already existed. It was a tradition without a name, confused sometimes with architecture and other times with applied science, even on occasion misnamed machine art. It is the art of the structural engineer and it appears most clearly in bridges, tall buildings, and long-span roofs.

This new tradition arose with the Industrial Revolution and its new material, industrialized iron, which in turn brought forth new utilities such as the railroad. These events led directly to the creation of a new class of people, the modern engineers trained in special schools which themselves came into being only after the Industrial Revolution had made them a necessity.

Such developments are well known and almost everyone agrees that they have radically changed Western civilization over the past two hundred years. What is not so well known is that these developments led to a new type of art—entirely the work of engineers and of the engineering imagination. My major objective in this book is to define the new art form and to show that since the late eighteenth century some engineers have consciously practiced this art, that it is parallel to and fully independent from architecture, and that numerous engineering artists are creating such works in the contemporary world of the late twentieth century. It is a movement awaiting a vocabulary.

The Ideals of Structural Art

Although structural art is emphatically modern, it cannot be labeled as just another movement in modern art. For one thing, its forms and its ideals have changed little since they were first expressed by Thomas

Telford in 1812. It is not accidental that these ideals emerged in societies that were struggling with the consequences not only of industrial
revolutions but also of democratic ones. The tradition of structural art
is a democratic one.

In our own age when democratic ideals are continually being challenged by the claims of totalitarian societies, whether fascist or commu-
nist, the works of structural art provide evidence that the common life
flourishes best when the goals of freedom and discipline are held in
balance. The disciplines of structural art are efficiency and economy,
and its freedom lies in the potential it offers the individual designer
for the expression of a personal style motivated by the conscious aesthetic search for engineering elegance. These three leading ideals of
structural art—efficiency, economy, and elegance—which I shall illustrate throughout this book, can be briefly described at the outset.

First, because of the great cost of the new industrialized iron, the
engineers of the nineteenth century had to find ways to use it as efficiently as possible. For example, in their bridges, they had to find forms
that would carry heavier loads—the locomotive—than ever before with
a minimum amount of metal. Thus, from the beginning of the new
iron age, the first discipline put on the engineer was to use as few natural resources as possible. At the same time, these engineers were called
upon to build larger and larger structures—longer-span bridges, higher
towers, and wider-spanning roofs—all with less material. They struggled to find the limits of structure, to make new forms that would be
light and would show off their lightness. They began to stretch iron,
then steel, then reinforced concrete, just as medieval designers had
stretched stone into the skeletal Gothic cathedral.

After conservation of natural resources, there arose the ideal of
conservation of public resources. In Britain, which was the center for
early structural art, public works were under the scrutiny of Parliament,
and private works were usually under the control of shareholders and
industrialists. The engineer had, therefore, always to work under the
discipline of economy consistent with usefulness. What the growing
general public demanded was more utility for less money. Thus arose
the ideal of conservation of public resources. The great structures we
shall describe here came into being only because their designers learned
how to build them for less money. Moreover, working with political
and business leaders was a continuing and intrinsic part of the activity

of these artists. They created not alone in a laboratory or a garret but under the harsh economic stimulus of the construction site.

Curiously enough, whenever public officials or industrialists decided deliberately to build monuments where cost would be secondary to prestige this art form did not flourish. Economy has always been a prerequisite to creativity in structural art. Again and again we shall find that the best designers matured under the discipline of extreme economy. At times, when approaching the limits of structure late in their careers, they might encounter unforeseen difficulties which increased costs. But their ideas and their styles developed under competitive cost controls. Economy is a spur, not an obstacle, to creativity in structural art.

Minimal materials and costs may be necessary, but they are not, of course, sufficient. Too many ugly structures result from minimal design to support any simple formula connecting efficiency and economy to elegance. Rather, a third ideal must control the final design: the conscious aesthetic motivation of the engineer. A major goal of this book is to show the freedom that engineers actually have to express a personal style without compromising the disciplines of efficiency and economy. Beginning with Telford's 1812 essay on bridges, modern structural artists have been conscious of, and have written about, the aesthetic ideals that guided their works. Thus, this tradition of structural art took shape verbally as it did visually. The elements of the new art form were, then, efficiency (minimum materials), economy (minimum cost), and elegance (maximum aesthetic expression). These elements underlie modern civilized life.

Civilization requires civic or city life, and city life forms around civil works: for water, transportation, and shelter. The quality of the public city life depends, therefore, on the quality of such civil works as aqueducts, bridges, towers, terminals, and meeting halls: their efficiency of design, their economy of construction, and the visual appeal of their completed forms. At their best, these civil works function reliably, cost the public as little as possible, and, when sensitively designed, become works of art. But the modern world is filled with examples of works that are faulty, excessively costly, and often ponderously ugly.

Such need not be the case. If the general public and the engineers themselves see the extent and the potential of structural art, then public works in the late twentieth century can, more than ever, be efficient, economical, and elegant.

The History of Structural Art

I shall demonstrate the potential of structural art through its history, and have divided the book into two parts to reflect the two major historical periods. The first part of the book traces the history of structural art up to the completion of the Eiffel Tower, the last great work of iron, and the second describes the developments springing from the use of steel and concrete and concludes with a series of the late-twentieth-century works. The historical narrative begins in Britain toward the end of the eighteenth century. Here we can see how the rise of new forms is connected directly to the use of new materials in solving the transport problems posed by industrialization. The transportation networks—canals, roads, and railways—accelerated the pace of technological developments, leading to urbanization and further industrial change. As cities grew more crowded, office buildings became higher, and train terminals of longer span and bridges of truly immense proportions began to be economically feasible.

The second period of structural art begins in the 1880s, when steel prices dropped and reinforced concrete was developed. Engineers soon began to explore new forms with these materials, so that even before the cataclysm of 1914, a bewildering variety of structures arose at a dizzying pace. But the maturity of new forms in steel and concrete came only afterward, when Western civilization careened from one world war to another through boom, inflation, and depression. During this period, movements in art and architecture proclaimed solutions to city decay, focusing on the menace or promise of technology.

The best known of these movements was the German Bauhaus, whose aim was to "avoid mankind's enslavement by the machine" by integrating architecture and machine production, and by getting the artist away from art for art's sake and the businessman away from business as an end in itself.[2] The new architect, in the words of the Bauhaus founder, Walter Gropius, would be "a coordinating organizer, whose business is to resolve all formal, technical, sociological, and commercial problems" and whose work leads from buildings to streets, to cities, and "eventually into the wider field of regional and national planning."[3] The Bauhaus and other such movements barely recognized the tradition of structural art. For example, in a classic work defining the Bauhaus, Gropius included forty-five illustrations, not one of which shows any work of structural art. Furthermore, in describing the comprehensive education given to the new architect, Gropius noted that there were no courses offered in steel or concrete construction.[4] Although Gropius and others stimulated new thinking about technology and design, they did it from the perspective of architecture rather than structure. Indeed, the great influence of such architects on post–World War II ideas about building has tended to obscure the tradition of structural art. In addition to the common confusion between structural art and architecture, there arose a misconception about the relationship of structure to science and to machine art. Therefore, I must say something about what this new engineering art is not, before showing historically what it is.

Engineering and Science

The confusion of structural art with science assumes that engineering, being applied science, merely puts into practice the ideas and discoveries of the scientist. The honor of creative genius and the precedence in innovation belong to the scientist; the engineer is merely the technician, following orders from above. This idea is a common twentieth-century fallacy. It was articulated, for example, by Vannevar Bush, wartime director of the Office of Scientific Research and Development, in his influential report to President Truman which led to the establishment of the National Science Foundation. Bush summarized his ideas vigorously:

> Basic research leads to new knowledge. It provides scientific capital. It creates the fund from which the practical applications of knowledge must be drawn. New products and new processes do not appear full-grown. They are founded on new principles and new conceptions, which in turn are painstakingly developed by research in the purest realms of science.
>
> Today it is truer than ever that basic research is the pacemaker of technological progress. In the nineteenth century, Yankee mechanical ingenuity building largely upon the basic discoveries of European scientists, could greatly advance the technical arts.[5]

Not only is Bush's history of Yankee ingenuity inaccurate, but so is his general belief that "basic research is the pacemaker of technological progress." In a 1973 conference, leading historians of technology presented papers on the subject "The Interaction of Science and Technology in the Industrial Age." The conference summarized the wide variety of studies by then completed and "overwhelmingly, the group agreed in disagreeing with the conventional view (of Bush) that technology was applied science."[6]

There is a fundamental difference between science and technology. Engineering or technology[7] is the making of things that did not previously exist, whereas science is the discovering of things that have long existed. Technological results are forms that exist only because people want to make them, whereas scientific results are formulations of what exists independently of human intentions. Technology deals with the artificial, science with the natural.

Science and technology are best viewed as parallel activities, each one at times drawing on the resources of the other, but more often developing independently. An example of this independence is the fact that of the vast number of technological inventions made since World War II for the military, only about 0.3 percent can be traced to scientific discoveries; the remainder developed independently, from design stimuli within the technological community itself.[8] A leading British scholar recently concluded that there is "very little indication of any clear or close links between basic scientific research and the great mass of technical developments." Having considered a wide variety of case studies, ranging from chemistry in Britain to structures in the United States, he observed that "science seems to accumulate mainly on the basis of past science, and technology primarily on the basis of past technology."[9] In our present context, it is essential that we make the distinction between science and technology, so that we can focus on the true sources of engineering originality.

From the fundamental difference mentioned earlier flow a number of other crucial differences. Science works always to achieve general theories that unify knowledge. Every specific natural event, to be scientifically satisfying, must ultimately be related to a general formulation. Engineering, in contrast, works always to create specific objects within a category of type. Each design, to be technologically satisfying, must be unique and relate only to the special theory appropriate to its category. It is this uniqueness that makes structural art possible. Were engineering works merely the reflections of general scientific discoveries, they would lose their meaning as expressions of the style of individual designers. The fact that these works need not—indeed, in some cases should not—be based on general theories is apparent from concrete studies in the history of technology. I give here two illustrations.

Robert Maillart, the Swiss bridge designer, developed in 1923 a limited theory for one of his arched bridge types which violated in principle the general mathematical theory of structures and thereby infuriated many Swiss academics between the wars. But Maillart's limited theory worked well for that special type of form. Within that category type, Maillart's theory was useful and had the virtue of great simplicity; he developed the theory to suit the form, not the form to suit the theory. In the United States, by contrast, some of our best engineers understood the general theory well, but not understanding Maillart's specific ideas, they failed to see how new designs could arise. They were trapped in a view of an engineering analysis which was so complex that it obscured new design possibilities. Today the undue reliance on complex computer analyses can have the same limiting effect on design.

A second, even more dramatic example occurred with suspension bridge design at the same time. A new and more general theory of analysis became fashionable in the 1920s. Imbued with the idea that more general theories would automatically give more complete insight into bridge performance, all leading designers of the period used that theory, which obscured rather than clarified understanding and helped cause the defective design for a series of major bridges in the 1930s and the Tacoma Narrows Bridge collapse of 1940.[10]

Such examples show how this new perspective on engineering design as an activity independent of basic science suggests a new type of research, basic to a design profession, where historical, humanistic study is as important as the development of scientific analyses.

Structures and Machines

Related to the fallacy that technology is applied science is the fallacy that technology involves only machines. This one-sided view dominated Jacques Ellul's frequently cited *Technological Society,* allowing him to portray the modern world as both mechanistic and demonic, without personality, without art, and without hope.[11] Crucial to Ellul's argument was his insistence on defining technology (or, in French, *la technique*) as "the one best way," the super-rational means by which one inevitably arrives at the single optimum solution to each problem. There is no possibility, in this view, for individuals to express their own personalities except, as Ellul puts it, by adding useless decoration to the machine. Only by compromising function or adding cost, two sides of the same thing, could the engineer inject any art. Ellul strongly ridiculed the idea of machine art, put forward by artists, architects, and critics between the wars. Like many other writers, Ellul argued that this art was merely symbolic of a machine age and did not at all reflect the efficiency of the "one best way."

But technology is not just machines. There are two sides to technology: structures—the static, local, and permanent works—and machines—the dynamic, universal, and transitory ones. The Eiffel Tower (figure 1.1), Seattle's covered stadium (the Kingdome), and the Brooklyn Bridge (see figure 1.2, p.18) are structures; they were designed to resist loads with minimum movement and to stand as long as their societies stand. By contrast, elevators, air conditioners, and cars are machines; they only work when they move and are continually replaced as they wear out or are made obsolete by newer models. Technology has always meant both structures and machines; they are its two sides.[12]

The civilized world requires both sides of technology. Structures stand for continuity, tradition, and protection of society; machines for change, mobility, and risk. There is a constant tension between these two types of objects—between the extremes of a frozen society where structure dominates and a frantic society dominated by machinery. Yet structures must be built by machines and most only can be built because of machines. Modern city buildings would be almost useless without elevators, and very few bridges would ever have been built without the pressure of railroads and automobiles. In the same way, machines

the pressure of railroads and automobiles. In the same way, machines require structure to hold them together and would be useless without structures in which or on which to operate.

As intimately connected as they are, structures and machines must function differently, they come into being by different social means, and they symbolize two distinctly different types of designs. Structures must not move perceptibly, are custom-built for one specific locale, and are typically designed by one individual. Machines, on the other hand, only work when they move, are made to be used widely, and are in the late twentieth century typically designed by teams of engineers. General statements about technology are frequently meaningless unless this basic distinction is first made.

In addition to the two types of objects, technology can be thought of as including two types of systems: networks and processes, which are extensions of structures and machines respectively. Networks—such as canals, roadways, railways, electric lines, and airways—are immovable conduits distributing things. The network is a distributor not a convertor. Processes, on the other hand, are systems that change the state of things—such as internal combustion, oil refining, water treatment, and electric power generation. These are dynamic systems, characterized by change and related intimately to machines such as engines, pumps, reactors, and turbines. Networks are static systems characterized by their permanence, and depend for their operation upon such structures as aqueducts, bridges, dams, airports, power plants, and transmission towers.[13]

I shall consider only structures, but it should be clear that they lose meaning if we forget their complementary relationship to machines. The Eiffel Tower is mainly lost to the general public without its elevators; the Kingdome would be useless without electric lights and air conditioning; and the Brooklyn Bridge was built by the use of all kinds of machinery and serves today as a major route for cars.

FIGURE 1.1
The Eiffel Tower, Paris, 1889, by Gustave Eiffel. When built for the Paris exhibition of 1889, this 300-meter-high iron tower was the highest man-made structure in the world. Its shape expresses visually the engineer's ideal for resisting the forces of wind.

13

Structures and Architecture

The modern world tends to classify towers, stadiums, and even bridges as architecture. This represents yet another, albeit more subtle, fallacy similar to the confusion of technology with applied science and with machines. Here even the word is a problem because "architect" does come from the Greek word meaning chief technician. But, beginning with the Industrial Revolution, structure has become an art form separate from architecture. The visible forms of the Eiffel Tower, the King-dome, and the Brooklyn Bridge result directly from technological ideas and from the experience and imagination of individual structural engineers. Sometimes the engineers have worked with architects just as with mechanical or electrical engineers, but the forms have come from structural engineering ideas.

Structural designers give the form to objects that are of relatively large scale and of single use, and these designers see forms as the means of controlling the forces of nature to be resisted. Architectural designers, on the other hand, give form to objects that are of relatively small scale and of complex human use, and these designers see forms as the means of controlling the spaces to be used by people. The prototypical engineering form—the public bridge—requires no architect. The prototypical architectural form—the private house—requires no engineer. We have seen that scientists and engineers develop their ideas in parallel and sometimes with much mutual discussion; and that engineers of structure must rely on engineers of machinery just to get their works built. Similarly, structural engineers and architects learn from each other and sometimes collaborate fruitfully, especially when, as with tall buildings, large scale goes together with complex use. But the two types of designers act predominantly in different spheres.

The works of structural art have sprung from the imagination of engineers who have, for the most part, come from a new type of school—the polytechnical school, unheard of prior to the late eighteenth century. Engineers organized new professional societies, worked with new materials, and stimulated political thinkers to devise new images of future society.[14] Their schools developed curricula that decidedly cut whatever bond had previously existed between those who made architectural forms and those who began to make—out of industrial-

14

ized metal and later from reinforced concrete—the new engineering forms by which we everywhere recognize the modern world. For these forms the ideas inherited from the masonry world of antiquity no longer applied; new ideas were essential in order to build with the new materials. But as these new ideas broke so radically with conventional taste, they were rejected by the cultural establishment. This is, of course, a classic problem in the history of art: new forms often offend the academics. In this case, it was beaux-arts against structural arts. The skeletal metal of the nineteenth century offended most architects and cultural leaders. New buildings and city bridges suffered from valiant attempts to cover up or contort their structure into some reflection of stone form. In the twentieth century, the use of reinforced concrete led to similar attempts. Although some people were able to see the potential for lightness and new forms, most architects tried gamely to make concrete look like stone or, later on, like the emerging abstractions of modern art. There was a deep sense that engineering alone was insufficient.

The conservative, plodding, hip-booted technicians might be, as the architect Le Corbusier said, "healthy and virile, active and useful, balanced and happy in their work, but only the architect, by his arrangement of forms, realizes an order which is a pure creation of his spirit . . . it is then that we experience the sense of beauty."[15] The belief that the happy engineer, like the noble savage, gives us useful things but only the architect can make them into art is one that ignores the centrality of aesthetics to the structural artist. True, the engineering structure is only one part of the design of such architectural works as a private house, a school, or a hospital; but in towers, bridges, free-spanning roofs, and many types of industrial buildings, aesthetic considerations provide important criteria for the engineer's design. The best of such engineering works are examples of structural art, and they have appeared with enough frequency to justify the identification of structural art as a mature tradition with a unique character. That character has three dimensions.

The Three Dimensions of Structure

Its first dimension is a scientific one. Each working structure or machine must perform in accordance with the laws of nature. In this sense, then, technology becomes part of the natural world. Methods of analysis useful to scientists for explaining natural phenomena are often useful to engineers for describing the behavior of their artificial creations. It is this similarity of method that helps to feed the fallacy that engineering is applied science. But scientists seek to discover pre-existing form and explain its behavior by inventing formulas, whereas engineers want to invent forms, using pre-existing formulas to check their designs. Because the forms studied by scientists are so different from those of engineers, the methods of analysis will differ; yet, because both sets of forms exist in the natural world, both must obey the same natural laws. This scientific dimension is measured by efficiency.

Technological forms live also in the social world. Their forms are shaped by the patterns of politics and economics as well as by the laws of nature. The second dimension of technology is a social one. In the past or in primitive places of the present, completed structures and machines might, in their most elementary forms, be merely the products of a single person; in the civilized modern world, however, these technological forms are the products of a society. The public must support them, either through public taxation or through private commerce. Economy measures the social dimension of structure.

Technological objects visually dominate our industrial, urban landscape. They are among the most powerful symbols of the modern age. Structures and machines define our environment. The locomotive of the nineteenth century has given way to the automobile and airplane of the twentieth. Large-scale complexes that include structures and machines become major public issues. Power plants, weapons systems, refineries, river works—all have come to symbolize the promises and problems of industrial civilization.

The Golden Gate, the George Washington, and the Verrazano bridges carry on the traditions set by the Brooklyn Bridge. The Chicago Hancock and Sears towers, and the New York Woolworth, Empire

16

State, and World Trade Center towers—all bring the promise of the Eiffel Tower into the utility of city office and apartment buildings. The Astrodome, the Kingdome, and the Superdome carry into the late twentieth century the vision of huge permanently covered meeting spaces first dramatized by the 1851 Crystal Palace in London and the 1889 Gallery of Machines in Paris.

Nearly every American knows something about these immense twentieth-century structures, and modern cities repeatedly publicize themselves by visual reference to these works. As Montgomery Schuyler, the first American critic of structure, wrote in the nineteenth century for the opening of the Brooklyn Bridge (figure 1.2), "It so happens that the work which is likely to be our most durable monument, and to convey some knowledge of us to the most remote posterity, is a work of bare utility; not a shrine, not a fortress, not a palace but a bridge. This is in itself characteristic of our time."[16] So it is that the third dimension of technology is symbolic, and it is, of course, this dimension that opens up the possibility for the new engineering to be structural art. Although there can be no measure for a symbolic dimension, we recognize a symbol by its elegance and its expressive power.

There are three types of designers who work with forms in space: the engineer, the architect, and the sculptor. In making a form, each designer must consider the three dimensions or criteria we have discussed. The first, or scientific criterion, essentially comes down to making structures with a minimum of materials and yet with enough resistance to loads and environment so that they will last. This efficiency–endurance analysis is arbitrated by the concern for safety. The second, or social criterion, comprises mainly analyses of costs as compared to the usefulness of the forms by society. Such cost–benefit analyses are set in the context of politics. Finally, the third criterion, the symbolic, consists of studies in appearance, along with a consideration of how elegance can be achieved within the constraints set by the scientific and social criteria. This is the aesthetic–ethical basis upon which the individual designer builds his work.

For the structural designer the scientific criterion is primary (as is the social criterion for the architect and the symbolic criterion for the sculptor). Yet the structural designer must balance the primary criterion with the other two.[17] It is true that all structural art springs from the central ideal of artificial forms controlling natural forces. Structural

FIGURE 1.2
The Brooklyn Bridge over the East River, New York, 1883, by John A. Roebling. When completed, this steel-cable suspension bridge was the longest-spanning structure in the world. Its diagonal stays express Roebling's idea of how a flexible bridge must be stiffened to prevent failure due to oscillations from wind.

forms will, however, never get built if they do not gain some social acceptance. The will of the designer is never enough. Finally, the designer must think aesthetically for structural form to become structural art. All of the leading artists of structure thought about the appearance of their designs. These engineers consciously made aesthetic choices to arrive at their final designs. Their writings about aesthetics show that they did not base design only on the scientific and social criteria of efficiency and economy. Within those two constraints, they found the freedom to invent form. It was precisely the austere discipline of minimizing materials and costs that gave them the license to create new images that could be built and endure.

Structural Art and Society

Most people would agree that the ideals of structural art coincide with those of an urban society: conservation of natural resources, minimization of public expenditures, and the creation of a more visually appealing environment. As the history of structural art shows, some engineers have already turned these ideals into realities. But these are isolated cases; how might they become the rule instead of the exception? We can address this question historically, by identifying the central ideas that have been associated with great structural art. These ideas reflect each of the three dimensions: the scientific, social, and symbolic.

The leading scientific idea might be stated as that of reducing analysis. In structural art, this idea has coexisted with the opposite tendency to overemphasize analysis, which today is typified by the heavy use of the computer for structural calculations. One striking example comes from the design of thin concrete vaults—thin shell roofs. Here, the major advances between 1955 and 1980—a time of intense analytic developments—were achieved, not by performing complex analyses using computers, but rather by reducing analysis to very simple ideas based on observed physical behavior. Roof vaults characterize this advance and they carry forward the central scientific idea in structural art: the analyst of the form, being also the creator of the form, is free to change shapes so that analytic complexity disappears.

The form controls the forces; and the more clearly the designer can visualize those forces the surer he is of his form. The great early and mid-twentieth-century structural artists such as Robert Maillart and Pier Luigi Nervi have all written forcefully against the urge to complicate analysis. We shall see the same arguments put forth by the best designers in the late twentieth century. When the form is well chosen, its analysis becomes astoundingly simple. The computer, of course, has become more and more useful as a time saver for routine calculations that come after the design is set. It is also increasingly valuable in aiding the designer through computer graphics. But like any machine, while it can reduce human labor, it cannot substitute for human creativity.

Turning to the social dimension, a leading idea that has come out of structural art involves what might be called the economy of public design competitions. Design quality arises from the stimulus of competing designs for the same project rather than from complex regulations imposed upon a single designer. Thus, governments could insure better designs by relinquishing some of their control on who designs and on what forms are chosen, and by giving this control to an informed public. It is not enough for the public merely to protest the building of ugly, expensive designs. A positive activity is essential, and that can only come about when the public sees the alternative designs that are possible for a project. The idea and meaning of alternative designs can best be illustrated by the history of modern bridges, but it applies as well to all other works of structure.

Although there is little tradition in the United States for design competitions in structure, such a tradition is firmly rooted elsewhere, with results that are both politically and aesthetically spectacular. Switzerland has the longest and most intensive tradition of bridge design competitions, and it is no coincidence that, by nearly common consent, the two greatest bridge designers of the twentieth century were Swiss: Robert Maillart (1872–1940), who designed in concrete, and Othmar Ammann (1879–1966), designer of the George Washington and Verrazano bridges, who designed in steel. That Switzerland, one-sixth the size of Colorado, and with fewer people than New York City, could achieve such world prominence is due to the centrality of economics and aesthetics for both their engineering teachers and their practicing designers, a centrality which is encouraged by the design competitions. Maillart's thin concrete arches in Switzerland were the least expensive proposals in design competitions, and they were later to provide the main focus for the first art museum exhibition ever devoted exclusively to the work of one engineer: The New York City Museum of Modern Art's 1947 exhibition on Maillart's structures. Othmar Ammann has been similarly honored; his centennial was celebrated by symposia both in Boston and in New York and by an exhibition held in Switzerland. Both Maillart and Ammann wrote articulately on the appearance as well as on the economy of bridges. They are prime examples of structural artists.

This Swiss bridge tradition continues today with a large number of striking new bridges in concrete that follow Maillart in principle if not in imitative detail. The most impressive post–World War II works are those of Christian Menn, whose long-span arches and cantilevers extend the new technique of prestressing to its limits, as Maillart's three-hinged and deck-stiffened arches did earlier with reinforced concrete. Design competitions stimulated these engineers and also educated the general public. Such competitions must be accepted by political authorities, must be judged by engineers whose opinions will be debated in the public press, and must be controlled by carefully drawn rules.

Once again, it is false images of engineering that keep us from insisting on following our normal instinct for open competitions. The American politics of public works falsely compares the engineering designer either to a medical doctor or to a building contractor. Supporters of the first comparison argue that you would never hold a competition to decide on who will remove your appendix; rather, you would choose professionals on the basis of reputation and then let them alone to do the skilled work for which they are trained. Similarly, if an already built bridge develops cracks, the solution is to hire a consultant who has a sound reputation for diagnosing and rehabilitating such defective works. But design is not the same kind of activity as diagnosis and rehabilitation. It needs more chances to exercise than there are chances to build, and it is stimulated by competition. However frustrating it may be to lose a competition, the activity is healthy and maturing, especially when even the losers are compensated financially, as they often are in Switzerland.

For proponents of the second false comparison, design competitions are to be run just as building competitions in which the lowest bid for *design* cost gets the design contract. In American public structures, design and construction are legally distinct activities. The cost of design is normally well below 10 percent of the cost of construction. Therefore, a brilliant engineer might spend more on a design which, as can often happen, will cost the owners substantially less overall. By the same token, an engineer who cuts his design fee to get the job may have to make a more conservative design which could easily cost the owner more in overall costs. Hence, large amounts of potential savings to the public are lost by a foolish policy of saving a little during the first stage of a project.

In one type of Swiss design competition, a small number of designers are invited to compete, some of their costs are covered, and they get additional prize funds in the order recommended by the jury. The winner usually gets the commission for the detailed design. Only several such competitions a year are needed to stimulate the entire profession and to show the general public the numerous possibilities available as good solutions to any one problem. This method of design award opens up the political process to local people far more than does the cumbersome and largely negative one of protest, legal action, and negation of building that so dominates public action in the late-twentieth-century America.

Properly defined design competitions reveal truths about society that are otherwise difficult to define. The resulting designs, therefore, became unique symbols of their time and place. This brings us to the third leading idea that has been associated with great structural art—the idea that its materials and forms possess a particular symbolic significance. Perceptive painters, poets, and writers have recognized in structural art a new type of symbol—first in metal and then in concrete—which fits mysteriously closely both to the engineering possibilities and to the possibilities inherent in democracy. The thinness and openness of the Eiffel Tower, Brooklyn Bridge, and Maillart's arches, as well as the stark contrast between their forms and their surroundings, have a deep affinity to both the political traditions and era in which they arose. They symbolize the artificial rather than the natural, the democratic rather than the autocratic and the transparent rather than the impenetrable.

The primary reason that the Eiffel Tower and the Brooklyn Bridge became dominant symbols was that their forms were new, transparent, and accessible to the general public. Contrast these to the 1884 Washington Monument and the 1831 London Bridge, two solid masonry structures that in their costly and monumental quality remind us of pre-industrial imperial eras rather than the democratic times in which they actually were built. Stone is a natural material; since the industrial revolution its use for structure has implied great cost and hence restriction to the wealthy. Moreover, its solidity, its inability easily to carry shifting loads, and its consequent massiveness imply heavy fortress-like forms.[18] Metal and concrete, properly designed, in every way contrast with stone. They are artificially made materials. Their forms reflect directly the inner springs of creativity emerging from contemporary industrial societies.

These forms imply a democratic rather than an autocratic life. When structure and form are one, the result is a lightness, even a fragility, which closely parallels the essence of a free and open society. The workings of a democratic government are transparent, conducted in full public view, and although a democracy may be far from perfect, its form and its actual workings (its structure) are inseparable. Furthermore, the public must continually inspect its handiwork; constant maintenance and periodic renewal are essential to its exposed structure. Politicians do not have life tenure; they must be inspected, chastised and purified from time to time, and replaced when found corrupt or inept. So it is with the works of structural art. They, too, are subject to the weathering and fatigue of open use. They remind us that our institutions belong to us and not to some elite. If we let them deteriorate, as we flagrantly have in our older cities and transportation networks, then that outward sign betokens an inner corruption of the common life in a free democratic society.

These ideas about politics, about science, and about art both animate and integrate the historical account of engineering art to which we now turn for the substance of this book.

PART I

The Age of Iron

CHAPTER 2

THOMAS TELFORD AND THE NEW ART FORM

We saw in chapter 1 that there are two main periods of structural art. The first one followed on the heels of the Industrial Revolution, beginning in the late eighteenth century and spreading throughout the world for about the next one hundred years. The second period began in the late nineteenth century and continues to this day. The primary distinctions lie in the materials and the forms. In the first period, the material is iron and the forms tend to be visually complex; in the second, the materials are steel and concrete, and the forms tend to be visually simpler.

The Eiffel Tower and Brooklyn Bridge are structures that stand between the two periods. They were not technological breakthroughs but, as the last structural designs of the two most famous bridge builders of the nineteenth century, they were climaxes as well as promises. The primary motivation of each was to span unprecedented distances with iron, *the* material of the Industrial Revolution. It was because Eiffel and Roebling created new forms in iron, on a new scale, and in permanent locations, that their works characterize the modern world. Although, perhaps obvious, it is nonetheless crucial that such structures could not have appeared before the Industrial Revolution, because industrialized iron did not then exist. The tower and the bridge, therefore, were not in the 1880s just portents of the future; they were also culminations of the past. The material of Eiffel's tower was iron, not steel, so in this respect it belongs to the first period, but its form set the direction for new forms in steel. Conversely, Roebling's bridge was the first major one to use steel rope for its cables, but the vertical suspenders and diagonal stays of its form looked back to the more complex forms of the past. The two structures will be discussed further in chapters 4 to 6, particularly how they follow from the developments considered here, lead to the developments taken up in the second part of this book, and exemplify the ideals of structural art which are our focus throughout.

The Second Iron Age

In looking at the first period, the major question we must ask is what happened during the Industrial Revolution to make possible the new art form of structure. The central material fact of the Industrial Revolution is iron. The new methods of producing that ancient material preceded and were essential to the most famous technological development of eighteenth-century Britain: the steam engine. And, without these new methods, and hence cheap and plentiful iron, developments in industry could not have been sufficient to merit the term "revolution."[1] The new methods involved replacing charcoal with coke in the smelting process. Using the energy powerhouse of coal in place of the far weaker store in wood, the iron founders of the West Midlands could begin to supply iron for machines and structures previously made of wood. Thus coal replaced wood in the process of iron making and in turn iron replaced wood for the products. In both cases, a far denser and stronger material supplanted the softer organic substance that had

FIGURE 2.1

The Iron Bridge over the Severn River, Coalbrookdale, England, 1779, by Abraham Darby III. The first major structure ever built of iron, this 100-foot-span, cast-iron arch bridge, being semicircular, has form and details of earlier non-metal arches. Two of the arch rings are incomplete, being discontinued as they meet the horizontal deck.

held together the technology of earlier civilizations. A nonrenewable resource replaced a renewable one; that is the primary ecological fact of the Industrial Revolution. Society thus began to mine its geological capital rather than fell its agricultural income. At the same time, the immediate power that was available increased enormously and centralized production became more and more economical. In this way, by the late eighteenth century, the development of industrialized iron came to define the course of technology and of society as a whole.

The most enduring symbol of the eighteenth-century rise in iron production is Iron Bridge (figure 2.1), built in 1779 by Abraham Darby III from cast-iron pieces. When it proved to be the only bridge in the

Severn River region to survive the disastrous 1795 Severn River flood, Thomas Telford, the founding president of the world's first civil engineering society, turned from masonry to metal and began to create the first series of iron bridges that demonstrated unequivocally the personal style of a structural artist. It was clear to Telford that Iron Bridge had survived that flood undamaged precisely because of the key property of iron, its high strength. Early cast iron was about five times as strong as wood and hence required one-fifth the amount of material to carry the same load. This drastic reduction in quantity of material allowed the design to let more water flow past the bridge during a flood. Masonry bridges acted as dams, building up water pressure that easily destroyed stone works. Wooden bridges, as well, had a damming effect and moreover were susceptible to breaks in joints and to flotation.

The visual lightness and the strength displayed by Iron Bridge stimulated Telford and others around the turn of the century to think about the new material and new forms. At first, of course, they still thought in terms of stone or wood structures, and many designers tried merely to put the new material into the old forms. Iron Bridge itself has the semicircular form typical of stone arches and its joined pieces are reminiscent of timberwork.[2] But for Telford the new material also provoked a different type of thinking. More than any contemporary, Telford saw the possibilities for a new visual world of iron, because he focused always on objects rather than theories, on economy of field construction rather than the business of designing structures, and on large-scale, public works rather than private architecture for the aristocracy.

Thomas Telford and Bridge Art

Telford was born in Glendinning, Scotland, in 1757. He began his career as a mason, and in 1778 helped build a three-span masonry arch bridge at Langhold. In 1782, he left Scotland for London to find a larger scope for his energies. In London, he worked as a draftsman in an architect's office, and between 1784 and 1787 he did alterations on the Shrewsbury Castle in Shropshire. Along with this architectural work, as a county surveyor from 1787 he designed his first bridge, three stone arch spans built at Montford and completed in 1792. By that time his talent for large-scale works began to be recognized; and, when the directors of the proposed Ellesmere Canal offered him the chance to carry out this immense project, Telford accepted the position, writing later:

> Feeling in myself a stronger disposition for executing works of importance and magnitude than for details of house architecture I did not hesitate to accept their offer, and from that time directed my attention solely to Civil Engineering.[3]

This reflection might be called the first self-conscious statement of the new engineering, fully disconnected from architecture and yet intimately related to the Industrial Revolution. Telford's decision led directly to the most impressive metal monument of eighteenth-century design still standing today: the aqueduct at Llangollen known as Pont-y-Cysyllte, completed in 1805 and functioning today with the original cast iron still fully intact.

From 1795 on, Telford worked with cast-iron structures, but it was in the Bonar Bridge design in 1810 that his ideas matured to the point where a new form emerged.[4] For this bridge over the Dornoch Firth in Scotland, Telford proposed a 150-foot-span cast-iron arch. He chose this wide span rather than the normal two-span masonry solution of earlier times in part because of flood and ice dangers. But more important were his design criteria: "to improve the principles of constructing iron bridges, also their external appearance . . . [and] to save a very considerable portion of iron and consequently weight."[5] Telford thus stated the central ideas of this new tradition—efficiency in materials, economy for construction, and appearance of the final form—and they have remained those of all structural artists ever since.

Telford's iron arch bridges were not the only such works at this time nor were they the longest spanning ones. The 1796 Sunderland Bridge spanned 236 feet, and John Rennie—Telford's only rival as Britain's finest bridge designer of the period—designed the 1819 Southwark Bridge with a central cast-iron arch span of 240 feet.[6] But what sets Telford apart is his distinct personal style; his iron arches are more visually attractive than those of his contemporaries, and they are also

FIGURE 2.2

The Craigellachie Bridge over the River Spey, Elgin, Scotland. 1814, by Thomas Telford. This flat 150-foot-span, cast-iron arch is the oldest surviving bridge of a type representing the first modern metal bridge forms. The arch, made of trussed elements having a constant depth, is fully continuous between abutments.

technically superior. A recent compilation of cast-iron bridges built between 1779 and 1871 lists the bridges in order of their technical quality. Of the top nine listed, eight are by Telford.[7] Of those eight, five are still standing today.

The oldest surviving bridge of the Bonar type is the 1814 Craigellachie Bridge (figure 2.2). Its arch is a flat circular profile of constant depth made up of two curved pieces connected by X-braces and radial struts. The thin roadway has a slight vertical curve and is joined to the arch by thin diagonal members whose general direction is radial. The whole form is light and open, the iron structure is the visible form, and the arch is made of standard pieces throughout its curved length. Although some of the visual elements derive from wooden bridges, the overall design as first conceived by Telford in 1810 represents a new form and one appropriate to cast iron.

There is no doubt as to Telford's aesthetic intention. He wrote with feeling about his Scottish landscape and about the beautiful Llangollen setting for the Welsh aqueduct.[8] He was closely enough connected to the architects of his day to absorb their love of the picturesque and to sense the significance of setting to a structural form. But he was the first civil engineer consciously to move away from the old canons of architectural taste. He did not write about the old architectural ideas of proportion, symmetry, and rhythm, but rather about the new engineering problems of construction, weight, and foundations. He was thinking all the time about appearance and landscape and form but, for Telford, the possibility for beauty must come internally from what the technical and economic constraints suggest, rather than externally from the images and formulations refined over centuries in the architecture of masonry.

Telford and the Limits of Structure

Cast iron liberated the imagination of Telford and others. It literally founded the modern engineering profession by forcing a group of designers to think deeply about structure at a new scale. Telford was first stimulated to think about very long-span bridges when in 1799 the Houses of Parliament appointed a select committee to investigate numerous proposals for the much-needed new London Bridge.[9] It had been proposed to span the Thames in one span to allow shipping to pass beneath. The lightness and the strength of cast iron suggested the solution. Of the many proposals, Thomas Telford's 1800 design for a cast-iron arch of 600 feet in span impressed the committee the most. There followed an extensive feasibility investigation which involved nearly every major user of cast iron in the emerging profession of engineering. Those consulted included various university professors, James Watt, John Wilkinson, the famous iron founder, and John Rennie. Although the consensus was that Telford's immense and elegant design could be built, Parliament never acted on it. This design was the earliest forerunner of Eiffel's tower and Roebling's bridge, and it foreshadowed the drama of each. Its proposed lace work of iron and great height would have dominated London visually as Eiffel's work was to dominate

THE AGE OF IRON

Paris nearly a century later; and the undoubted spectacle of seeing a city while crossing a bridge anticipated the visual excitement of Roebling's central elevated walkway to Brooklyn. It was, however, just this height, which had so stimulated Telford's imagination, that led to the great cost of the bridge approaches and also, presumably, to the parliamentary neglect. Entrusted with the eventual construction of both the Waterloo (1817) and London (1831) bridges, John Rennie fell back on older Parisian examples of multiarch stone works and thus reinforced the prevailing attitude that masonry was the proper city material. Needless to say, such stone posturing did not appeal to Telford.

Despite its importance, Telford's London bridge design was not truly modern in form. Influenced, perhaps, by the Sunderland design of 1796 (itself stimulated by ideas from Thomas Paine), Telford imagined a series of parallel arched elements, somewhat similar to the three paralleled arches in Iron Bridge, only very flat. Although his bold design stimulated others to propose long-span arches, Telford himself departed from this Iron Bridge-type precedent and developed the different form of the Bonar type in 1810. In his autobiography, Telford never mentioned the Thames bridge design, nor was any illustration included in his *Atlas of Works*. He did briefly refer to it in his 1812 "Bridge" article but gave no drawing of it, preferring instead to emphasize his Bonar Bridge and his 1811 proposal for a Bonar-type 500-foot arch over the Menai Straits.

After 1800, Telford turned his energies to the outlying regions, where he could proceed to develop new forms in response to the new industrial needs. In 1803 he became engineer to the commissioner for roads and bridges in the highlands of Scotland. It was in this position that—with the Bonar and the Craigellachie—he began to design what we have characterized as the first set of iron bridges to show the integration of technological soundness and handsome form. From the highlands of Scotland, Telford would move to the hills of Wales and to the outer limits of structure, not with the arch but with the cable, not with cast iron but with wrought iron.

The second iron age began in the foundry and was first made visible by arches of cast pieces designed and assembled in ways related to stone arches. Wrought iron, on the other hand, came from the forge, and first found major structural use in the chains of early-nineteenth-century suspension bridges. Cast iron, like stone, is far better in compression (squeezing together) than in tension (pulling apart); it is more impervious to weather than is wrought iron. Therefore, the obvious replacement for stone in arch bridges was cast iron, and the obvious material for the cables in the new suspension bridges was wrought iron.

The first three decades of the new century saw the suspension bridge come from the rope-hung exotica of South America and China to the heart of the Industrial Revolution. Britain led the way. The single greatest work of this period was Telford's 580-foot-span bridge, completed in 1826 over the Menai Straits in northwest Wales (figure 2.3). His was the first British bridge to be indisputably the longest span in the world.[10] It is the most important work in Telford's remarkable career, and it stands today as a symbol of the great aspirations of pre-Victorian Britain. Its design and its subsequent history reflect both the promise and the perils of an industrial world.

The bridge was over the most difficult section of the Holyhead Road connecting London to the Dublin ferry in Holyhead, on the is-

---

FIGURE 2.3

The Menai Bridge over the Menai Straits, Wales, 1826, by Thomas Telford. This 580-foot-span, wrought-iron, chain-suspension bridge was the longest-spanning structure in the world when completed.

land of Anglesey. The overall project for an improved connection between London and Dublin, spurred by the 1800 union of Ireland with Britain, was given to Telford in 1810, and the bridge design was accepted by Parliament in 1817. Nine years later, on January 30, 1826, the London mail coach galloped across the first bridge to span directly over an open reach of ocean.[11]

But the bridge was doing some galloping of its own. Telford's resident engineer, W. A. Provis, had noted undulations from gusting wind just before the bridge opened.[12] Telford then added transverse bracing, which cut down the movement. No significant motion occurred until ten years later, two years after Telford's death. In January 1836, the bridgekeeper reported large oscillations to Provis, who recommended a longitudinal stiffening of the roadway. Sadly, no action resulted, and in 1839 a gale tore part of the roadway loose. This severe damage to both carriageways was rapidly repaired and Provis then designed a stiffening of the roadway that lasted over half a century. A steel deck replaced the original roadway in 1893 and the entire bridge span was rehabilitated in 1940.

Telford's writings in the 1820s and Provis's field observations show a clear awareness of how horizontal wind can cause extensive vertical motion in a suspension bridge. Telford realized that a longitudinal stiffening of the deck would reduce that danger, but he felt unjustified in adding that costly provision until such time as it might become unavoidable. Had he been alive in 1836, it seems plausible that the bridgekeeper's report would have led Telford to make those changes, his great prestige insuring their implementation. It is thus possible that no severe damage would ever have arisen and that Menai could have been regarded as a full success.

As we shall see, great structural artists have always learned from the full-scale performance of their own works and the works of others. Roebling changed his Niagara Falls bridge design *while the bridge was under construction,* after he heard of the failure of the Wheeling Bridge in 1854. The birth of prestressing, the most revolutionary structural idea of the twentieth century, can be traced back directly to Eugène Freyssinet's 1910 bridge at Le Veurdre, which after completion would have collapsed into the Allier River had the designer not applied emergency jacking by night to save it. Othmar Ammann, designer of the great New York bridges from the George Washington to Verrazano, wrote in 1953 that "the Tacoma Narrows bridge failure has given us invaluable information. . . . It has shown [that] every new structure which projects into new fields of magnitude involves new problems for the solution of which neither theory nor practical experience furnish an adequate guide. It is then that we must rely largely on judgement and if, as a result, errors or failures occur, we must accept them as a price for human progress."[13]

All of these structural artists worked at the limits of structure. These limits are just what stimulate imagination and are a primary basis for the aesthetics of this new art form. This was certainly true in Telford's case, and with undeniable results. Of all the suspension bridges completed before Telford's death, none were built as well as Telford's and none had such a strong influence aesthetically on subsequent design. In addition to Menai, Telford designed the 380-foot-span Conway suspension bridge also completed in 1826 and standing in good condition today.

Art and Politics

Menai is the first major work of structural art visually to symbolize, in its thinness, the lightness of the new engineering and the demands of the new politics. The bridge was contemporaneous with the Reform Bill of 1832, the primary effect of which was to give representation to industrial cities such as Birmingham, Manchester, Leeds, and Sheffield. Politics was being directly influenced by the Industrial Revolution. Spreading the franchise more widely went together with spreading materials more thinly. Both actions called forth new forms.

In politics as in structure the risky idea of new forms proved exciting to the new designers. No one better exemplified the connection between the two spheres than Thomas Paine. His two primary interests were structure and politics; he termed *The Rights of Man* his "political bridge." Paine's designs for iron bridges had considerable short-term influence in both Britain and America, where his elegant models encouraged some designers to think of long spans with thin metal sections. His design stimulated in part the longest eighteenth-century iron arch in Britain, built at Sunderland, even though its final design was fully the work of other men.[14] Paine's major importance to engineering history lies, however, not in his technical influence, but rather in the connection he made between technology and politics, both by seeing his political writings as bridges and by emphasizing in his life the revolutionary impulses of reformer in society and in metal. He saw himself breaking with the past both in politics and in structural design.[15]

The new designers broke with the centuries-old tradition of solid stone structure. At the same time, the electoral reforms began to break the long tradition of monarchical and aristocratic political structures. In both cases, breaking with tradition meant taking risks. The daring light metal structures beginning to appear early in the century reflected the risks that the postrevolutionary societies began to take, risks that brought a public ethic—conservation of public resources—into coincidence with a professional aesthetic—light appearance. Of those using the new material, Telford was the first consciously to think in these new structural terms—the aesthetic of thinness going together with the ethic of the conservation of materials and money.

Telford's Aesthetic

Telford took a strong stand for the independence of engineering, both from the visual maxims of eighteenth-century architecture and from the mathematical ideals of eighteenth-century science. Ornamental facades and scientific abstractions, coming from the elite academics rather than from the provincial building sites, violated his instinctive sense of form. One of his writings shows Telford's aesthetic thinking; unique in Telford's own time but closely similar to writings by later structural artists, the section on "Bridge" for the *Edinburgh Encyclopedia* was written in 1812. In 1813, several of his bridge reports were printed in the *House of Commons Reports*. [16]

In the "Bridge" article, Telford critically reviewed previous iron arch bridges: Iron Bridge, Buildwas, Sunderland, the 1800 Boston

Bridge of John Rennie, the 1805 bridge at Bristol, and his own 1810 Bonar Bridge design. He began his discussion by noting that iron bridges were "unquestionably a late invention of British artists," and that the main problem with Iron Bridge was that "more skill than that of the mere ironmaster was required." His use of the word "artist" is pre-romantic and hence cannot have the same meaning as we would give it today. But, for Telford, the word does mean someone dedicated to both skill and beauty. His article moves effortlessly back and forth between technical discussion of connections and member sizes and criticism of appearance; he sees no separation between use and beauty. This 1812 article is the first treatise by an engineer on structural art.

Telford described how the iron circles between the ribs and the deck both in Iron Bridge at Coalbrookdale and at Sunderland are the wrong form and are wasteful of material. The two higher circular ribs at Coalbrookdale do not carry the load well and they have "a mutilated appearance." In Rennie's Boston bridge, which had cracked badly when built, Telford observed that "the ribs, in springing from the perpendicular faces of the masonry of the abutment, have also a crippled appearance." He went on to observe that at Bristol "the supporting pillars [between road and arch] are still placed perpendicularly [vertically]; . . . which, as the arch has more curvature, has still a worse effect than at Boston."

All of these aesthetic objections Telford had sought to overcome in his Bonar bridge design. This design involves a single arch span, supported by a masonry face cut perpendicular to the arch slope, and in the spandrels, instead of circles or upright pillars, "lozenge, or rather triangular forms are introduced . . . [to keep] the points of pressure in the direction of the radius . . . this disposition of the iron work, especially in the spandrels, also greatly improves the general appearance."[17] For him it possessed the basic virtue of being a technical and an aesthetic improvement, and that integration is the central motive of all structural artists.

As we have seen, Telford separated engineering from architecture as early as 1793, but nevertheless always retained an interest in the latter. In an 1813 article in the *Edinburgh Encyclopedia* on "Civil architecture," he emphasized that the primary visual purpose of architecture was to express its load-carrying function.[18] For Telford, it was the laws of nature and the needs of society that gave stimulus to form, not preconceived aesthetic rules. Yet many writers on aesthetics believed then and believe now that forms arising from laws of natural science, or from social necessity, cannot be art. "We are in the presence of a work of art only when it has no preponderant instrumental use, and when its technical and rational foundations are not preeminent." This mid-twentieth-century view of art historian George Kubler—a view excluding useful objects and rationally based forms—has its origin in the philosophy of Immanuel Kant. As Kubler puts it, "Kant . . . said . . . that the necessary cannot be judged beautiful, but only right or consistent. In short, a work of art is as useless as a tool is useful."[19]

Kubler took an eighteenth-century viewpoint that separated fine and useful arts and that defined the process of artistic production, in Kant's words, as "purposeness without a purpose." The artist must be both original and disciplined (have purposeness) but he must not merely follow rules from society or laws of nature. Furthermore, the goal of the artist, in Kant's view, is the communication of aesthetic ideas through sensible forms, "and these aesthetic ideas are fictional, requiring works of art to be things which are 'in their own right, for their own sake.' "[20] Art is for the sake of art. Kant's thinking was necessarily uninfluenced by the Industrial Revolution. It was easy for him to see art (in our sense of the word) as fine art and useful art as merely craft.

Telford, and succeeding structural artists, recognized intuitively that the new materials changed radically the old separation between the fine and useful arts (art and craft). Structure would begin, with Telford, to liberate the imagination and take its place with the other plastic or visual arts of painting, sculpture, and architecture. It would begin to communicate aesthetic ideas and to show how an aesthetically designed object can at the same time be a useful work. Structure would, after the introduction of cast iron, show how preeminent rational foundations could communicate the artist's aesthetic ideas while actually enhancing instrumental use of safely conveying people across wild ravines.[21]

The major artistic results from the Industrial Revolution were structures which expressed the aesthetic idea that the constraints of society—uses—and the constraints of nature—rational foundations—were the proper stimuli to imaginative form in a world forever changed. Today many would dispute this idea, arguing that in fact the constraints of society and nature must be transcended if art is to arise. The genius must be freed from ordinary rules, allowed to express himself through an unfettered imagination and an "artistic" life. Telford was not such a genius and his works, nearly all of which still serve their intended purpose, certainly do not reflect uselessness. Moreover, Telford was the most technically sound of the pioneering designers as well as the one who gave most weight to aesthetics. He is the first modern engineer to show that a concern for aesthetics does not compromise technical quality but rather can improve it. We have already argued that the aesthetic motivation in a structural artist seems in fact to stimulate efficient designs. It remains for us to explore how it can be that such designs can be both art and technology.

The two usual objections to the idea that technology can be art might be rephrased as questions. First, even if beautiful, are such designs merely the result of the meticulous application of science, dictated by their rational foundations, and devoid of any personality? Second, do not the pressures for economy, society's overriding constraint, make the expression of aesthetic ideas impossible, and is not the form merely a result of a drive for maximum profit to both the owner and the builder? What can an artistic designer hope to express of his imaginative and emotional longings when burdened by such considerations? These two questions can properly be answered only by exploring the sense in which a structural artist is constrained by scientific laws and social patterns. Again Telford provides us with the beginnings of an answer. The second question is simply an example of the general belief that design always converges to the most economical solution, economy being the society's quantitative measure. We shall take the question up in chapter 6.

Science and Engineering

The first of the two questions brings us back to the problem of whether technology is applied science. Does technological innovation follow directly from basic scientific discovery? As already indicated, we can derive some insights from Telford, his designs, and his writings.

Telford had little use for the science of his day, was untrained in mathematical formulations, and made few if any calculations for his designs. He was reputed to have no knowledge even of geometry, let alone the calculus invented in the seventeenth century by Newton and Leibnitz.[22] It seems incredible today that without any mathematical analysis someone would seriously guarantee a 600-foot-span arch, over two and one-half times the span of any previous European bridge. Even more remarkable is the fine performance of his numerous extant iron bridges whose forms did not come from mathematical analyses. When saying that science had little influence on Telford, I mean two distinct ideas: first, that discoveries of nature's laws by people like Galileo and Newton did not play any role in Telford's designing, and, second, that Telford did not use in his design work the mathematical formulations devised by such researchers. Thus, science here means new discoveries and new methodologies *developed independently of design imperatives.* On the other hand, Telford directed innumerable tests on structural elements which he designed, and he also carefully observed the behavior of structures in service.

The clearest statement of Telford's ideas on science appears, perhaps, in the second part of the three-part "Bridge" article in the 1814 *Edinburgh Encyclopedia.* This second part, entitled "Theory of Bridges," was not actually written by Telford but at his request by Alexander Nimmo (1783–1832), one of his Scottish protégés.[23] The ideas it expresses are fully consonant with Telford's own. Telford had met Nimmo when the latter was rector of an academy in Inverness. Telford hired him to work on the Highland roads and in 1809 recommended him for a government appointment as an engineer in Ireland. There Nimmo designed a series of fine stone bridges which, according to Ruddock, are the equal of any of the French designs of the previous century. Nimmo was fully conversant in the science and mathematics of structural theory and had wide practical experience. His writing reflects this background but is enlivened by a firm belief that mathematical theory does little for the practical designer.

Nimmo's article begins with Newton by implying that even Britain's most eminent scientist had had little if any positive influence on engineering. Nimmo concedes that "it was only [after] Newton had opened the path of true mechanical science, that . . . arches attracted the attention of mathematicians." But, he continues, "we are much inclined to doubt whether the greater part of their speculations have been of any value to the practical bridge builder."[24] Near the end of the article he discusses the errors in Newton's speculation on the flow of water around a bridge pier. In between these references to the great scientist, Nimmo simultaneously presents an essentially correct exposition of the principles of bridge design and conducts a polemic against the idea that scientific research has aided the practicing designer. He argues that the calculus is needless, that theoretical analyses impede design ideas, and that high precision in calculation is worthless.

Throughout the article Nimmo discusses proper form, which for him usually involves thinner structures. Thus the rejection of scientific theory goes together with a recommendation for design efficiency. Nimmo does give an arch theory, but one that is both computationally simple and visually oriented. It is based upon ideas empirically known to the Romans and used extensively by Telford and his generation. These ideas did not, therefore, come from the scientific revolution. Rather, as Nimmo is at pains to show, those eighteenth-century scientific refinements were more of a distraction than an inspiration to designers. He notes, for example, that the overemphasis on refining the mathematical form of an arch profile (parabola, catenary, circle, etc.) led analysts to neglect the importance of the foundations. "If the deductions of the theory were to be followed . . . they may lead . . . to the proposing of weakness instead of strength, and craziness instead of stability. . . . Give the modern engineer only a sure foundation, he will raise a structure as durable as the materials of which it is composed."[25] The scientific studies have "led to no one useful practical result" because they have necessarily been constricted to the arch profile—which can be treated mathematically—and, in the meantime, "as to the thickness of archstones, side walls, and piers, the horizontal section or ground plan of the bridge, the manner of filling up its haunches, of forming the joints, of connecting it with the abutments, wing walls, etc., we are still left in the dark."[26] Scientific theory constricts vision and leaves out most of the practical problems.[27] All structural artists since Telford have argued this thesis and its corollary that the simplification of analyses liberates the imagination.

It would be wrong to assume that Telford's distrust of scientific studies led him to avoid all insights afforded by mathematics. For the Menai Bridge, he carefully considered the opinion of Davies Gilbert

THE AGE OF IRON

that the sag of the chains be increased from 34 feet (Telford's original design) to 50 feet (based on Gilbert's calculations). Gilbert, later to become president of the Royal Society, was a Holyhead Road commissioner. When Telford had presented his plans in 1820, Gilbert thought the chains too flat and set about to develop a mathematical theory which he later published in 1826.[28] In the final design Telford did increase the sag, although only to 43 feet, and he gave credit to Gilbert for having influenced his design. Thus the scientific study followed the design and did not stimulate ideas on form, but it did influence the final detailed work. In other words, it was Telford's engineering design that stimulated Gilbert's scientific research. Art proceeded science in the development of engineering structure.

A recent study of Telford's highland roads and bridges concluded that "the whole enterprise shows Telford's great virtue as an engineer, his concern for economy, not in the short run, but in the long term. . . . Functional but transcending merely functional, the bridges epitomise the grandeur of Telford's conception . . . [and] for Craigellachie we can adopt [the poet] Robert Southey's quotation about Bonar Bridge, 'As I went along the road by the side of the water I could see no bridge; at last I came in sight of something like a spider's web in the air—if this be it, thought I, it will never do! But presently I came upon it, and oh, it is the finest thing that ever was made by God or Man!' "[29]

This response to the "grandeur of Telford's conception" prefigures similar reactions to Brooklyn Bridge, the Eiffel Tower, and all other masterpieces of structural art. Telford had begun the new tradition with roadway bridges and canal aqueducts; the following generation of structural artists would continue it for the next major result of the new iron age: the railroad.

CHAPTER 3

BRUNEL, STEPHENSON,

AND RAILWAY FORMS

The Problem of Form

If iron was the maker of the Industrial Revolution, the iron horse was its mover. Darby's material and Watt's machine combined to accelerate wildly the pace of industrialization and urbanization in the twenty-five years between the completion of Telford's Menai Bridge and the 1851 opening of the Crystal Palace. Two British engineers, Robert Stephenson (1803–1859) and I. K. Brunel (1806–1859), dominated this period as Telford and Rennie had done the previous one.

Iron structure had moved out of the narrow confines of arch bridges and into a broader realm which included factories, public buildings, ships, and, above all, everything associated with railroads. As the centerpiece of the Great Exhibition, the Crystal Palace dramatized along its 1,848-foot length the visual power of huge open spaces framed with light, standardized, and prefabricated iron pieces. The structure and the form seemed one; the traditional "architecture" was relegated to exterior trimming. Significantly, the designer was a gardener, not an architect.

But such a building was an anomaly in nineteenth-century Britain. Even in industrial Manchester all the important buildings were of stone. An illustrated plan of the city in 1857 was surrounded by etchings of fifty-one civic, religious, and commercial buildings, all but one of which have facades of stone, and none of which shows the possibilities for new building forms with exposed structure.[1]

While Manchester and other cities were building in stone from the wealth made possible by iron, engineers designed a bewildering array of structures to accommodate the railroads. The leaders, Stephenson and Brunel, were both artists in iron structure but they were caught up in the frenzy of the railroad to such an extent that neither would stop long enough to reflect deeply on structural form. Whereas Telford had worked with the restricted idea of cast-iron arch bridges for thirty-five years, the two younger men experimented with a wide variety of forms, while at the same time developing railway machinery and designing whole systems of transport. Brunel, in particular, with restless energy, pursued so many enterprises in this age of railway mania that his astounding talent for inventing form never matured beyond his brilliant early works. Brunel was almost like someone from another and more technologically advanced planet suddenly set down in a backward land and overwhelmed by the opportunity of introducing new ideas.

The lives and careers of Stephenson and Brunel were in many ways parallel: both had distinguished engineer fathers; both, like Telford and Rennie, had no formal engineering education; and both died within a month of each other at a relatively young age. Both men created record-breaking spans that call forth comparisons to Telford's designs. Such comparisons are valid. But, because Stephenson and Brunel had to consider the new engineering problem of the locomotive load, they also came up with very different solutions and invented very different forms. The new machine forced structural engineers to change ancient ideas about form because for the first time in history, a heavy and dynamic load had to be supported by a light metal form. For Telford and all before him, the primary load had been the dead weight of the structure itself. The problem of design had been the subtle relationship between the form of structure and the forces within it due to its own dead weight; and the size of those forces in turn depended on the form. This led Telford to design cast-iron arches which, like masonry, resist compression well.

The idea of arch form is severely disrupted if a large load, such as a locomotive, can move about on the structure. Moreover, since the railroad must be nearly level, almost like canal viaducts, girders or trusses were often more practical than arches. Such forms, under locomotive loads, must resist tension and vibrations. The danger of cast-iron girders for railway loading was tragically demonstrated when, in May 1847, Stephenson's cast-iron girder bridge over the Dee River at Chester collapsed with a passenger train on it.[2] Such events stimulated the search for new forms in wrought iron. Both Stephenson and Brunel set about to find such forms and, even though they did not fully succeed, their struggles did produce two great bridges, which characterize the end of British dominance in nineteenth-century structural art.

Robert Stephenson

Stephenson's father, George Stephenson (1781–1849), rose from being an uneducated mine worker in Newcastle to becoming the designer of the world's first successful steam railway in 1825. He worked closely with his son, designing everything from locomotives to rail bridges. Many of their early iron bridges reflect Telford's arch forms, but in his last and greatest works Robert Stephenson struck out on his own and created the straight tubular form. Both major examples of this form appeared, symbolically enough, next to the two monumental Telford suspension bridges, one at Conway in 1849 and one at Menai in 1850. Robert Stephenson's last request was that he be buried next to Thomas Telford, and so he was. To this day his remains lie next to those of his mentor, in Wales and Westminster.

Stephenson's struggle with form succeeded technically but not aesthetically. In the Britannia Bridge at Menai, the two vertical-wall iron girders were integrated by horizontal plates top and bottom to form a hollow box through which the trains ran. The straight horizontal iron box appears to be a solid mass carried by three straight vertical two-eyed stone towers looming over 200 feet above the water.

These towers reflect Stephenson's uncertainty; he had initially planned to build a suspension bridge with a very stiff horizontal deck to prevent oscillations such as those from wind observed on Telford's Menai Bridge and those from the dynamic hammering of locomotive wheels.[3] In the end, the deck was stiff enough not to require cables even though the towers still stand ready to receive a suspension system. This extra, unused security characterized both the immense industrial wealth in Britain up to the Great Exhibition and the inherent conservative temper of these early engineers. Economy was far less crucial than safety in an age when bridge failures were common and in a society grown wealthy beyond comparison. Stephenson's work has been compared to America's moon flight and proclaimed to be "not the product of the genius of the railway engineer alone, but of the collective mechanical genius of the English nation."[4]

The aesthetic defects of the Britannia Bridge are rooted in the fact that structural art does not flourish when the constraint of economy is removed. Stephenson's tubular bridges were based upon detailed testing but not on a need for minimum materials or low cost. The economic imperative of putting the rail line in service quickly overrode the structural engineer's goal for construction economy.

The history of the Britannia Bridge does, however, exemplify one major feature of structural art, namely, that new designs precede new theories. The Britannia Bridge, like Telford's Menai Bridge before it, shows that "the work of the civil engineer involved not the application of existing theoretical knowledge but the design and development of techniques that provided empirical knowledge"[5] from which later developments could arise.

Also instructive are the contrasts between Telford's Bonar Bridge and Stephenson's Britannia Bridge. Telford had developed his mature iron arch form for the Bonar Bridge in 1810 after working with the cast-iron arch form for over fifteen years. Stephenson brought out the tubular form for his immense Menai design without earlier works to guide him. Telford had to produce an inexpensive design for his highlands bridge, and thus he had to think of economy as he developed his form. But, more essentially, Telford wanted lightness, and he therefore sought to make light structures that were as safe as they were inexpensive. Stephenson seems not to have thought visually in this way. The aesthetic goal of lightness was not, for him, a primary goal. Yet it is in fact crucial to structural art; for the greatest structural artists, the goal of visual lightness is as primary as those of safety and economy.

If we turn now to Brunel, we can see how his aesthetic ideas, being more focused on visually thin structure, directed his work toward designs of even greater technical merit than those of his contemporary.

Isambard Kingdom Brunel

No character in the history of engineering fits so well the popular image of genius as does Isambard Kingdom Brunel. Even his outlandish name, combining his English and French heritage, prophetically signaled someone without peer.

In yet another parallel with Stephenson, Brunel was the son of one of Britain's foremost engineers. When Tsar Alexander had invited Marc Brunel (1769–1849) to Russia in 1821, the Duke of Wellington intervened to keep him in England.[6] Isambard was born in 1806 at Portsea, England, where he grew up. After studying mathematics and watchmaking in Paris for three years, he returned to England, where at age sixteen he began his engineering career, working with his father. In 1824 young Brunel went to work on his father's greatest project, the boring of a tunnel under the Thames. He rose quickly to the position of resident engineer on this monumental construction, but in January 1828 was seriously injured as part of the tunnel gave way. He recovered slowly, and in 1829 his family sent him for recuperation to Clifton, high on the limestone cliffs overlooking the Avon Gorge leading to Bristol.

That his parents would have chosen this dramatic site for his convalescence can only be regarded as providential because it went together with young Brunel's exuberant imagination and the extraordinary coincidence of a bridge competition there in 1829. Brunel, with no previous bridge experience, proceeded to make four different designs, each of a suspension bridge with a central span far greater than any previous bridge anywhere of any type (spans from 870 to 916 feet). For this reason, the bridge commission felt uncertain about judging the twenty-two designs submitted, and it asked Thomas Telford, then seventy-two, to be the judge. Telford rejected all twenty-two designs; he considered it wrong for the span to exceed that of his Menai Bridge. Undoubtedly, he was as much concerned about wind oscillations as about his retention of a world's record.[7] Telford then made his own design, which included huge Gothic towers down into the valley. Brunel sharply objected to this design in a letter to the commission. Eventually, the commissioners agreed with Brunel's objections. They held a second competition in 1831 and, after some further discussions, gave the design to Brunel. Work began on June 21, 1831, but was suspended when political riots in Bristol made it impossible to raise funds. By 1843 both towers had been completed, but the bridge was not finally built until 1864, five years after Brunel's death.

With the bridge construction at a halt, the youthful Brunel turned to railroads and between 1833 and 1841 directed the design, construction, and operation of the longest major rail line in the world, the Great Western Railway between London and Bristol. It was a grandiose project: of broad gauge, it contained the world's longest railway tunnel (nearly 2 miles) and the world's longest spanning brick arched bridge at Maidenhead. In 1854 Brunel designed and built Paddington Station, the London terminal for his railway, and in 1859 he completed the Saltash Bridge near Plymouth for the extension of that rail line from Bristol to Exeter to Cornwall.

Brunel's virtuosity as an artist in structure shows in these vastly different types of construction, for example, in the light, elegant, intersecting iron vaults over the Paddington train platforms (figure 3.1). But his relatively short life and his extraordinarily various mechanical engineering designs did not allow him the time to carry his structural ideas as far as Telford had carried his. It was, in particular, the frantic activity always associated with modern machinery that distracted Brunel and even led to his premature death. Brunel not only laid out entire rail lines, but he designed the rails, the switching, and the station with buildings, and he thought deeply about locomotive design. At the same time, he began designing the world's largest iron ships; these proved both technically too far ahead of their time and financially disastrous.[8]

FIGURE 3.1

Paddington Station Roof, London, 1854, by Isambard Kingdom Brunel. This iron arch roof shows Brunel's use of metal in the design of intersecting vaults for covering the train shed at the London terminus for his Great Western Railway.

Unfortunately, Brunel usually invested his own money in the ventures for which he was the designer.

It is typical of the fundamental distinction between the two sides of technology—structures and machines—that whereas the former are static and permanent, the latter are dynamic and transient. Barely a trace remains of Brunel's major machinery—the ships and the locomotives—and none are currently in use.[9] Most of his major structures, on the other hand, still stand and serve their purpose as well today as they did over a century and a third ago. The structures, of course, have needed maintenance, and over time some parts have been replaced; but, as with Telford's works, Brunel's structures are the permanent symbols of their age, the last great era of British world dominance in politics, science, machinery, and structures. It was in the 1850s that British dominance climaxed, and Brunel's works—in all their grandeur, self-confidence, and mixed success—characterize that climax.

If Telford was engineering's Bach—creating patiently and with unparalleled productivity—then Brunel was its Wagner. Telford was essentially a servant of the state, paid a fee to produce almost weekly a new design. Brunel was, by contrast, a private entrepreneur who designed entire networks. Telford's life holds little fascination apart from his works, whereas Brunel's life is ultimately as exciting as the objects he created. Telford belongs to a classic tradition, Brunel to the romantic age. No one thought of Telford, during his lifetime, as an artist in the same sense as they thought of Turner; yet Brunel struck his contemporaries as both a genius and an artist. He was, however, an engineering artist, a fact not well recognized then or now.

Because he was an engineering artist, Brunel's works were based upon meticulous detail, sound technical training in the field, a love of the visual objects of technology, and a clear understanding of politics. His biographer Rolt, among others, has compared his sketch books to those of Leonardo and his personality to that of Michelangelo, "to the genus of deep, violent, colossal, passionately striving natures." He has always been thought of in Britain as a Renaissance man. And yet, his biographer, Rolt, errs in stating that "he and his generation bequeathed a sum of knowledge which, like his great ship, had become too large and too complicated to be mastered any longer by one mind. . . . The result has been that while the collective sum of knowledge has continued to increase at a prodigious rate the individual sum has so seriously diminished."[10] Rolt, implying that only lesser men followed, or could follow, Brunel, limits his field of vision to Britain, where indeed Brunel had no successor; he misses the basic fact that, outside of Britain, Gustave Eiffel and numerous others who came after Brunel not only knew more than he but created greater and sometimes more beautiful works. This qualification having been made, however, it can be said that no other structural artist has attempted such a variety of works as Brunel or worked on such a scale.

The Tension between Structural Art and Business

Brunel's career illustrates a characteristic of structural artists in that many times their energy and imagination deflected their design talents away from buildings and bridges toward nonstructural designs. Nearly all of the greatest structural artists have been so inventive and many-sided as to involve themselves in ventures that led away from structural design.[11] The temptation into other areas is not motivated solely by artistic factors. It arises also because structural art is the prototypical art of an industrial–democratic revolution. As such, structural art politically symbolizes service to the building of a common life; its ethic is a servant ethic that eliminates the possibility of great financial profit. Brunel clearly recognized this and felt the paradox that his greatest works brought him his smallest financial return. As he put in his *Journal,* "One thing however is not right; all this mighty press brings me but little profit—I am not making money. I have made more by my Great Western shares than by all my professional work—what is my stock in trade and what has it cost and what is it worth?"[12] The dilemma of which Brunel speaks has existed since the Industrial Revolution, which coincides with the emergence of structural art.

In other arts, such as modern sculpture and painting, the rewards for success can be comparable to those in business: Picasso died a millionaire and Henry Moore's profit is immense. But no twentieth-century structural artist can make anything but a modest single professional fee from his best works. He therefore looks to other types of business in order to gain financial independence.[13] In the nineteenth century, Washington Roebling wrote about his father, John Roebling, the designer of the Brooklyn Bridge: "My father always held it as a necessity that a civil engineer (one of the poorest professions in regard to pay) should always, when possible, interest himself in a manufacturing position." The reason, of course, was not merely to leave design and make more money; on the contrary, "the rope business being established [John A. Roebling's wire rope manufacturing] . . . his ambition prompted him to greater efforts [bridge design]."[14]

In the best survey of civil engineering in nineteenth-century America, Daniel Calhoun emphasizes the fact that engineers came increasingly to see themselves as servants of business.[15] If so, this perception may account in part for the relative lack of structural artists in the United States, especially when compared to such small countries as Switzerland where the idea of design for the public welfare is stronger.

Brunel and Stephenson

As should already be obvious, despite certain similarities in their careers, there were great differences between Brunel and Stephenson. Samuel Smiles, the famous Victorian biographer of British engineers, contrasted Brunel and Stephenson together with their respective fathers: "The Stephensons were inventive, practical, and sagacious; the Brunels ingenious, imaginative, and daring." Smiles proceeds to generalize those traits in national terms. "The former were as thoroughly English in their characteristics as the latter perhaps were as thoroughly French."[16]

The contrast Smiles makes between the practical and the imaginative is valid in a certain business sense but not in the sense of structural art. In terms of business ventures, Brunel dared much and perhaps overextended himself. He simply tried too many different ventures at one time to be able to avoid, in some of them, disastrous failure. But in structural design, Brunel was as practical as Stephenson. In fact, in his structural art, Brunel's daring and sagacity reinforced each other. This conjunction of daring and sagacity, of the practical and the imaginative, is characteristic of all great structural art.

The difference between Brunel and Stephenson, then, is the difference between a not fully mature structural artist and one who, although more mature, was less artistic. This difference emerges when we compare the greatest bridge of Brunel—the Royal Albert Bridge at Saltash—with Stephenson's greatest bridge—the Britannia Bridge. Some of the aesthetic defects of the Britannia Bridge were evident in the comparison made earlier with Telford's Menai Bridge. The present comparison is even more direct and therefore even more revealing. Both Stephenson's and Brunel's bridges are for railway and both have essentially the same main-span lengths. Stephenson's Britannia Bridge, completed in 1850, has two main spans of 460 feet each and two side spans of 230 feet. Brunel's Royal Albert Bridge at Saltash has two main spans of 455 feet each and seventeen shorter approach spans ranging from 69.5 feet to 93 feet.

The first measure of comparison is the amount of material used for main spans. The Britannia main spans contain about 7,000 pounds of iron per foot of length whereas the Saltash main spans contain 4,700 pounds of iron per foot. Thus, the Brunel work uses substantially less material.[17] A second quantitative measure is cost. This measure is less precise because the locations are different, the time of construction not the same, and the total length and span lengths are different for the approaches. Nevertheless per foot of single track, the Brunel bridge cost about half that of the Stephenson bridge. Thus the lighter work was also the cheaper.[18]

The primary reason for the large differences in iron and in cost lies in the main structural form chosen. At Britannia, the span has solid walls and a total depth (from top to bottom of the box) ranging from 27 to 30 feet; at Saltash, the span is open and the depth (distance between top tube and bottom chain) is about 62 feet at midspan. The greater depth at Saltash means that less material is needed; the solid wall at Britannia puts extra material where it is not needed. Both engineers had Telford as their model, and both believed that such long spans required a suspension bridge. Yet they both knew that the suspension form needed extra stiffening for a locomotive loading. Stephenson's practical approach to this problem was to invent a hollow box form for the railway. He saw this at first only as the stiffened deck of a suspension bridge, but detailed tests convinced him later that no cables were needed and the deck could stand alone. Brunel's daring approach was to imagine a new form in which the arch tube could stiffen the cables and where the cables could tie together the arch ends.[19] In both bridges the towers rise well above the roadway; but at Saltash their function is to connect the arch and cables, whereas at Britannia, standing free above the hollow tubes, they serve no purpose.

Finally, the Saltash span shows visually how the loads are carried: by compression down the arch and tension up the cables (figure 3.2). In the Britannia span, such a visual statement is missing; it looks equally stiff from end to end (figure 3.3). The Saltash is a highly expressive form; the Britannia hides its form in deference to a uniformity which its designer argued was suited to construction. But the justification for construction suitability lies in economy, and the Saltash, as we have seen, was less costly.

In appearance the two works could hardly be more different, considering their similarity of scale and use. A comparison of the three major visual components common to all bridges—the supports, the span, and the approaches—shows this difference. In the Britannia, the

FIGURE 3.2

The Saltash Bridge over the Tamar River near Plymouth, England, 1859, by Isambard Kingdom Brunel. The two main spans of 455 feet each are carried by a combination of tubular arch and chain cable. The structure is lighter and was less costly than the Britannia Bridge.

FIGURE 3.3

The Britannia Bridge over the Menai Straits, Wales, 1850, by Robert Stephenson. Stephenson initially planned a suspension bridge with cables, passing through the holes near the tower tops, to support the stiff wrought-iron tubes through which the trains traveled. Tests proved the tubes to be so strong that no cables were needed. The two main spans are each 460 feet. The tubes burned in 1970, and the bridge has since been rebuilt in different form.

supporting towers are purely vertical, extend well above the girders, and are given a decorative cornice. In Saltash, the towers extend only to meet the span and they have no decoration. As for the span itself, at Britannia the girders are visually solid and give no expression of structure. At Saltash the expression of structure is pronounced but ambiguous: the form is complicated by being in effect two distinct forms, the arch and the cable. The span, however, is open and all parts are clearly articulated: the horizontal deck, the vertical suspenders, and the two spanning elements, arch and cable. The abrupt change between main spans and approaches sets off the Saltash arch-cable although the visually continuous horizontal deck girders do express some integration of the many spans. At Britannia, the massive stone entrances signal a complete break between approaches and main spans, as well as emphasizing the decorative vision of this bridge as a national monument, a vision the immense sculpted lions on the approaches confirm.

The Saltash stands for the daring, experimental, even nautical verve so central to the rise of Britain as a world power; the Britannia characterizes the type of self-conscious symbol that great powers often build when their dominance is already on the wane. Saltash is a strong visual stimulant, inelegant and idiosyncratic; Britannia deadens the art of structure, despite the abstract elegance of its composition. As we shall see later, forms like the Britannia appealed to many twentieth-century designers as they struggled to come to terms with technology. But when they followed such nonstructural directions, their works, too, tended to be wasteful of material and costly to build.

There is another symbolism to these two bridges, though it resides more in the personalities of the two designers than in the physical structure of the works. For all the differences of character that had resulted in two such different bridges, and for all their almost continuous public confrontation and debate on engineering issues, Brunel and Stephenson maintained a steadfast friendship throughout their lives.

> "It is very delightful," Brunel had written after an evening spent with Stephenson in May 1846, "in the midst of our incessant personal professional contests, carried to the extreme limit of fair opposition, to meet him on a perfectly friendly footing and discuss engineering points." When Stephenson had needed his support and advice at the floating of the first huge tube of his Britannia Bridge across the Menai, Brunel had waived all his engagements and hurried north to be at his friend's side.[20]

This private friendship in the face of public rivalry seems to reflect the view that these two men had of their work, and the context into which they put it, and thereby, to express the ethic of dedication to public welfare necessary to the structural artist.

To follow the progress of structural art through the age of iron, we must turn now to France, where the greatest of all engineers in iron was beginning his career as Robert Stephenson and Isambard Kingdom Brunel were ending theirs.

CHAPTER 4

GUSTAVE EIFFEL

AND THE CRESCENT

BRIDGE

The Tower and the Industrial Fair

Just as Britain had demonstrated her national superiority with the Great Exhibition of 1851, so France in 1855 put on a Paris exposition patterned after that of her rival. A second one followed in 1867, a third in 1878, and in 1884 planning began for a fourth one to commemorate the centenary of the opening of the Etats Généraux on May 5, 1789.

The eighteenth century had ended with two transforming European revolutions, France's political revolution and Britain's industrial one. Together these events seemed to promise a boundlessly improving future, and it was this future that the industrial fairs served to portray. The 1889 fair represented, in addition, France's desire to recapture something of her eighteenth-century glory. In contrast to Britain, which in the 1880s could still consider itself the greatest nation on earth, the French felt defeated, depressed, and dishonored. Surpassed economically by Britain, and in 1870 devastated militarily by Bismarck's new Germany, France could only look back to the period before 1814, when it had been the great European power. As the end of the nineteenth century approached, that longing for greatness remained.

Georges Berger, general manager of the 1889 exposition, expressed this sense of France's desire to recapture its past glory: "We will show our sons what their fathers have accomplished in the space of a century through progress in knowledge, love of work and respect for liberty." Together, science, technology, and politics had, in Berger's view, led society to new heights. As he put it, "We will give them a view from the summit of the steep slope that has been climbed since the dark ages." Not only was the Eiffel Tower to be climbed by every Parisian visitor, as Berger imagined, but to be built it had also to climb up on itself. It was to be the perfect symbol of the new world view, its lightness of form a contrast to the dark ages. Finally, the fair was to show that "the law of progress is immortal, just as progress itself is infinite."[1]

Such was the promotional language of 1889. The tower has continuously provoked aesthetic responses—some of it in the form of fine poetry and impressive painting—because Eiffel designed it to be a beautiful object with no historic precedent prior to the Industrial Revolution.

Structure and Architecture

To the shrill criticisms of the tower as "useless . . . monstrous . . . baroque, mercantile . . . dizzily ridiculous . . . like a gigantic factory chimney,"[2] Gustave Eiffel (1832–1923) responded carefully and profoundly: "The first principle of architectural beauty is that the essential lines of a construction be determined by a perfect appropriateness to its use." He was not referring to the architecture of the past or even of his own time; this we can see immediately by his definition of "use." For Eiffel, use meant primarily the tower's ability to carry loads. "What was the main obstacle I had to overcome in designing the tower?" he continued. "Its resistance to wind, and I submit that the curves of its four piers as produced by our calculations, rising from an enormous base and narrowing toward the top, will give a great impression of strength and beauty."[3]

In designing the tower, Eiffel integrated form and function in a new way. For Eiffel, as for all structural artists, function or use was to be narrowly defined as the carrying of the large loads. Such problems of load and scale had already been experienced by Telford, Brunel, and Stephenson. Function was, therefore, not defined by human use in the sense of living, working, meeting, and worshiping. These more complex uses were and are the functions for which architects create forms. The more that loads play a role in design, the more a work approaches the category of pure structure.

The validity of this distinction in terms of function between structure and architecture depends upon another distinction between the two, that of scale. As Eiffel put it, "there is an attraction and a charm inherent in the colossal that is not subject to ordinary theories of art. . . . The tower will be the tallest edifice ever raised by man. Will it not therefore be imposing in its own way?"[4] Eiffel saw clearly that the new materials and the new structural forms defined a new art form. Large scale and narrowly defined use are thus the principles upon which structural art depend. The small scale of the private house and its complex human use make it a prototypical work of architecture; the long span of a bridge and the rise of a tower combined with their heavy loads make them prototypical of the engineer's art.

But as works of art structures must have a conscious symbolic meaning, as well as an obvious response to the function of physical loads. This, too, Eiffel recognized, as is apparent in his defense of the tower: "It seems to me that this Eiffel Tower is worthy of being treated with respect, if only because it will show that we are not simply an amusing people, but also the country of engineers and builders who are called upon all over the world to construct bridges, viaducts, train stations and the great monuments of modern industry."[5] The tower was thus, in Eiffel's mind, the great symbol of a revived France—not the flounce of the Folies Bergères but the forge of the industrial future.

Thus Eiffel described his tower by identifying the three principles of structural art: large scale, narrowly defined use, and the embodiment of social values and aesthetic ideas. Scale implies a scientific approach to form because of the great risks encountered; use implies a social ethic related to cost and utility; and, finally, the ability of a structure to express ideas implies that it is symbolic in the same sense as any other type of work of art: consciously symbolic.

All of these principles depend upon the technical skill of the designer, and the simple fact is that no contemporary structural engineer had a greater skill than Eiffel. The tower climaxed a career which was, on purely technical grounds, the most impressive anywhere. As with Telford, Stephenson, and Brunel, the permanent results of Eiffel's work are both the most visually impressive and the most technically refined structures of their age. To see these results in Eiffel's designs, we need to have a brief picture of his career and to look more closely at a few of the many spectacular structures upon which he drew for the completion of his tower.

Gustave Eiffel

Eiffel was born in Dijon on December 15, 1832, and was raised in a middle-class family. In 1852, he failed the examination for entrance into the prestigious public Ecole Polytechnique in Paris. Undeterred, he enrolled in the private Ecole Centrale des Arts et Manufactures, from which he graduated in 1855 with a degree in chemical engineering. A family feud prevented him from entering his uncle's vinegar business in Dijon, so he took a job with a firm that designed and built railway equipment.[6] It was by chance, therefore, that he landed in the great industry of the period and that his energy became directed toward its new material, iron. In 1858, he was sent to Bordeaux to build a 1600-foot-long, seven-span, cast-iron bridge across the dangerous Garonne river. His careful calculations combined with an inventive construction scheme brought the bridge to completion on schedule in 1860.

By 1867, he had left the railway firm and established himself both as a designer and as a builder with a factory for metal construction in a Parisian suburb. His business quickly grew to international proportions; by 1885, he had built hundreds of major iron structures including bridges, railway stations, exhibition halls, gas works, reservoirs, cranes, factories, and department stores. He had become France's leading engineer in iron.[7] Aside from a profitable business, however, he had designed and built a series of structures that showed his aesthetic ideas, even if the art world paid him no attention. As Le Corbusier put it years later, Eiffel "was pained by not being seen as a creator of beauty. . . . His calculations were always inspired by an admirable instinct for proportion, his goal was elegance."[8]

The 1851 Crystal Palace and the 1867 Paris Exhibition

For the 1867 fair, Eiffel was asked to design the Machinery Hall, the largest part of the immense Central Pavilion, France's version of the Crystal Palace. The contrast between the Machinery Hall and the Crystal Palace is striking, and central to a recognition of why structural art in iron reached its climax in France rather than Britain. Visually the 1867 hall could not compare to the 1851 British structure, but technically it was far more significant. For the Machinery Hall, Eiffel prepared a 110-page report on iron arch design which included one of the first full sets of computations on arch behavior.[9] This structure, the largest of its kind at the time, was 1,608 feet long and 1,266 feet wide, and was made in one huge ellipse with seven concentric galleries. The outside gallery roof carried Eiffel's arches over the hall of machines. They spanned 115 feet, and rose only 20 feet. The arches of the central nave of the Crystal Palace had only spanned 72 feet, but they had risen about 36 feet. In concept, these British semicircular arches were not structural. Rather, they reflected forms antedating the Industrial Revolution. Even in their material—wood—they were not modern.[10] Eiffel's arches, on the other hand, were flat, nearly parabolic, and of wrought iron, demonstrating visually the potential for structural art. By comparison, the Crystal Palace was as primitive in its structure as Iron Bridge. But, just as Iron Bridge had symbolized a new manufacturing process for bridges, so the Crystal Palace took on a similar meaning for buildings. Its hundreds of standardized pieces bolted together stimulated architects to try and imagine an aesthetic in iron that might compete with the accepted taste in stone. These designers could not succeed because the Crystal Palace was not structural art.

Eiffel explained years later why this was so. "The English engineers have almost entirely bypassed calculations and they fix dimensions of their members by trial and error and by experiments . . . and small-scale models." By such means Eiffel continued, "the English went ahead of us in their practice, but we have had the honor, in France, to surpass them by far in the theory and to create methods which opened up a sure path to progress, disengaged from all empiricism."[11] This is a contrast radically different from that which Samuel Smiles made between Stephenson as British and Brunel as French. Smiles had contrasted the empiricism of Stephenson to the daring of Brunel, viewing the former as more reliable and hence preferable. Eiffel, however, found French theory more reliable than British empiricism because that theory "permits exact calculations [from which come] structures which are much lighter and at the same time are stronger than those built earlier."

Eiffel's motive for theory is therefore aesthetic, economic and technical: to build structures which are lighter, cheaper, and stronger *at the same time*. He believed that the "sure path to progress" came from combining theory with practice and not in by-passing theory by trial and error and numerous tests. Eiffel did not mean that scientific theory would be the stimulus to better design; rather, he meant that calculation was essential to design because, as he put it, "at the start [of modern structural design], designers multiplied the number of load-carrying members and thus complicated their structural systems; today, on the other hand, there is the tendency to simplify them as much as possible, because the more a system is simple, the more one is sure of how the loads will be carried." Calculations, therefore, are justified only when they lead to simpler systems and lighter members. Theory has no other significance; everything is secondary to the final built object. Calculations are a means to progress, but progress itself is read in the final forms. To see the progress Eiffel made we shall look at three of his many bridges. In these are both the origins of the Paris tower and the seminal ideas for twentieth-century structural art.

Span and Tower

Between 1867 and 1869, Eiffel constructed four viaducts along the rail line between Gannat and Commentry in the Massif Central west of Vichy. Of the four, the viaduct at Rouzat (figure 4.1) is visually the most striking and accessible since the highway passes directly under as it crosses the Sioule River about 200 feet below the railway.[12] Three 200-foot-span trellis girders carry the rails, and two 200-foot-high metal towers support the girders. These were among the first high towers in iron. But even more significant than their height is their form. At the

FIGURE 4.1

The Rouzat Viaduct over the Sioule River, near Gannat, France, 1869, by Gustave Eiffel. Two 59-meter-high wrought-iron towers support three 60-meter-span trellis girders to carry a single track rail line. The towers, curving outward at the base to reduce wind loading, show the beginning of Eiffel's design style which culminated in the Eiffel Tower twenty years later.

base the towers spread out in a curve to meet masonry foundations. Here, for the first time, Eiffel used the iron towers to reflect visually the influence of the lateral wind loads.

There is only a single rail line at Rouzat and, therefore, the viaduct is both very high and very narrow. The structure is inherently weakest in the lateral direction; it is in danger of tipping sideways, especially when a train is on the structure and the winds are high. This type of danger shook the industrialized world in 1879 when the high narrow railway over the Firth of Tay in Scotland blew over in a high wind, killing all seventy-five of the people on the train that was crossing.[13] Eiffel, already fully aware of this type of problem in 1867, provided lateral stiffness on all four viaducts by shaping the vertical towers. Here is the beginning of an evolution of form that climaxed on the Champs de Mars twenty years later. Eiffel also developed a new way of constructing the girders by building them horizontally out from the high cliffs over the towers to join in the center. In this way he could avoid all scaffolding in the deep valley. This construction idea, not seen in the final form, nevertheless played a central role in Eiffel's structural art because it made the viaducts economical.

The First Crescent Bridge: Douro

In 1875, the Royal Portuguese Railway opened an international competition for the construction of a bridge over the Douro River near Oporto. The eight different designs submitted with builders' fixed prices give a summary of long-span bridge ideas developed up to 1875.[14] The shorter spans and river towers of two of the designs made them more expensive than comparable designs with longer spans. The other six designs, with roughly the same 525-foot center span, show a wide variety of forms and a wide range of prices.

The two simplest forms were priced the lowest. Of the two, Eiffel's crescent arch is undeniably the more elegant form; it was also the less expensive, being a full 31 percent below the other. The Douro competition confirmed the fact that Eiffel, at age forty-three, was the lead-

FIGURE 4.2
The Pia Maria Bridge over the Douro River, Oporto, Portugal, 1877, by Gustave Eiffel. This 160-meter-span, wrought-iron, crescent-shaped arch rises 42.5 meters at its crown. Eiffel bid his design 31 percent below the next bidder in an international design-construction competition.

ing bridge designer in Europe. It also shows that the more beautiful form coincides with the most useful structure, that is, the structure providing the required utility with the least cost. In fact, Eiffel's design has also proven to be durable: the bridge stands today in fine condition after over a century of continuous use.

Comparing Eiffel's design (figure 4.2) with the next lowest bid (figure 4.3), we note that his horizontal trellis girders are shallower because their spans between supports are less than half of those in the other design. The price Eiffel paid for shorter spans is in the four extra vertical members. The two of these over the arch are very short and therefore cost little. It was a serious defect of the competing design

FIGURE 4.3
The Pia Maria Bridge, next lowest bid design, 1875. This design requires heavier horizontal trellis girders, and the gabled arch is used only to support the girder at midspan.

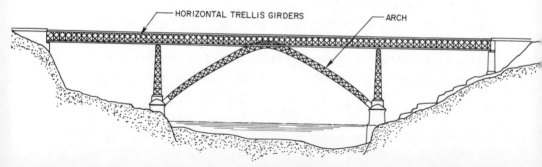

that it did not use such vertical members to reduce the girder spans over the arch. Had it done so the arch form would have changed also. In the competing design, the arch merely replaced a vertical tower at midspan; Eiffel, in contrast, designed the arch to provide a more continuous, and therefore much more efficient, support of the rail line.

But the major virtue of Eiffel's form is the use of hinged supports for the arch. These permitted the arch to be economically constructed, as we shall illustrate in the Garabit viaduct. Along with the reduced girder materials, it was this construction procedure that mainly accounted for the low cost of design. Moreover, the wide lateral spreading of Eiffel's arches in plan not only gives a greater lateral stiffness than the competing design, but also makes the crescent form visually more striking. The form gets narrower but deeper as it rises from the hinges. Such an idea is highly rational, but it is unique to Eiffel. It is a mark of his style to give three-dimensional variation to structures whose overall form is largely two dimensional. The form is handsome in pure profile (its two-dimensional aspect), but in addition it provides visual surprise and delight from different perspectives (its three-dimensional aspect).

The Second Crescent: Garabit

These two visual aspects—simple profile together with complexity as seen by changing perspective—reach a high point of expression in Eiffel's last major bridge. In late 1878, Eiffel was approached by Léon Boyer (1851–1886), a young engineer from Florac in the Massif Central. Boyer asked if Eiffel could repeat his Douro bridge at Garabit, over a far deeper valley, for the rail line from Neussargues to Marvejols, 17 kilometers south of St. Flour.[15] The state engineers had first proposed to build the rail line down into the valley and back up again, but Boyer had urged them to get Eiffel to build a high viaduct which would, Boyer estimated, save about 2 million francs. They agreed, and on June 14, 1879, Eiffel signed a contract which included the judgment that he was the most qualified engineer to do such a work.[16] This judg-

FIGURE 4.4

The Garabit Viaduct over the Truyère River, near St. Flour, France, 1884, by Gustave Eiffel. This 165-meter-span, wrought-iron crescent was the world's longest arch span when completed. The two-hinged arch is separated visually from the thin horizontal girder, unlike the Douro crescent.

ment was explicitly written in to justify not holding a competition for such a work. Almost exactly one hundred years later, the same type of judgment, this time in Switzerland, would justify the construction of a new form in prestressed concrete which would rival Eiffel's forms in technical, economic, and aesthetic quality. The intervening hundred years mark the growing maturity of the new art form announced by the wilderness Garabit and its urban counterpart, the Paris tower.

The development of Eiffel's style can be seen by comparing Garabit (figure 4.4) with Douro. In describing the Douro crescent form, Théophile Seyrig, Eiffel's engineer, wrote in 1878 that a form was sought that would be "at the same time the most graceful and the best suited to the load-carrying necessities." Moreover, by choosing the crescent form with hinges at the supports, "the calculations were markedly simplified and all those who have once made complete arch calculations know that such an advantage is not to be disdained."[17] Simplicity of calculation, graceful form, and suitability to the necessities of load, all went together in the evolution of the new crescent form. In Garabit, these ideas were extended as its higher arch was given a slightly different form and the intermediate railway supports were moved closer to the center of the arch span. This was done to improve the arch loading, while at the same time making the trellis girder spans equal on either side of the highest tower.

The most obvious difference between Douro and Garabit lies in the center of the span; whereas in the former, the horizontal trellis girder is interrupted, in the latter, Eiffel kept that girder visually continuous and structurally distinct. In part, this difference arises because at Garabit the railway is much higher above the valley than it is at Douro. The flatter Douro form leads to higher forces; therefore, dropping the arch fully below the railway as at Garabit would have increased the forces noticeably. Nevertheless, the Douro form is less satisfactory because it superimposes the arch on the girders without integrating the two visually. Any increased costs at Douro for an even flatter arch would have had no effect on the competition outcome. Douro was the best example of structural art in iron arch bridges built up to 1877; Garabit is the greatest work of structural art ever built in iron arch form and the masterpiece of Eiffel's bridge career.[18]

JOHN ROEBLING AND THE SUSPENSION BRIDGE

The first American structural artist to attract international attention, and the only nineteenth-century structural engineer after Telford to rival Eiffel, was John Augustus Roebling (1806–1869). Although a generation older than Eiffel, Roebling's career did not properly end until his son managed to complete Brooklyn Bridge just six years before Eiffel finished his tower. Roebling and Eiffel took iron in opposite directions; the former hung structures in flexible suspension, the latter framed them in rigid arches. Both initially gained international fame by creating in wilderness settings new forms for railway bridges and both ended their structural careers with unique designs in their countries' most important cities. Yet Roebling and his ideas belong to his time—that of Stephenson and Brunel—because, to a far greater extent than Eiffel, he had to struggle with form and to do it largely empirically on the basis of field experience. In this regard, he may be compared with his best-known contemporary engineer, Brunel.

Brunel and Roebling

Both Brunel and Roebling were born in 1806, and both were trained abroad: Brunel in France, Roebling in his native Germany. Both married in 1836, and by 1841 both had established major new enterprises: Brunel, the Great Western Railway, and Roebling, a wire rope manufacturing plant. Both completed world famous railway bridges in the 1850s, and the greatest spanning bridge design of each was built posthumously. Both men proposed grand schemes for immense works, based on elegant, detailed, and carefully thought out plans. None of their structures failed and the greatest of these still serve their intended purposes.

But similar as the two men were, their differences are of even greater significance. Brunel, rising rapidly to prominence, was a national figure by 1841, at which time Roebling was still an unknown state employee with not a single design realized. Brunel designed a staggering variety of structures while promoting vast projects in rail lines, giant ships, and terminals; Roebling, by contrast, had as early as 1826 set his design imagination on one type of structure only, and everything he subsequently did was directed toward that single-minded goal. In personality, Brunel was outwardly ebullient but inwardly pessimistic; Roebling appeared always to be the stolid, glowering German, whereas inwardly he seethed with an almost inchoate romantic idealism. Brunel followed a famous engineering father; Roebling fathered a remarkable engineering son. Brunel's structures, for all their imaginative flair, characterize the end of an era both in the choice of form and in the dominance of Great Britain. Roebling's works, on the other hand, signaled the beginning of a clear understanding of suspension bridge behavior and the advent of the United States as a technological and political power.

But of all the contrasts, the most central lies in their ideas on structural design as an art form. Roebling consciously wrote about his structures from an aesthetic point of view, as did Telford and Eiffel. Possibly Brunel, had he lived as long as Roebling, might also have reflected on appearance and symbolism, but his style as seen in the works themselves was not as developed as Roebling's, and would have given him less to draw upon for such ideas. By the end of Brunel's life, the great ships overwhelmed his imagination, leaving Saltash in their wake. In the last years of his life, Roebling had his wire rope factory so well organized that he could spend his time at bridge sites concentrating on design and construction. Brunel's nonstructural businesses submerged his talent for structural design, whereas Roebling's powerful design motive disciplined his business ventures.

The Immigrant Engineer

Roebling was born in Mühlhausen, midway between Göttingen and Erfurt, in the year Napoleon defeated the Prussians at nearby Jena. He grew up in a middle-class family, and showed, early, a talent for mathematics, as well as a restless independence. His studies concluded in 1826, when he received an engineer's diploma from the Royal Polytechnical Institute in Berlin, founded only sixteen years earlier. Roebling was as well educated in engineering as anyone of his generation, and had far more formal training than nearly all of his British or American contemporaries.

After a few years in the Westphalian road service, he became convinced that his future lay elsewhere. On May 11, 1831, following the unsuccessful 1830 revolution in Europe and subsequent repressions, Roebling with his brother and a small band of German emigrants left Mühlhausen and headed for America. They arrived in Philadelphia on August 6 and after several months founded a German farming community near Pittsburgh, calling it Saxonburg. John Roebling was the leader, but for him farming was only a means to the end of practicing his profession of bridge design.

In 1837, Roebling became an American citizen. Bored with farming, he took a job as an engineer for the state of Pennsylvania, building dams and locks, and surveying line for a prospective railroad route. He soon became principal assistant to the chief engineer of the state. At Johnstown, Pennsylvania, Roebling became familiar with the newly constructed Portage Railroad, where long canal boats were hauled up mountains by hemp ropes. He successfully replaced hemp with iron wire rope and, in the summer of 1841, he established a factory for wire rope at Saxonburg.

Having won an 1844 competition, Roebling built his first suspension bridge, which carried a canal over the Allegheny River. By 1849, when he moved his factory to Trenton, New Jersey, he was a success at both factory production and bridge building. Roebling's first suspension bridge for a roadway was built in Pittsburgh, over the Monongahela River in 1845. His next major works were the 821-foot-span Niagara Falls rail and road suspension bridge completed in 1855, and the Cincinnati suspension bridge, begun in 1856, which was interrupted by the Civil War and eventually completed in 1866.

In March of 1857, Roebling wrote a letter to Horace Greeley, published in the *Tribune,* announcing his intention to build a bridge over the East River. Greeley himself had proposed a bridge in the *Tribune* as early as 1849. In April of 1867, a charter was finally granted by the New York legislature, and in September of that year Roebling presented his plan in Brooklyn. The statement with which his written proposal began is perhaps his most noted; it claims, among other things, that "the great towers . . . will be ranked as national monuments. . . . As a great work of art, and a successful specimen of advanced bridge engineering, this structure will forever testify to the energy, enterprise, and wealth of that community which shall secure its erection."[1]

In February of 1869, Roebling presented his plans to a consulting board that included the president of the newly reconstituted American Society of Civil Engineers, William Jarvis McAlpine, and Henry Latrobe, son and namesake of the architect chosen by Thomas Jefferson to rebuild Washington, D.C., after its burning by the British in 1812. On June 28, 1869, Roebling's foot was crushed by a ferry boat while he was surveying for the bridge, and he died of lockjaw on July 22. His eldest son, Washington A. Roebling, became chief engineer for the bridge at age thirty-two.

Roebling at the Limit of Structure

Roebling's last three major designs—those at Niagara, Cincinnati, and Brooklyn—were each as close to the limit of scale as any other works in the nineteenth century. In other words, like Telford's Menai Bridge, they were about as light as possible, yet safe and enduring. We shall begin by considering the first of those three designs—and the only one not still standing—the Niagara River Railway suspension bridge (figure 5.1).

In his report on the bridge, which was published in Great Britain, Roebling noted that the total cost was under £80,000 and made the startling claim that "the same object accomplished in Europe would have cost one million pounds, without serving a better purpose or insuring greater safety."[2] This stupendous difference, a factor of over ten,

---

FIGURE 5.1

The Niagara River Bridge near Niagara Falls, 1855, by John A. Roebling. This 821-foot-span, iron-wire, rope suspension bridge carried a single track railroad on its upper level and a carriageway on the lower level. Its numerous stays in various directions reflect Roebling's empirical efforts to prevent oscillations. This was the only major suspension bridge to carry successfully a railroad for an extended period. It was removed in 1897.

is not without justification when the cost of this bridge is compared to the Britannia Bridge completed just six years earlier.[3]

Roebling further stated that the total weight of the bridge was less than 1,000 tons.[4] If all this is taken to be the weight between towers (a high estimate), then the weight per foot would be 2,430 pounds compared to 7,000 pounds at Britannia, even for its much shorter spans. Thus, Roebling's design is considerably cheaper and lighter than Britannia. Yet, Roebling claimed that his structure did not sink under loads any more than did the tubular bridge form; specifically he stated that his bridge was as stiff as Stephenson's Conway Bridge.[5]

The price Roebling paid for this lightness and economy lay in the necessity to use wood in the deck and in the restriction of locomotive speed to 3 miles per hour. Still, the Niagara Bridge confounded nearly all engineering judgment of the age, which held that suspension bridges could never sustain railway traffic. For 42 years the bridge served well, although it needed much maintenance. A few more thousand dollars put into the initial work would have saved much of that maintenance cost later on.[6] The bridge was removed when railroad loadings so increased as to make it no longer economical to maintain.

The Niagara Bridge was a technical tour de force never again to be repeated. It showed Roebling's talent for successfully completing a work of huge proportions with a minimum of resources. As he put it himself, he was "in a country where the engineer's task is to make the most out of the least."[7] But although the Niagara Bridge was a technical triumph, it was not an aesthetic masterpiece. It was, however, an essential proving ground for Roebling's last two major works because it showed him just how far he dared go. When the bridge was nearing completion, he got word that the Wheeling bridge of his principal rival, Charles Ellet (1810–1862), had blown down in a wind storm. Failure of this 1,010-foot span, then the longest in the world, dramatized the fact that, as Roebling put it, "a number of such fairy creations are still hovering about the country, only waiting for a rough blow to be demolished."[8]

However, Roebling himself was not so sure how light he could make the Niagara Bridge without exceeding its limits; upon hearing of the Wheeling failure, he immediately wrote his chief engineer in Trenton, "I shall want for this bridge at least another coil of rope . . . *as soon as you possibly can do it,* send it by Rail Road. . . . I am anxious however to secure the new floor well by stays."[9] The italics are Roebling's. He was, as usual, at the construction site to follow the entire field operation.

The profile of the bridge shows all sorts of stays tied between the bridge deck and the floor of the valley. This strange array of cables gives the bridge an uncertain look. It visually expresses the empirical nature of the structure, having a kind of reverse support. Roebling had reached the limit and now he could safely, in his own mind, go to longer spans, in somewhat less harsh environments, and dedicated to the supreme goal of structural engineers—to unite beauty and utility in urban public works.

The Ohio River Bridge

In 1846 Roebling had proposed a bridge over the Ohio River at Cincinnati with two 788-foot suspension spans connected at mid-river by a gigantic stone pier 200 feet high.[10] Ten years later, and after the successful completion of the Niagara Bridge, Roebling began construction of a revised Cincinnati design crossing the river in one 1,057-foot suspension span, the longest in the world (figure 5.2). The two other bridges over 1,000 feet in span (neither of Roebling's design)—the one at Wheeling and the 1851 Niagara River carriageway suspension bridge—were both destroyed in wind storms.[11]

It was in his final report to the bridge directors in 1867 that Roebling for the first time in a more coherent way let his ideals on aesthetics and symbolism flow into his technical writing. His Niagara Bridge had stood up against all predictions of failure, his Ohio River design was now completed, and his greatest design had suddenly become politically possible thanks to the terrible ice blockages during the winter of 1866–67 in the East River between Manhattan and Brooklyn. Roebling was now internationally recognized as America's foremost bridge designer. The Cincinnati Bridge report would be, as it sadly turned out, his valedictory on structural art.[12]

FIGURE 5.2

The Cincinnati Bridge over the Ohio River, 1866, by John A. Roebling. When this 1057-foot-span, iron-wire, cable suspension structure was completed it was the longest-spanning bridge in the world. Roebling's mature style shows here in the impressive stone towers and the light, suspended span with stays radiating from the tower tops. This was the prototype for his Brooklyn Bridge design.

Roebling's Ideals

Woven into the Cincinnati report are Roebling's ideals for structural design, and supporting those a set of ideals for mid-nineteenth-century American society. In his general remarks, Roebling announced "that nation which attains to the highest perfection in its skillful production and application to the various arts of life, will rank also highest in the scale of social advancement and political power." He proclaimed technology as the basis for social welfare and not merely for material welfare for, as he continued, "the material forms the basis of the mental and the spiritual; without it the mind may conceive, but cannot execute."[13]

However naive Roebling's connection between material and spiritual may sound, it is the fundamental premise for his work and cannot be dismissed, the more so because the material basis becomes spiritual through an ethic central to structural art. Roebling immediately defined this ethic with the statement that "where strength is to be combined with lightness and elegance, nature never wastes heavy cumbrous masses." It is an ethic of using the least resources and it is expressed, for Roebling, by "the architects of the Middle Ages [who] fully illustrated this fact by their beautiful buttresses and flying arches, combinations of great strength and stability, executed with the least amount of material." It is the visual expression of lightness and strength which can lead to works of art, but there must also be an integration of form. In suspension bridges with a thin, spanning deck structure, Roebling argued, "the elevation of the bridge floor would be too light in appearance, as compared to the massiveness of the towers." But when diagonal stays and floor trusses are added, then "the whole has a pleasing effect, and at the same time presents strong and reassuring proportions, which inspire confidence."[14] In other words, lightness alone is not sufficient for appearance; the two major parts, tower and deck, must be related to one another by stays to give an overall impression of both unity and confidence. Had this judgment been seriously contemplated sixty years later, engineers could have avoided a whole series of faulty suspension bridge designs culminating in the incredible thinness of the deck in the first Tacoma Narrows Suspension Bridge, which collapsed in 1940.

Roebling proceeded to discuss the imposing stone towers, which he noted should not be highly ornamental but rather "of simplicity, massiveness, and strength." He then announced a major ideal. "Public works should educate public taste. . . . In the erection of public edifices, therefore, some expense may and ought to be incurred in order to satisfy the artistic aspirations of a young and growing community." This may seem, in our age, to be a call for expensive ornament, but Roebling was referring to expense in design thinking rather than in construction materials. He made this clear in describing his tower design: "the mass is not solid but divided into two parts . . . the central projecting part forming a buttress. This feature of buttresses is preserved throughout the whole height, not only on account of appearance, but also for the sake of strength, to save material, and to reduce the weight upon the foundation." His design attains its visual power by combining use (reduced materials) and beauty (buttress form), and as such follows the lead, as Roebling himself emphasized, of "medieval architecture [which] is distinguished for its remarkable lightness and great strength at the same time, owing to the judicious use of the buttress."[15]

How utterly different is this reaction to the Gothic from the pious facade-making that dominated so much of the so-called Gothic revival of the same period. Much of the Gothic revival merely consisted of building lovely reminders of an imagined past as a protest against the industrial world. Roebling, by contrast, was able to imagine how new spiritual ideals might arise from the industrial world. For him, the Gothic was not a form to copy, but a design ideal to study.[16] He saw in the Gothic the ethic of conservation which underlay the aesthetic of structural art.

Once again, this time in describing the two cables themselves, Roebling observed that wrapping the seven strands (each with 740 wires) into each of the cables "gives them the appearance of solid cylinders; it has a pleasing effect, and its solid aspect inspires confidence."[17] Finally, in summarizing his completed work, Roebling announced again a general ideal for design: "the present age is emphatically an age of usefulness. The useful goes before the ornamental. At the time when Grecian culture was shaping the human mind, the reverse was the accepted rule; first the ornamental, then the useful." He concluded from this contrast that "the general interests of mankind are more promoted by the present than it was by the ancient maxim."[18] Here is the midcentury contrast between the structural ideal and the architectural fashion. While Roebling was studying the making of iron wire and the effects of wind on suspension structures, his architectural colleagues were traveling to Greece to copy down the old forms for use in new facades.

Much of the protest against technology then and now sees in it only a crass materialism. This is why Roebling took the time to defend his age and to proclaim the virtues of industry. "No matter what may be charged against the material tendencies of the present age, it is through material advancements alone that a higher culture of the masses can be attained." For Roebling, the construction of expensive opera houses, palaces, banks, and so on, will never bring the "higher culture of the masses" that the building of the railroad will. The one merely uses up materials to express wealth, whereas the other allows "the works of industry [to] be soon broadcast over the surface of the earth, [so that] want will disappear."[19]

Of course, as words alone these are indistinguishable from the loud praises so often sung in Roebling's time for the glories of technology. They only stand out because of Roebling's works. When words and works go together, each is enriched by the other. Roebling was building not just for a profit; indeed it is unlikely that he made much money from his bridges. Nor was he writing just for publicity. He did both building and writing to express his ideals for society: that the spirit can be uplifted by understanding technology and by creating out of it superior works that people can afford, that they can openly use, and that they can aesthetically enjoy. That is the meaning of technology, and that is the want to be satisfied: not just material needs but "a higher spiritual culture."[20]

This view allowed Roebling to appreciate both the French Gothic and British industrialized iron. With respect to the latter, he stated that "Telford's successful accomplishment of the old Menai suspension bridge . . . was the great feat of those days" and that it was "to the genius of the late Robert Stephenson [that] we owe the tubular bridge, while it was reserved for the ingenuity of Brunel, Jun. to illustrate an apparent perfection by the construction of the Saltash Bridge." However, he continues, "these have now ceased to serve us as models."[21] Roebling's reaction to the great works of the recent past is that found in all artists of the front rank. These artists are stimulated by, and learn from, their antecedents, but in their mature works they are on their own. At the time of his Cincinnati report, Roebling had reached his full stature. Four months later he submitted his plans for the proposed East River Bridge, and with that design his career ended. Yet, when completed in 1883, the Brooklyn Bridge (figure 5.3) would open up a new period in structural engineering, and it would symbolize, along with Eiffel's tower, a new period in history—a period in which the technological world was to become the central dominating aspect of human life.

FIGURE 5.3

The Brooklyn Bridge as seen from the central elevated walkway. The vertical suspenders and the diagonal stays create a mesh of steel through which pedestrians can see changing perspectives of the city as they walk above the traffic and between the civic centers of Manhattan and Brooklyn.

THE BRIDGE AND
THE TOWER

The period between the Franco-Prussian War and the turn of the century—the climax of the eighteenth-century Enlightenment, to some historians—produced a series of visible and permanent symbols that more than ever before stretched structure to its limits. Among them, the Eiffel Tower and the Brooklyn Bridge are the most obvious, but there are others, including the Washington Monument, the Garabit Viaduct, the Eads Bridge, the Firth of Forth Bridge, and the first skyscrapers of Chicago. These symbols all serve to characterize their age. They stand for certain realities of modern life, and symbolize an artistic as well as a rationalistic vision of the technological world.

Yet the symbolic nature of these structures has been misunderstood by most twentieth-century writers. These writers have looked at designed objects and called them products of science, they have looked at the works of trained engineers and called them architecture, they have looked at structure and called it machine art.

To correct this view, we must understand, first, that the tower and the bridge are firmly rooted in the physical and social reality of Parisian and New York soil—both literally, in their triumph over the muck of the Seine and East River, and figuratively in their conflict with French artistic reactionaries and American urban bribery. Their significance cannot be abstracted from these realities. These two works have stood while millions upon millions of people have walked delightedly within their structure or have ridden through them, viewing the continuously changing city patterns through webbings of metal.

Climax and Enlightenment

The twentieth-century misunderstandings of structural art stem, to some extent, from the ideals of the eighteenth-century Enlightenment. The Enlightenment had expressed a faith in the gradual progress of science, education, and reform.[1] By the 1880s these ideals had so permeated Western society that works of technology were incorrectly seen as flowing from scientific discovery. Moreover, it was assumed that the vastly expanded knowledge acquired through education in the scientific method would so enshrine reason above emotion that politics would be reformed along lines of peace, prosperity, and justice. In this vision, machinery played a pivotal role, as both the working physical model of science and the central image for a rational, efficient, and unarguably fair society.

The tower and the bridge seemed to embody those Enlightenment ideals. Moreover, both Eiffel and Roebling talked about science; they themselves had the best of educations; and at least Roebling saw his works as promises for a new utopia. Yet, when we look at the writings of those engineers beginning with Telford, we detect another set of ideals. These ideals place building over discovery, and feeling alongside of reason; they reflect a deep reverence for changeless laws of wind and gravity and the persistent necessity to deal with political facts. In short, these structural artists were seeking to combine passion and reason in order to create new forms out of the new material of the Industrial Revolution.

Experience with, and a knowledge of, the political realities was in every way crucial to structural engineers. Whereas machine engineers could invent and produce so long as some private financier would listen, structural engineers could do nothing without direct political activity. Legislatures were, if not always the financiers, at least the police and the judges. Telford, Eiffel, Roebling, and the rest had to know intimately how political decisions came about and how civic leaders thought. Moreover, they and their followers in the twentieth century had a hearty distrust of science-oriented academic engineering. This was so because for the structural artists knowledge is built primarily upon experience with specific constructed objects, and only secondarily upon theoretical generalizations. Their theories came from generalizing common traits found in completed structures; they did not create their structures by finding particular applications for general theories.

Roebling, Eiffel, and all later structural artists believed firmly in scientific education; they did not make the mistake of the British in so denigrating academic research as to be blinded to its constructive role in training engineers.[2] But as much as Eiffel praised French theory, he did not wait for a formalization of the mathematics of arches; nor did Roebling wait for a metallurgical determination of the properties of drawn iron wires. When academic research resulted in some new idea, they were alive to its possibilities; but their designs cannot be explained by reference to such research.

Finally, all structural artists agreed that their works had beauty and that they were obliged to think aesthetically. They did not have any special vocabulary for expressing their aesthetic ideals; often they used the word architectural to mean visual or artistic. Moreover, before the twentieth century, structural artists frequently resorted to some decoration, as a bow to the architectural fashions of their day. But their designs were rapidly shedding such anachronisms. In the Brooklyn Bridge, Roebling decidedly treated the entire work as one unified engineering form of which every detail came from his own pen. There was no aesthetic collaboration at all in his works. Eiffel's tower is more complex because there are decorative features which he requested his architect to install on the bare form. But, in discussing his design, Eiffel never referred to those features; he argued the tower's aesthetics solely on the basis of its pure engineering form. And it is clear that it is in its engineering form that the art of the tower lies. Without its decorative arches and arcades, the tower would still be one of the two greatest works of structural art of its period—even though some people would undoubtedly be appalled at its pure form.

To some, this hypothetical tower with its ornament removed, might seem too simple and crude to be a work of art; it might seem to be a mere reflection of scientific laws. The Brooklyn Bridge—its towers in particular so thoroughly condemned by the critic Montgomery Schuyler—might also seem too primitive, too much a work of empirical applied science, to contain all the complexity of design in a Rodin statue, for example, or a Cézanne landscape. Therefore, we need to look carefully, and with as little technical jargon as possible, into why both the tower and the bridge are as sophisticated, complex, and personal as any sculpture or painting of the period. We must go to the heart of structural form.

Function Follows Form

The first principle of structural art is that the form controls the forces. In general terms, this means that function follows form and not the reverse, which had been so appealing as a principle to writers on building in the nineteenth century. Specifically for the Eiffel Tower this means that the loads of wind and weight are dependent upon the designer's choice of form, and that even for the same load the forces within the structure depend upon that form.

The blowing force of the wind is, of course, a scientific fact to be discovered, but the actual pressure on the structure is a combination of that blowing force and the area of the metal surface. If the tower were widened near the top, the horizontal force due to wind would be larger and the danger of tipping over greater. Moreover, forces high up are more dangerous than the ones low down. Thus a form whose exposed surface decreases as it rises will have its wind forces reduced. Each change in form, therefore, changes the load, and it is the load (the "action" in Newton's law) which causes forces in the metal pieces and on the foundations beneath the ground (the "reactions" in Newton's law).

But that is not all. The forces also depend upon the form in a different way. If the legs of the tower spread, its resistance to wind load increases; that is, for the same wind load, the size of the forces on the metal will be less in direct ratio to the spreading. It is harder to push over someone whose legs are spread in the direction of the push. Thus, form changes both actions and reactions, and the Eiffel Tower, by spreading at its base, reduces the forces both in the metal pieces above ground and in the foundations below.[3]

If all of these factors could be accurately calculated, then could we not rationally determine a single optimum form for the wind? Those people who see the engineer as applied scientist would claim that such automatic results preclude aesthetic choice and, with Kant, would say that useful objects can only be right or consistent, not beautiful. But judging a form "right" requires some measure against which to compare different forms and by which to identify the right one. This would be most obviously the amount of iron required. However, the undecorated tower cannot be reduced to mere iron because its foundations require masonry, which is also crucial to rightness. If the legs of the tower are spread wider, the vertical reactions are less and hence less masonry is needed. But increasing the spread increases both the amount of metal required to connect the legs and also the amount of surface against which the wind acts. These factors all interact to increase the complexity of the problem. As this example makes clear, we cannot readily devise a measure of "rightness." There are always at least two different materials in any such structure—metal and masonry—and thus, in principle, no single measure of rightness can be devised on the basis of minimum materials. Moreover, the above arguments derive from wind loads only; but there are always gravity loads as well, which further complicate any attempt to find a basic definition of rightness.

The principle of "function follows form" therefore means that there is no absolute scientific basis for judging the correctness of any form. If the Eiffel Tower were only 10 meters high, and not 300 meters, then wind would be irrelevant to the design and only gravity would control it. In that case, it might be possible to establish a basis for correctness but such a small scale puts the object out of the range of structural art. Engineers are not needed and the principles of structural art are inapplicable.

At the scale of structural art there is, therefore, more than one material and more than one load. We may still ask, cannot these be reduced to some single measure? To begin with the materials, we may postulate that the single measure could be cost and that the cheapest—rather than, for example, the lightest—structure would be the most correct.

The Uncertainty of Cost

If metal and masonry are given fixed prices, then, as the form changes the relative quantities of materials used, it is possible that one form will emerge as the least expensive and hence (according to the measure of cost) the most correct. But it is in principle impossible to determine the least expensive design because cost is a social measure and not a scientific one. Cost depends not upon some laws of nature but rather upon patterns in society; it depends upon time and place. By contrast, the quantities of materials can be found simply by measuring the dimensions of the structure. Therefore, these quantities are scientific in the same sense that properties of water are scientific, inasmuch as they can be accurately predicted by anyone anywhere at any time. It is always possible to say that certain types of designs will be very costly compared to other types, but it is never possible to say that one design will be the cheapest regardless of its social setting. Of the many related reasons for the uncertainty in cost, two will illustrate the idea: labor costs and contractor's bidding.

Labor costs vary from place to place because of supply and demand. Even where the hourly wages are rigidly standardized by central law or by union power, the actual labor cost of putting metal pieces together in the field will still vary enormously. This is so because the same number of people working in different places are productive to different degrees, depending on various factors, including the cultural traditions they bring to their work. This is even true in machine production in factories,[4] and it is much more obviously the case for the building of structures in the field.

Uncertainty in cost also arises when, as is usually the case, there are competitive bids for construction. It is impossible to predict what the lowest bid will be. As the scale of the structure increases, so does the uncertainty of this prediction. Where different designs are competitively bid for the same work, it is possible to proclaim after the fact that one design was the cheapest, but it is in principle impossible to predict ahead of time which one that will be. The bid will be heavily conditioned by the regional economic conditions characterized by the degree to which contractors are busy. In other words, whether bids are high or low depends upon whether the contractors are "hungry" or "well fed." Cost, therefore, cannot be used in structural engineering as a means for predicting an optimum design.

As these examples show, cost is uncertain. It is not, however, mere guesswork. Telford, Eiffel, and Roebling all developed their forms under the stimulus of winning competitions in which their designs were cheapest. But they did not win every competition they entered, and a few of their works cost far more than they themselves estimated.[5]

Often it is argued that innovative ideas will cost more when first put into practice and only with time will come down in price. However, new ideas in structure almost always come along with competitive bids. Telford's Bonar bridge, Eiffel's Douro, and Roebling's Niagara were all the least expensive proposals, and we shall see this trend continue into the twentieth century. The impetus for new form comes from the need to create inexpensive structures, and this empirical fact leads to the second principle of structural art: minimum cost (economy) is an essential discipline for the creation of structural art. Economy stimulates creativity. Without the discipline of cost there can be no structural art.

Economy and Creativity

Every major artist we shall discuss in this book worked under conditions of extreme economy. Where some of their fellow designers such as Stephenson at the Britannia Bridge were given extra budgets for ornament or "architectural effects" the resulting structures are inferior as structural art. This principle does not mean that all works of structural art were the cheapest possible solutions to the problem posed, but it does mean that every new form in the two-century history of structural art has arisen under constraints that did not permit added-on elements of cost intended for "beauty."

The Eiffel Tower was probably the least expensive solution proposed for the 1889 fair. There was no cost competition, so no one can ever be sure. But all the ideas for form which reached a climax in the tower were worked out in Eiffel's viaducts, and these were designed under strict constraints of economy. For example, Eiffel's first crescent arch bridge, the Douro, was dramatically cheaper than all its international competitors. The same line of development explains the Brooklyn Bridge, which could not have been designed by Roebling without the formative experiences of his numerous suspension aqueducts and bridges, culminating in the Niagara structure. Nearly everything Roebling had done up to the Civil War was built only because it was the least expensive solution that its owners could find.

These two principles of form and economy go together with a third one pertaining more directly to aesthetics and art: that of the single designer's personality being central to his completed works. Up to this point, we have consistently credited work discussed to a single designer, and yet we know that many people worked on each of these large structures. In some cases, these people even worked on design. Are not these large works, then, the product of a team of collaborators? Is it not inaccurate to say that Eiffel designed the tower, when others did most of the design work? The answer to this question is crucial to the case for structural art, because in all other art forms (but not in all other forms of technology) we can unhesitatingly credit each of the greatest works to one single artist.

Structural Art and the Artist

The question of who really designed the Eiffel Tower has been the object of serious debate. The facts are well documented. On June 6, 1884, Maurice Koechlin (1856–1946), a young Swiss engineer in Eiffel's employ, sketched a proposed 300-meter tower for the 1889 fair. On May 20, 1885, Eiffel presented this idea publicly to the Society of French Civil Engineers. Eiffel himself was to credit Koechlin with the preliminary ideas for design.[6] However, in a compact 1949 history of civil engineering written by Hans Straub, the Swiss engineer, Koechlin is called the actual designer of the Eiffel Tower.[7] Koechlin gave the original 1884 sketch to his alma mater, the Federal Technological Institute in Zurich, where it remains on display.

We could find many examples parallel to this, both in Eiffel's works and in those of other structural artists, all of whom had talented employees who were capable of doing designs on their own. It is, therefore, of no small value to pursue the case of Koechlin in some detail, to show conclusively that Eiffel, and not his chief office engineer, was the true creator of the new forms in iron for which succeeding generations have regularly credited him. First of all, we may ask what kind of a designer Koechlin was. Was he capable of the tower design? Our answer cannot be fully satisfactory because there has been no detailed study of his works, but we can at least try to show whether Koechlin's long career gives any other evidence to support the contention that he had the independence of vision to create such a tower.

Koechlin studied in Zurich under Carl Culmann, about whom we shall have more to say later, and graduated in 1877. For two years he worked for a railway company in Paris, and in 1879 he joined the Eiffel firm, where he remained until the late 1930s. He was quickly made chief of the structural section, so that by 1880 he was directing the calculations for the Garabit. He was not with Eiffel at the time of the Douro design, so he could have had nothing to do with the crescent form development. Neither he nor anyone has claimed that he was the designer of any Eiffel work prior to the tower. It appears that in all cases of works during the 1880s he ran the office in which all the calculations were made.

Following the completion of the tower and Eiffel's subsequent retirement from the firm, Koechlin remained and must have then assumed more responsibility for the concepts of succeeding structures. Yet there is no evidence after 1889 of any designs similar to the tower, or of any further development of the forms produced in the 1880s. In short, the firm appears to have produced no structural art after the tower, even though Koechlin remained for another half century. This does not prove that Koechlin did not design the tower, but it does not help make the case that he did. Without Eiffel the firm did not create structural art.

Moreover, with each of Eiffel's major developments there is a different name: Nordling worked with him at Rouzat,[8] Seyrig at Douro, and Koechlin on the tower. Little if anything has been written on Nordling's other designs. Seyrig left Eiffel's firm shortly after the Douro design, and competed with him on competitions in the early 1880s. Seyrig's independent designs show significant differences from Eiffel's and do not indicate that he was a front rank artist.[9] The common factor in all of Eiffel's major works is Eiffel himself and, while he gave credit to his associates, he also described the development of the ideas as his own.

In 1900, Eiffel described the origins of the tower as leading directly from Rouzat to Garabit, and finally to a new system of higher towers in which the four legs are spread more widely and made to stand without connections to each other near the base.[10] There is no question of crediting anyone else with these developments; it is clear from Eiffel's writing that they resulted from his own ideas; and those ideas explain the form of the tower. Therefore, when Eiffel credits Koechlin with the design of the tower, what he means is that Koechlin took his (Eiffel's) own ideas and applied them to the well-known problem of a 1,000-foot-high tower (already proposed in England by Trevethick in 1832, and in America by Clarke, Reeves and Co. in 1874). Koechlin did the detailed work, but Eiffel had had the idea, had already developed the forms, and had the experience to direct the entire project, as well as the personality to achieve the final result.

There are many examples of great artists early in their careers working for other great artists and doing designs which sometimes are difficult to attribute to one or the other. But the question of who is an artist is eventually settled by what the younger person does later and on his own.[11] Koechlin was a distinguished engineer, but he was not a structural artist.[12]

The Eiffel–Koechlin relationship suggests, in answer to our earlier question, that a work of structural art comes from the mind of a single artist. It would be premature to expand upon that idea before discussing the history of this art form since the Eiffel Tower. Still, several preliminary ideas, already suggested by the bridge and the tower, should be reviewed briefly before moving to a discussion of the works of the twentieth century. These ideas have to do with possible misunderstandings about function and form, about economy and creativity, and about personality and art.

Preliminary Ideas on Structural Art

Eiffel said that the tower's function was to resist the wind loads. But he could have designed a form, even at that height, whose function was different. The world's tallest structure before the tower replaced it was the 1884 Washington Monument, a monument that has a form *not* influenced by wind loads. The Washington structure is a solid masonry obelisk, 555-feet high, with a hollowed core for access. With its thick stone walls, the monument is physically what it appears to be visually, a solid heavy shaft, whose function is to carry its own dead weight vertically into the ground. The highest winds ever recorded in the region have no influence on the dimensions of a structure with a form such as this, a solid form that defines its dead weight function.[13] When we come to skyscrapers we shall see how this question of form will control the manner in which the wind and the weight enter into the design.

Turning next to the idea of economy, it is important to reiterate that this essential constraint applies to overall cost, and not just to any one of the individual components of cost—design, construction, and maintenance. Too often these are separately funded and hence the overall cost may be confused with only one or two of these essential elements. It is often true that a substantial outlay for design will result in such a reduction in the other two costs as to permit a lower overall cost. The extraordinary care that Telford lavished on his designs was directly responsible for the sound performance of his works both as inexpensive constructions and as durable monuments. Roebling too worked with meticulous care, and his designs included detailed drawings of construction methods. Eiffel had over five thousand drawings made of all the parts of the tower, and this great preconstruction expense literally made possible the smooth and extraordinarily swift building sequence.

As we shall later discuss in more detail, twentieth-century practice has tended to separate design from construction to such an extent that the cost of design is often a determining factor in the choice of form. What people often fail to realize is that inexpensive construction is not the inevitable result of cheap design. Design normally costs well below 10 percent of construction on the relatively large scale works of structural art. Therefore, a 100 percent increase in design cost could easily be justified by a 10 percent saving in construction cost. This is especially the case when the designer thinks through the construction sequence to fit it to design ideas. Eiffel's use of hinges in the Garabit arch not only controlled the forces but also simplified construction, by permitting adjustments as the arches were suspended from the banks. Roebling's cable-spinning method made his bridges both better designed and cheaper to build. His method was so sound that although developed in the 1840s for small aqueducts, it was used in the 1980s for the world's largest span over the Humber in Britain. Creativity is therefore related to low overall cost, and that cost sometimes requires higher than average design expenses. Clear thought in concept will always benefit economy in construction.

Finally, structural artists have usually done their best works without any aesthetic collaboration on design. However, these artists do on occasion work with other artists, and the collaborative results can sometimes be of high quality. In discussing skyscrapers, we shall find such collaboration between architect and structural engineer. It is usually possible to argue that one or the other makes the form; of interest to us here are those cases in which engineers rather than architects have designed new forms for tall buildings. In such cases, the engineer's ideas were so strong that the collaborating architect chose to use them directly as primary visual material. Yet other cases of engineers creating new forms for tall buildings involved not collaboration but rather an engineer becoming drawn to building design to such an extent that he began to act as architect and engineer together. Both patterns were evident in Chicago, where the skyscraper took its earliest structural form.

PART II

The New Age of Steel and Concrete

CHAPTER 7

JENNEY, ROOT, AND THE FIRST CHICAGO SCHOOL

The Office Tower

In the 1880s there arose in Chicago and elsewhere a large number of office buildings of ten to sixteen stories, which at the time seemed so high that the buildings acquired the name skyscrapers. But while the new height of these nineteenth-century buildings reflected the new technical, economic, and aesthetic conditions of the time, they were not yet of a scale to carry structure to its limits and thus to qualify as structural art. These buildings did stimulate architects and writers to think about city design in the light of these new conditions.

The new technical conditions were metal beams and columns supported by reinforced concrete foundations; the economic factors involved the rapidly increasing bureaucratization of business, which lead to an explosion in office space within the city; and the aesthetic conditions are characterized by the ideas of the French architectural theorist, Eugène Viollet-le-Duc (1814–1879). It is necessary to explore each of these conditions with respect to Chicago building in the 1880s because it is here that much of the writing about modern engineering and architecture starts. Also, several clarifications are in order, as discussions of these buildings have often confused structural art with architectural art.

The new metal and concrete techniques used in the Chicago skyscrapers laid the engineering basis for later uses at much greater scales; but for 16-story buildings the engineering stimulus was too slight to call forth any major imaginative structural art. As is the case in architecture, the need for light, for usable space, and for rentable amenities took priority over the structure. The studies for opening up the exterior walls were more significant than those for supporting it.

The aesthetic ideas of Viollet-le-Duc came to Chicago through the publication of his *Entretiens (Lectures)* in 1863 and 1872 and their translations into English in 1875 and 1881. The timing was uncanny and the influence profound. Viollet-le-Duc had developed a theory of building which emphasized the importance of construction and structure to architectural expression. His theory arose out of his extensive studies in Gothic architecture. What made him of such influence was his application of the theory to nineteenth-century building, transmuting the light Gothic masonry skeleton into a new metal structure, and moreover providing a serious rationale for the nineteenth-century aesthetic delight in Gothic by invoking the technical instead of the purely visual meaning of form.

The Gothic as Nostalgia

The *Entretiens* were the centerpiece in the intellectual debate on nineteenth-century building and Gothic form. Medieval Gothic expressed for the first time in history the visual potential of structure designed

100

at its limits. This fundamental fact escaped the notice of Gothic revivalists, largely because they were uninterested in technology. Moreover, as the revival continued on into the mid-nineteenth century, it became increasingly an idealistic reaction to modern industry. By the time collegiate Gothic began to educate the American elite at the turn of the century in America, the stony facades of the Gothic revival clearly expressed a longing for a supposed past where unity of life and purpose had saved populations from the disintegration so obvious in the late nineteenth century to such writers as Henry Adams and Ralph Adams Cram, the noted Gothic revival architect. Cram wrote in an introduction to Adams's *Mont-Saint-Michel and Chartres,* "To live for a day in the world that built Chartres Cathedral, even if it makes the living in a world that creates the 'Black Country' of England or an Iron City of America less a thing of joy and gladness than before, equally opens up the far prospect of another thirteenth century in the times that are to come and urges to ardent action toward its attainment."[1] Cram's implication, clearly, is that joy and beauty explain the Gothic whereas modern industrial structure is ugly and merely utilitarian. Such a view is based as much upon a misunderstanding of Gothic form as it is upon a superficial study of modern structure.

Henry Adams had sensed accurately that the primary fact of modern life was technology; and he had dramatized his insight by an image he first came upon in Chicago. There, in 1893, at the World Columbian Exposition, he had stood in the Hall of Machinery and felt, as he put it, the immense emotional force of the dynamo. For Adams the dynamo was an image for Chicago, and Chicago, in turn, was "the first expression of American thought as a unity." It revolted him as he "sat down helpless before a mechanical sequence."[2] Motion, force, and the restless energy of conquering a new land had broken into Adams's Boston Brahmin existence.

Then, in 1900 at the next great exposition, held in Paris, Adams came upon the contrast that explained Chicago. Again he saw the dynamo, but now "as he grew accustomed to the great gallery of machines, he began to feel the forty-foot dynamo as a moral force, much as the early Christians felt the cross . . . before the end, one began to pray to [the dynamo]."[3] This led him to contrast the dynamo with the Virgin (Notre Dame), Chicago with Chartres, the modern with the medieval. Adams perceived the Gothic cathedral as an expression of unity; yet at the exhibition he seems to have focused only on the dynamo, overlooking the unity expressed by the soaring Eiffel Tower, which in 1900 was again the centerpiece for the fair. In the same way, his deep studies of medieval life (he gave the first course in America on medieval studies at Harvard where he taught in the 1870s) focused on the Gothic monument without exploring its commercial and technological bases.[4]

Adams and many others saw only one half of each age: they missed the dynamism of the thirteenth century as much as they overlooked the motionless structures defining the new era of metal. The dynamo and the Virgin, as contrasting symbols, are balanced by the modern tower and the medieval trade. The Chicago of the late nineteenth century was in fact close in spirit and in commerce to the Paris of the thirteenth century, for Chicago is more than mere commerce and the Gothic more than nostalgia. Both pioneered the structural art of the time. Both show that beautiful form can go together with beautiful structure. The skyscrapers of Chicago were indeed "the first expression of American thought as a unity" and symbolize, along with Roebling's bridges, a major American talent for combining use with beauty.

The Skyscraper and the Cathedral

The similarities between modern Chicago and medieval northern France are well documented. Carl Condit, America's leading historian of building, identified the "most radical transformation of the structural art since the development of the Gothic . . . in the twelfth century . . . [as] the complete iron framing or skeletal construction."[5] This transformation took place largely in Chicago between 1879 and 1893. As one example, Condit cites the 1891 second Leiter Building (now the Sears Roebuck Building) whose "long west elevation is developed directly out of the structural system behind it, much as the isolated buttresses of the Gothic cathedral serve as the primary visual elements in its indissoluble unity of structure and form."[6]

Condit's phrase, the "indissoluable unity of structure and form," suggests a connection between the ideas of Gothic and those of modern structural art in metal form which writers on the Gothic have sensed as well. A leading architectural historian, Robert Branner, observed that the cathedrals "were to their contemporaries like skyscrapers turned inside out, with story after story towering up to the vaults."[7] The skeletal meaning has to do not only with the use of minimum materials to achieve an unprecedented scale but also with the social milieu within which these large works arose. Branner sets the medieval stage by emphasizing that "Gothic style was essentially urban. The cathedral dominated all, a marker to be seen from afar."[8] The skyscrapers came into being with the urbanization of Chicago and other American cities. Moreover, as Branner continued, "the Gothic evolved at a time of profound social and economic change. Trade and industry revived, commerce brought communications. The dissemination of the style . . . was not unlike the exploration of an industrial technique."[9] Such a description fits late-nineteenth-century Chicago with remarkable accuracy. Chicago experienced a vast population influx and great social and economic change; it was a center of trade and commerce for the Midwest, and it became the major American inland communication center. Furthermore, both the cathedrals and the skyscrapers were originally stimulated by the scourge of urban organization, fire. In northern France, fire had destroyed the older churches as well as the wooden towns,[10] and of course the rise of Chicago and the appearance of high buildings is dated from the great fire of 1871.

Fire posed a serious threat to late-nineteenth-century Chicago and to the small medieval towns of northern France because, compared to the more settled cities of their respective eras, they were less carefully built and of less durable materials. Today tourists think of Paris, and even Chartres and Amiens, as centers of high culture, but in the twelfth century they were less so. Thus, the Gothic style arose in a relatively barren, out-of-the-way landscape.[11] Writing from the center of Rennaissance culture, the Italian, Giorgio Vasari (1511–1574), characterized Gothic in a way that clearly reflects his prejudice against northern France—a prejudice not so very different from that of some modern northeastern writers against the midwest: "Then new architects arose who created that style of building for their barbarous nations which we call Gothic and produced some works which are ridiculous to our modern eyes but appeared admirable to theirs."[12] Indeed, this quotation reveals the origin of the term "gothic." Notre Dame de Paris, Chartres, Bourges, and the rest were barbarian works; they symbolized a nontraditional urban middle class, made wealthy by commerce. The cities competed with each other to have the highest buildings as symbols of civic growth. All this, even as late as the sixteenth century, seemed barbarian to the more sophisticated inheritors of long tradition and older wealth.

The Gothic cathedrals, of course, expressed also a new image of religious life, and certainly they cannot be understood without starting from the standpoint of medieval Christianity; but the religious life they expressed was itself more multifaceted than its cloistered revival in the nineteenth century assumed. The cathedrals have given us a record of medieval life defined in terms of technique, of politics, and of art. The cathedrals express the complete spirit of the thirteenth century better than anything else left to us, but it takes some study to see through their antiquarian tracery to the substance of their structure. Modern towers and spans also express our spirit as shown in technique, politics, and art. In Chicago we can see this expression best during the period between the fire and the 1893 Columbian exposition, and again eighty years later under similar conditions of rapid urban construction.

The First Chicago School

The development of the modern skyscraper, as with bridges, depended upon a special type of designer, strict economic constraints, and new functions to be controlled by new forms. It will come as no surprise to discover that the new designers were trained as civil engineers and that they invented new forms because their clients insisted on the discipline of economy. The Bostonian investor, Peter Brooks, expressed this discipline in an 1881 letter to his architect, John Root: "I prefer to have a plain structure . . . with a flat roof . . . and well braced by iron rods if needed. The building throughout is to be for use and not for ornament. Its beauty will be in its all-adaptation to its use."[13] This was Boston's prescription for the hinterland Chicago. It was a prescription that Brooks felt was appropriate to Chicago, but would most likely not have applied to his home city. Nevertheless, such criteria have produced the finest examples of urban skyscrapers. The two designers most responsible for carrying Brooks's ideals into practice were William Le Baron Jenney (1832–1907) and John Wellborn Root (1850–1891). Both came to Chicago with degrees in civil engineering, so, like Roebling a half century before, they were technically trained far beyond most of their fellow designers. In Chicago, they became the chief technicians, and hence the architects, for the most striking buildings of their era. They were drawn to Chicago by the vast potential for new designing, just as thirteenth-century technicians had been drawn to northern France from all over the realm.

William Le Baron Jenney

Jenney was born in Massachusetts, studied at the Lawrence Scientific School, and in 1853 entered the Ecole Centrale des Arts et Manufactures in Paris. He graduated in 1856, one year after Gustave Eiffel. From 1861 to 1866, Jenney served in the Union Army as a civil engineer, rising to the rank of major. He came to Chicago before the fire in 1867, and the next year opened an architectural office which he ran the rest of his life.[14]

Three buildings established Jenney's reputation as the pioneering designer of skeletal city buildings. The first Leiter Building of 1879 marked the beginning of skeletal urban form whose facade consisted only of glass and structure. There was almost no ornament. According to a contemporary critic, this emphasis on pure structure was "largely influenced by . . . the works of Viollet-le-Duc."[15] Jenney knew of these works from his Paris years, and he stressed their importance to his employees. His second major work was the Home Insurance Company Building of 1884 which, according to Condit, "was the major progenitor of the true skyscraper, the first adequate solution to the problem of large-scale urban construction."[16] Here, for the first time, the structure was the form, although some extraneous detailing marred the appearance. Such details disappeared on the third of Jenney's major works, the second Leiter Building of 1891, referred to earlier in connection with Gothic form. The building is not a skyscraper, being only eight stories high and over 400 feet in length, but its facade is so clearly its structure that it signals the possibilities for great height. The strongly expressed and widely spaced vertical columns are direct forerunners of the late-twentieth-century Chicago skyscraper. In fact, this building was later bought by Sears Roebuck, whose 1,454-foot-high tower of 1974 has the same basic facade: widely spaced main columns between which lighter columns frame the expanses of glass.

Jenney was aware that he was creating new forms but he was evidently not excited by new architectural ideas. He remained an engineer doing architecture. It was the younger Root who carried Jenney's ideas further and with more self-consciousness.

John Wellborn Root

Born in 1850, Root grew up in Georgia until 1864, when, at the height of the Civil War, he was sent to live with business friends of the family in Liverpool. Unlike so many nineteenth-century architects, his foreign experience was thus neither in sophisticated Paris nor in classical Rome or Greece, but, rather, in a commercial city. There, at the height of British supremacy, Root absorbed the stone and iron atmosphere of the Industrial Revolution.[17] After the war, Root came back to his family's new home in New York, and took a degree in civil engineering at New York University. He had always wanted to be an architect, but in 1866 there were no such schools in the United States so Root did the next closest thing, graduating fifth in his class in 1869.

After holding several jobs in New York, he moved to Chicago in early 1872, just three months after the great fire. There he worked for the architect Peter B. Wight (1838–1925), who years later described Root as an exponent of the principles of Viollet-le-Duc. According to Wight, Root judged a building "architectural" or "nonarchitectural" based on the extent to which the "fabric impressed him with a strong sense of structural reality."[18] In mid-1873, another of Wight's young architects, Daniel H. Burnham (1846–1912), convinced Root to join him in partnership. Thus formed the most productive partnership in the first Chicago school. Burnham and Root survived the chaotic "dark years" of Chicago building in the mid 1870s, and in 1880 began to get commissions for commercial buildings. From 1880 to Root's death in 1891, the firm designed twenty-seven major buildings in downtown Chicago and over two hundred buildings all told.

If Jenney was an engineer doing architecture, then Root was an architect who did engineering. Because of his technical training, Root approached the two Chicago engineering problems—marshland sub-soil and metal superstructure—without any hesitation. He invented the concrete foundation reinforced with a grillage of steel rails, and he was the first designer to use the metal skeleton as the complete wall structure.[19] But architectural considerations were important as well. Root tried to accommodate the new utilitarian edicts from Boston clients such as Peter Brooks to the old ideals of urban elegance. He thought of the tall city building in terms of a set of specific functions: well-lit office space, practical circulation, easily maintained spaces, structure, and so on.[20] But the buildings also had a second important function—the general ideal of visual design—about which Root had far more concern than Jenney. Root tended to give greater priority to the specific functions than to the visual design. The danger in this, of course, is that the overall design may end up as mere stylistic facade, as merely another specific function included last. This was, in fact, Root's weakness.

As has been mentioned, from the perspective of structural art a sixteen-story building is normally of too small a scale to give the structure precedence in the overall design. The first Chicago school explored the use of structure and some buildings expressed structure, but they found empirically that structure was usually unsatisfying as the primary visual element in design. Root was perhaps the first designer to discover that a well-designed sixteen-story building could reflect a new visual idea without either denying the structure or expressing it prominently.

Root, as the culmination of the first Chicago school, helped to prepare the way for others, two-thirds of a century later, to show how, as the scale increased, structural art could for the first time become a primary element in new city building.

Root and Sullivan

Louis Sullivan (1856–1924), and not John Root, usually gets the gold medal from historians. With regard to Sullivan's first skyscraper, Hugh Morrison wrote, "the problem had been solved, a new need had called forth a new form."[21] And Condit calls Sullivan's approach the higher functionalism of "psychological as well as utilitarian statement."[22] Nevertheless, Root's work is more profound and, for our study of structural art, more revealing.

Sullivan, born in Boston and educated largely on his own in Philadelphia, arrived in Chicago in 1873, a year after Root, worked briefly for Jenney, and went to Paris in 1874. The following year he returned to Chicago for good. In 1879, he joined the office of Dankmar Adler, a self-educated engineer, and in 1881 they formed the firm of Adler and Sullivan which lasted until Adler dissolved it in 1895. Sullivan was subsequently unable to sustain a practice; he died almost unknown in 1924. Frank Lloyd Wright, who had started his career in Sullivan's office, helped revive Sullivan's fame by getting him to write his autobiography, published in 1922.

For Sullivan, the idea of the skyscraper was the expression of vertical form, which he achieved through columns on the facade. We can see why Root is more central to the history of structural art by contrasting Sullivan's Wainwright Building of 1891 in St. Louis with Root's Monadnock in Chicago, completed the following year. The Wainwright facade (figure 7.1) consists of a heavy two-story base, from which spring closely spaced seven-story columns which end in a richly decorated horizontal band surmounted by a flat overhanging roof. Every other column in this ten-story building is in fact nonstructural. Moreover, the columns are fully disconnected visually from the base, where the horizontal spandrels and vertical columns are flush. Above the base, the highly ornamented spandrels are set back from the columns to emphasize the vertical over the horizontal. In contrast, the facade of Root's Monadnock (figure 7.2) is an undecorated wall pierced by windows from base to roof. The slightly spreading base expresses a widened foundation where the strong masonry must meet, below grade, the relatively weak Chicago marshland. The flat

FIGURE 7.1

The Wainwright Building, St. Louis, Missouri, 1891, by Louis Sullivan. The strong vertical expression is achieved by seven-story columns of which only every other one is structural. The lower two floors are visually cut off from the upper columns by a horizontal band.

FIGURE 7.2
The Monadnock Building, Chicago, 1892, by John W. Root. The facade is an undecorated wall with windows.

cornice is without ornament and the overhang smoothly curves out from it.

Sullivan expressed the vertical supports in a building whose facade is nearly as wide as it is high, whereas Root has designed a facade whose verticality is fully continuous and expresses what it needs to be, a wall with openings. Sullivan's facade reflects an aesthetic that disregards the relative unimportance of vertical structure. Root's facade expresses clearly the facade as wall. Root did not pretend that structure defined a sixteen-story facade, whereas Sullivan demonstrated that modern structure could be used just as mainstream nineteenth-century architects used the classical orders. Sullivan's facade is a variation on the classical plinth, colonnade, and entablature formula.[23] His ideas were decorative even if his building was for the new office building function.

Root's form is original and rational in the sense of showing visually what it does protectively. At the scale of Monadnock, the wall is a weather protection and a source of light; it need not be a structure. Sullivan's form is decorative and less rational. If the first Chicago school is parallel to the high Gothic, then Root is its climax and Sullivan its florid aftermath.

Sullivan may have been, as Morrison claimed, the prophet of modern architecture, but Root was closer to structural art. Architectural art, so closely connected to the small scale, has tried, as Sullivan did, to humanize the larger scale by making it appear to be something that its utilitarian function did not require. This is what Condit perhaps means by "the higher functionalism of psychological statement." In house and small office design such statement is emotionally satisfying to many, but as the scale increases this uplift becomes harder and harder to achieve short of mere fashion or costly facade.

The first Chicago school had recognized by the 1890s that structure was relatively neutral at the scale of the sixteen-story building. For Sullivan, this neutrality was not enough; his urge to express and to decorate was strong as was his instinct for personal statement. He began the tradition of playing with form and pretending that it was structure. The real beginning of structural art in high buildings had to await the period after World War II, with the second Chicago school and its buildings of truly immense height.

CHAPTER 8

BIG STEEL BRIDGES FROM EADS TO AMMANN

Skyscrapers and Bridges

When the Chicago architects of the 1880s needed structural help they turned more and more to bridge engineers and especially to those who had railroad experience. Railway building was the training school for American structural engineering with steel. The rapid spread of the continental network at midcentury reached a peak after the Civil War. Certainly, by 1880 there were a number of experienced bridge designers who had been forced, by working with large structures under the dual constraints of safety and economy, to develop a more rigorous scientific approach to design in steel. Two unique bridges, completed between 1874 and 1890, illustrate how designers struggled to build new forms appropriate to the newly economical steel. James Eads's St. Louis arches and Benjamin Baker's Firth of Forth cantilevers, each a piece of structural art, were created by designers who did only one such object. Like *Cavalleria Rusticana* and *I Pagliacci,* their composers left only one major object apiece, but in each case the work is so important that it can stand comparison to those of Roebling and Eiffel, just as the lone works of Mascagni and Leoncavallo can stand with the operas of Verdi and Puccini.

After describing the Eads and Forth bridges, we shall follow the works of America's three leading steel bridge designers: Gustav Lindenthal (1850–1935), Othmar Ammann (1879–1965), and David Steinman (1887–1960). Just as Chicago building was strongly influenced by the French ideas of Viollet-le-Duc, so the steel bridges brought to America ideas developed in the German-speaking regions of Central Europe. Lindenthal was Austrian, Ammann German Swiss, and Steinman—the only one of the three born in the United States—had studied the German literature and translated major bridge treatises from German into English. Even Eads, whose principal assistants were German-trained, got the form for his St. Louis bridge from an earlier German work.

Chicago versus St. Louis: The Eads Bridge

The St. Louis Bridge was probably the first bridge in the United States to be completed explicitly as an object of civic art. The city consciously set out to create a monument to symbolize its aspirations of reestablishing economic dominance in the Middle West, in the face of Chicago's explosive growth.[1] In 1864, Gratz Brown, senator from Missouri, introduced into the United States Congress a bill stating that the work should be built "for the ages, of a material that shall defy time and of a style that will be equally a triumph of art and contribution to industrial development."[2]

The importance of the bridge was more than just symbolic. The bridge was to connect St. Louis both to the prosperous Northeast and to the expanding West by collecting together a network of railroads. In the years before the Civil War both St. Louis and Chicago had boomed, but the war cut St. Louis off from its natural river link to New

Orleans while reinforcing Chicago's rail connection to the Northeast. Moreover, rail lines coming through Chicago began to cross the Mississippi even before the war. It was clear to the residents of St. Louis that only a bridge could save their city.

But the bridge had to land on Illinois soil to the east, and that meant somehow cooperating with the state whose largest city was Chicago. Cooperation between competitors was not easy. In 1866, a Chicago entrepreneur named L. B. Boomer tried to get legal authority to build the bridge. After much controversy, the St. Louis and Illinois Bridge Company fought off Boomer's challenge. The company was renamed with Illinois first as a compromise, but St. Louis remained in control, and the design was to be done by one of St. Louis's civic leaders, James Buchanan Eads (1820–1889). Eads was not primarily a bridge designer. Having come penniless to St. Louis in 1833, he had by the 1840s established a successful business of salvaging boats sunk in the Mississippi. During the war he had designed and built for the Union army a fleet of iron ships which kept the river open for the North.

The design Eads presented to the bridge company in 1867 was clearly influenced by a three-arch railway bridge at Coblenz over the Rhine which he had seen several years before, but the differences were significant. Not only did Eads design arches that were 520 feet in span, over 50 percent longer than those at Coblenz, but he also decided to use steel rather than iron. Both in scale and in materials, Eads's design was unprecedented. Except in a few suspension bridges, no designer had exceeded 400 feet in span, and never had a major structure been built of steel. Moreover, Eads's design greatly improved the appearance of the arches by keeping them from coming above the roadway as they did at Coblenz.[3]

Eads's bold design did not go unchallenged. In early 1867, the bridge company hired a well-known bridge engineer, J. H. Linville, an associate of Andrew Carnegie's, to review Eads's preliminary plans. Linville found them foolhardy, unsafe, and impractical.[4] Although Eads easily convinced the bridge company that Linville was wrong, he soon faced a much more serious challenge from the Chicagoan, Boomer. The latter had hastily organized a meeting of well-known civil engineers in St. Louis. Calling itself "The Bridge Convention, St. Louis 1867," the group issued a general report, which never mentioned Eads or his design but was clearly aimed at discrediting both. It spoke of an "unqualified disapprobation of spans of 500 feet," and it proposed the design of truss spans for the bridge. The implication was clear that the arch was not a correct form for such a work and that had such a convention been held earlier, "the eccentricities of even the greatest minds would have been brought down to the consideration of the subject in its most practical form . . . [the Convention thus] would have restrained all tendency towards erratic but brilliant ideas."[5] This report looked authoritative and it complicated the bridge company's efforts to secure financing. More importantly, it stimulated Eads to write a detailed rebuttal, which appeared in May 1868, and which provides a fine contrast between the design imagination of an individual and the depersonalized analysis by a committee, which the Bridge Convention report represented.

From our point of view, the major differences between the convention's report and Eads's rebuttal are in the matters of aesthetics and history. The convention report is almost completely lacking in any historical perspective or in any concern for bridge appearance. It mentions in passing the Britannia and Niagara bridges, but only to note the recent progress in engineering and to emphasize the "danger that, under the incentives of these wonderful achievements, the engineer may be led either to attempt impossibilities or, what is more likely, to venture too far in an untried field."[6] It makes no mention of bridge appearance at all.

In his own report, Eads defended his venture into the untried 520-foot-span arches by a direct appeal to history and, in particular, to the works of the greatest metal arch designer up to that time, Thomas Telford. Eads described Roebling's Niagara suspension bridge as well as a recently designed Dutch truss bridge with a span of nearly 500 feet. He focused on Telford's 600-foot-span arch proposed for London and his 500-foot arch design for Menai, making the convention's concern about 500-foot spans seem foolish.

Even more central to our considerations of structural art is Eads's defense of his arch form. "We are too prone" he wrote, "to associate . . . the beautiful in architecture and engineering with the idea of costliness. . . . It is easy to prove, beyond any possibility of a question, that in no other form could the material in these members of your Bridge which impart to it the chief feature of its gracefulness be used with such economy."[7] Eads saw his design as being both graceful and economical at the same time, a basic ideal of the structural artist. It may be true that—like Telford at Menai, Eiffel with his tower, and Roebling in Brooklyn—Eads did underestimate the final costs, due to the unprecedented difficulties of sinking two midriver piers and of erecting long arches with such a new material as steel. But the convention could not predict any better; its design, using more metal, and five river piers instead of two, would almost certainly have been more costly than Eads's.

The eccentricities of Eads's mind went together with substantial engineering experience. And, although Eads lacked direct bridge experience, he compensated for this lack by hiring as his principal assistants Henry Flad (1824–1898) and Charles Pfeifer (1843–1883). Flad was a graduate of the Institute of Technology in Munich, and in 1896 would become the president of the American Society of Civil Engineers. He developed the construction procedure of cantilevering the arch halves held by cables from above, much the same procedure as Eiffel would use a few years later over the Douro. Pfeifer did the basic calculations for Eads, and he was later to write an important treatise on arches.[8] These German-born engineers provided Eads with the detailed structural experience he lacked, but they did not make the design itself. Carl Gayler, another German who worked for Eads, later said explicitly that Eads made the design decisions, and that those decisions frequently arose because of "the artist in Eads." Indeed, as Eads wrote in a report of 1870, "modifications in the general arrangement of the arches and in the details of their construction will considerably improve the architectural appearance of the Bridge and simplify its fabrication."[9] Although Eads's interest in this bridge first arose primarily from his entrepreneurial goals, once he had become immersed in the project the artist in him took over.

Eads never designed another bridge before or after.[10] His major technical works had been centered on the river, and part of his fascination with the bridge had been the challenge of setting foundations deep below its shifting sandy bottom. His last great work was the opening up of the New Orleans harbor through the construction of the South Pass jetties. His unique bridge was for St. Louis what Roebling's and Eiffel's designs were for New York and Paris. If Eads's design is less famous, that is due largely to the eclipse of his city as a major world

FIGURE 8.1

The Eads Bridge over the Mississippi River at St. Louis, 1874, by James B. Eads. The first major structure built of steel, its central 510-foot spans were the longest arches in the world. Eads believed his arch span to be far more elegant than trusses. A comparison with later nearby bridges supports his view.

metropolis. Yet when the bridge was built, the city saw it as the central symbol of a renaissance for "St. Louis the future Great City of the World."[11]

The St. Louis Bridge (figure 8.1) never served the number of railroads that had been anticipated, and today it no longer carries rail traffic. Yet it is still intact, and remains a symbol of the hopes expressed consciously by one of America's great cities. It can still stand visual comparison with any comparable structure because its designer was concerned with both aesthetics and economy. He did not entirely succeed in creating a fully used bridge just as St. Louis itself did not succeed in outpacing Chicago; but its arched forms still show, when compared to the newer St. Louis crossings, the correctness of Eads's 1868 judgment that "the superstructure [is] far more graceful and elegant than any form of truss-bridge yet constructed."[12]

The Forth Bridge

Grace and elegance may not generally characterize trusses, but the cantilever truss over the Firth of Forth in Scotland can fairly be called a work of art comparable to the Eads Bridge. Its design sprang from two sources: the Tay bridge collapse in late 1879 and the lifelong bridge studies of Benjamin Baker (1840–1907). Baker, the designer at Forth, like Eads did only one major bridge, and his last major work, like that of Eads, was a great river project—the damming of the Nile River at Assuan.[13] Although younger than Eads by twenty years, Baker first wrote publicly about bridge design in a series of articles under the title "Long-Span Railway Bridges" published in the British journal *Engineering*.[14] This treatise, running through ten issues of the new illustrated weekly journal, tried systematically to compare all metal bridge forms then in use or under study for railway loadings. Baker's conclusion was that for spans above 700 feet the cantilever was the most efficient, using the least metal in its superstructure. This conclusion was supported by Baker's own experience in working on the design of a series of long-span bridges between 1864 and 1871 while with John Fowler (1817–1898) in whose office he began in 1862. None of these bridges was built but when, in 1880, the firm of Fowler and Baker was asked to make a new Forth design, Baker had a clear idea of how he wanted to span the great estuary in steel.

The two great barriers to Scotland's east coast travel were the Firth of Forth just above Edinburgh, and the Firth of Tay below Dundee. It took the strong economic force of the railways to turn an ancient Scottish vision of bridge crossings into reality. Both crossings were first designed by Thomas Bouch (1822–1880) and put into construction in the 1870s. At the Forth, Bouch had designed a suspension bridge with two spans, each of 1,600 feet. When his Tay bridge collapsed in late 1879, the public lost confidence in Bouch and the foundation work for his structure at Forth ceased, his design was rejected, and a new design was requested of Fowler and Baker.

Baker's design for Forth also divided the work into two very long spans, there being high ground in the middle of the estuary. The free spans are 1,710 feet, over 100 feet more than Brooklyn Bridge, and the steel form rises 342 feet above the masonry piers, compared to the 276.5-foot height of the masonry towers of the Brooklyn Bridge. Baker's colossal structure carried into practice the conclusions of his 1867 articles, but visually his 1880 design is far more impressive than his 1867 sketches. The cantilever truss bridge at Quebec two decades later would exceed Baker's span but with a less handsome form and with less technical success.[15]

Baker, in the Forth Bridge, created a work of structural art by taking a known form—the cantilever bridge truss—and designing it in a unique, personal way. The cantilever idea was not originally Baker's, any more than the suspension idea was Roebling's. In 1867, Baker had clearly credited others with the idea and merely tried to show where it might best be used. By 1880, however, he had thought more about its detailed form, which shows in the final design Baker's concern for appearance. This is particularly evident in the bridge profile (figure 8.2) which he made into a single, smooth, three-span form with slight breaks only at the shore ends of the outer spans. Moreover, the smoothness is accentuated by the lower curved profile just meeting the roadway and following the relatively small suspended span's lower line. The light vertical profile gives way to an increasingly dense form as one moves more toward a foreshortened view. The inward slope of the metal piers becomes more apparent as one approaches a cross-sectional view. The Forth Bridge, like the Brooklyn Bridge, takes on radically different appearances as one moves around it. It has a simple profile but density of interior form that connects it to other structural art peers of the 1880s: Brooklyn, Garabit, and Eiffel's tower. All show simple profiles but complex sections. The complexity of Baker's design arose partly from the Tay disaster; he wanted to be certain that no wind would ever interfere with the service of his bridge. Hence the large lattice diagonals both in profile and section.

Like other structural artists, Baker reflected on aesthetics, especially after his bridge had been deplored by influential writers. William Morris, for one, thought the bridge horribly ugly.[16] People suggested that the use of decoration would have improved its otherwise crude look. This question was discussed in a major 1901 paper presented by Joseph Husband, a British civil engineer, to the Institute of Civil Engineers. Husband gave a detailed analysis of metal bridge aesthetics and highly praised Baker's Forth along with other bridges such as Telford's

FIGURE 8.2

The Forth Bridge over the Firth of Forth in Scotland, 1890, by Benjamin Baker. With two spans of 1710 feet, this steel cantilever bridge surpassed Brooklyn Bridge as the world's longest span. The steel structure rises 342 feet above the masonry piers. Although from a foreshortened view the bridge appears dense and massive, in profile it exhibits a surprising lightness.

Menai and Stephenson's Britannia.[17] Husband's 34-page paper provoked a lengthy and heated discussion, including some spirited comments by Baker himself—now Sir Benjamin Baker.[18] The discussion turned to the two basic questions of how a bridge form ought to relate to its function and of whether engineers should collaborate with architects. Baker responded to the first question by referring to the Britannia Bridge, which had been almost universally praised by the paper and its discussants. Baker was the only one who spoke historically. He noted that he did not admire the Britannia Bridge because he "could not understand the object of extending the piers high up above the tube." To find out why this had been done, he had looked into the records, where he had found Stephenson's report, with its ambiguous conclusion that the towers were there in case the tubes needed suspension

chains. This ambiguity of structural function was inconsistent with Baker's aesthetic sensitivity, which was based upon the principle "that fitness was the fundamental condition of beauty." The Britannia towers did not fit, and therefore the bridge was not admirable as a work of structural art.

As to collaboration between engineers and architects, Baker told of his design experience with the Assuan Dam where "the contract drawings had been . . . handed over to the architectural department . . . [and] when they came back they had been saturated with Egyptian temples." Baker told the contractors "not to take any notice whatever of architectural detail, because the dam was not to be an imitation of a temple 4,000 years old." On the Forth Bridge, Baker admitted no such details either, and there was no recorded architectural collaboration. Like his fellow structural artists, Baker made the form to suit his own image of the crossing. It has little refinement of detail but much strength of overall shape. The architectural knowledge of that period could have contributed nothing to his design, even though some perceptive architects did recognize its aesthetic power.

Like Eads's bridge, Baker's Forth design has stood, since its March 4, 1890, opening, as a masterpiece in steel design. Like Eads, Baker used tubular arch-shaped curves, and, like Eads, Baker never did another great bridge. At Baker's side when the Prince of Wales (later Edward VII) officially declared the bridge opened was Alexandre Gustave Eiffel whose tower had opened less than a year before. Eiffel, too, had finished his structural career; a new generation was beginning to prepare the new material for its prototypical twentieth-century use: highway bridges to serve the automobile.

The Transition: Gustav Lindenthal

Between the Civil War and World War I, the railroad reached its peak; it was the unchallenged emperor of land motion. The monuments it inspired included big steel bridges, vast city terminals, and, of course, thousands of miles of track, running all over the country and then converging like regimental files laying seige to the city.

This railroad era was also a time of urbanization; and the confrontation of rail and city posed one of the major technical and aesthetic puzzles of the Industrial Revolution. Between 1880 and 1920 the bridge designer who attacked this puzzle in the most direct and permanent way was Gustav Lindenthal (1850–1935). His Hell Gate Bridge, coming at the end of railroading's dominance, symbolized the era with all its pretension, ambiguity, and power. It is the most visible link in what was perhaps the mightiest single urban project of its time: the full rail connection between New England and New Jersey. It was the last grand scheme of the Eastern railroads before Henry Ford and his Michigan colleagues began to make obsolete the inflexible network of rails.

Many of the previous great bridges had influenced Lindenthal. He experimented with form as no structural artist before or since has done. His thorough German training, his forceful and magnetic personality, and, above all, his lifelong devotion to steel bridges, not only led to unusual designs, but also laid the basis for the modern forms that emerged fully in the 1920s, for it was in Lindenthal's design office that the two most prominent twentieth-century steel bridge designers got their practical training. Both Ammann and Steinman played major roles in the Hell Gate Bridge; their remarkable careers, which were to reach such heights in the 1930s, took off from Lindenthal's stolid, detailed Germanic fueling. More than anything else, however, Lindenthal raised the issue of engineering and art, and of bridges as works of structural art, with such insistence that his protégés could never again escape the fact that they were building, as Ammann put it with respect to Hell Gate, "a great bridge in a great city, [which] should be a work of art to which science lends its aid."[19]

Lindenthal did not quite reach the summit of structural art; he tended to separate aesthetics from structure, to prefer massive form to lightness, and to design many radically different forms rather than focusing on one or two. Nonetheless, Lindenthal remains a major figure—in his own right, as well as by virtue of his influence.

Gustav Lindenthal was born in Brünn, Austria (now Brno, Czechoslovakia) in 1850, studied engineering at the Polytechnical Institute in Dresden, Germany, and came to the United States in 1874. For a short while he worked in Philadelphia as a stonemason on the centennial buildings, but soon his design talent secured him a supervisory position on the construction of the two permanent fair buildings.[20] Thereafter he worked as a railroad bridge engineer until 1881, when he opened his own office in Pittsburgh. His designs were immediately recognized as being of unusual quality. His first two major works were in Pittsburgh: the replacement of Roebling's 1845 roadway suspension bridge over the Monongahela River, and a new Seventh Street bridge over the Allegheny River. These signaled Lindenthal's approach to design: each structure was different in form; each showed a strong, unusual profile; and each included a major element of visual design.

For his detailed explanation of the Monongahela Bridge, a two-span truss of the Saltash form, Lindenthal received a major prize from the American Society of Civil Engineers.[21] He gave as his first reason for the lens-shaped truss, "the pleasing appearance (for a city bridge) in comparison with the ordinary parallel chord truss"; his other three reasons were of a technical nature. The trusses of this bridge were of steel, which by 1882 had become less costly than wrought iron.

The Monongahela Bridge was opened on March 19, 1883, two

months prior to Brooklyn Bridge. Like Roebling, Lindenthal lavished considerable design care on the towers. But, unlike Roebling, Lindenthal saw the towers as having two separate parts: a visual and a structural. As good as Lindenthal was, he cannot be put in Roebling's class, because such dichotimization necessarily led less to integration and more to facades. In Lindenthal's description, the Monongahela towers "are built of cast-iron, the roofs being wrought iron; they support merely their own weight; they encase the steel posts, which, to the eye, would seem very slender supports, and would appear out of proportion in comparison with the heavy piers and high trusses." Instead of taking those awkward proportions as a basis for modifying the structure, Lindenthal used them as an excuse for hiding one major structural element, the towers. Thus, whereas for Roebling the integration of structure and form was the basis for design, for Lindenthal the two were separate questions. Aesthetics became disconnected from structure, and this attitude eventually led Lindenthal to consult with architects when his works became larger and more complex.

In 1888, Lindenthal made his first design proposal for the Hudson River crossing. This great span was his lifelong goal, comparable to Roebling's vision for the East River. His first design, to be built at Twenty-third Street, consisted of a 3,100-foot main span carrying rail lines as well as carriageways. It was an immense work; nothing so heavy has ever been built. The Pennsylvania Railroad eventually decided to tunnel under the river, and Lindenthal's scheme lay dormant until after World War I.

In 1902 and 1903, Lindenthal was bridge commissioner for the city of New York. He completed the already begun Williamsburg Bridge, planned the Queensboro and Manhattan bridges, and studied reconstruction for the Brooklyn Bridge. Here again, we see Lindenthal's diversity. The Queensboro he designed as a cantilever bridge with no suspended center span (unlike the Forth); his design was built and stands today a densely trussed form with a suspension bridge profile. For the Manhattan Bridge, Lindenthal designed an eyebar chain suspension bridge with slender towers. He strongly favored eyebars, the system used in Britain by Telford and Brunel, over the wire cables of Roebling. The design was changed after his tenure as commissioner ended, and the Manhattan was redesigned as a wire-cable bridge with fixed towers spreading at the base. For both the Queensboro and Manhattan bridges, Lindenthal called in an architect to collaborate on the design. According to his memoir, this was "probably the first time in American bridge history [that] an architect was called in to collaborate on the design."[22]

Between 1907 and 1917, he worked on the Hell Gate designs, and from 1914 to 1917 on a two-span continuous truss railway bridge over the Ohio River near Sciotoville, Ohio. Each span is 775 feet, the longest span trusses then built, and the bridge was called "perhaps the boldest continuous bridge in existence."[23] Lindenthal's 1922 paper on the bridge led to a second award from the American Society of Civil Engineers.

Throughout the early 1920s, Lindenthal tried to promote his gigantic design for the Hudson River bridge, but without success. That project was to be taken over by his former assistant chief engineer, Othmar Ammann; the location would change, and the form would be quite different. Lindenthal's forms stimulated younger designers but his vision was still rooted in the nineteenth century and in a Germanic massiveness, characterized best by his Hell Gate arch.

The Hell Gate Bridge

The Hell Gate Bridge is the most visible element of a complex network of tunnels, terminals, bridges, and track that runs from Connecticut through the Bronx, Queens, Brooklyn, and Manhattan to New Jersey. Various designs had been proposed to cross the deep 850-foot-wide channel by which the East River separates Long Island City from Wards Island. The first, in 1892, was a cantilever design over three spans. In 1904, Lindenthal proposed three new designs: a suspension bridge, a continuous truss, and another cantilever design.

In 1905, a rail line which had been planned was shifted, making a three-span solution less practical, and Lindenthal began to study single-span two-hinged arches. He made two proposals: one a crescent arch following Eiffel, the other a spandrel-braced arch following R. Krohn's 1898 Rhine bridges at Bonn and Düsseldorf.[24] Lindenthal pre-

FIGURE 8.3

The Hell Gate Bridge over the East River, New York, 1916, by Gustav Lindenthal. The long-est-spanning arch in the world when completed, this steel bridge was made to look massive by its stone towers and by the increased spacing of the two chords at the support. Structur-ally the towers serve no purpose; the arch is actually hinged at the abutments. Nearly all the load is carried by the lower chord. The arch spans 977.5 feet.

ferred the German type of arch, and his reasons reveal a predeliction for massiveness over lightness: the German over the French. As Ammann reported it, although "both designs are pleasing in appearance, the spandrel arch owing to its height increasing from the center toward the ends, is more expressive of rigidity than the crescent arch, the ends of which appear to be unnaturally slim in comparison with the great height at the center."[25]

The real meaning here is that the *idea* of making the bridge profile slim is unnatural to Lindenthal; Eiffel gave his tapered crescents visual and technical stability by widening them at the hinges. Lindenthal's spandrel-braced arch is a *trompe l'oeil*. It is a two-hinged arch, like the crescent, but visually it looks like a hingeless arch built continuously into the stone pylons (see figure 8.3). That gave it the expression

of rigidity. Lindenthal is, in principle, doing at Hell Gate just what he had done over the Monongahela a quarter of a century earlier: hiding the true structural form behind a nonstructural facade. In the Hell Gate Bridge the pylons hide the fact that the only part of the arch to receive support is the lower curved chord—the arch proper—while the upper chord merely ends in thin air behind the visual protection of the masonry. Visually, the arch is made up of two chords—as in the Eads bridge—with the spacing between them increasing toward the heavy abutments. In reality, the arch is primarily the lower chord with the upper chord serving only as bracing.[26] The aesthetic of a visual rigidity overpowers the structure of a slender arch.

Many agree with Carl Condit, America's leading building historian, who wrote that not one American arch "is superior to it in overall size and weight and in the power and dignity of its form." The connection of weight and dignity is what Lindenthal and the consulting architect, Henry Hornbostel, wanted to achieve. Condit continues, "the slender arch rib, with its massive but simply articulated stiffening truss, is the very expression of combined stability and energy; its enormous thrust is perfectly contained, in a visual sense, by the heavy masonry towers."[27]

This is the aesthetic of mass; an inheritance from the period before the Industrial Revolution, with its reliance on masonry for monumentality. The Hell Gate Bridge is a splendid attempt to make steel feel like stone. Lindenthal is a major figure because, like a few earlier designers and like some of his contemporaries, he carried structure to new limits. But he retreated from the aesthetic implications of these limits. His ambiguous forms do have an aesthetic power, but one that lies outside those principles of design that we here are calling structural art.

When a designer builds nonfunctional stone towers to visually contain arch forces, which in fact do not exist where they appear to exist, then the design is not an indissoluble union of structure and form but rather a massive frill. The imagination needed to make that integration is missing at Hell Gate. The principles that we shall summarize and make more formal in the epilogue do not admit the making of false images. Such images are appropriate at small scale and for intensive human uses; for structural art they are not.

Perhaps it is well at this point to emphasize two fairly obvious ideas. First, the Hell Gate has an aesthetic power, that is, its appearance moves some people; second, it is nonetheless defective as structural art. A nonsense verse whose lines are metrically perfect and well rhymed may sound beautiful to me but I will not understand its meaning. It falls outside any evaluation I might make as to its poetic art. This is what Benjamin Baker meant when he said he ceased to admire the Britannia Bridge the moment he could not make sense out of its form. The problem is similar at Hell Gate. Indeed, the difference between Baker's and Lindenthal's major designs are characterized by their reactions to the Britannia Bridge. In describing his Sciotoville design in 1922, Lindenthal began by extolling the Britannia Bridge and the genius of its designer. He does not see, as Baker did clearly, the basic design flaw in this otherwise remarkable work.[28] Lindenthal's influence was carried on into the late twentieth century, but with very different results, by his assistant chief engineer Ammann and his chief calculator Steinman. Both came closer to the ideal for structural art than did their mentor because both took history and aesthetics more as the engineer's responsibility.

Modern Steel Forms: Othmar Ammann

No twentieth-century engineer has left more of a mark on steel bridge design than Othmar Ammann. Taken as a whole, his designs, of which all but one stand in fine condition today, provide the best example of structural steel bridge art done in this century. Ammann surpassed Lindenthal partly because of his different heritage and partly because of his different vision. Although German speaking like his mentor, Ammann grew up and was educated in the Swiss tradition. This tradition exerted such a determinant influence on him that, even though all his designs were built in America, the Swiss correctly have always considered them representative of their nation. (The only Swiss postage stamp with an American work on it is a 1979 issue showing Ammann and his Verrazano Bridge of 1964.)

The modern Swiss engineering tradition began in 1855, with the founding of the Federal Polytechnical Institute in Zurich and the appointment of Carl Culmann (1821–1881) as its first professor of civil engineering. We shall trace this tradition up to the late twentieth century when we come to the works of Robert Maillart and Christian Menn. For now, we need only note the peculiarly Swiss, as opposed to German, features that set Ammann's work apart from that of the German-trained Lindenthal. Standing between Germany and France in a cultural as well as geographical sense, the Swiss tend to reflect a mediation between the two cultures. In structural engineering, they respect the thorough, detailed, and scientific analyses developed in Germany; indeed, Culmann was a German. But at the same time, they admire the lightness and elegance of the French designs. Culmann's philosophy of design came directly from French visual methods of analysis.

Ammann was to learn bridge design from Culmann's best student, Wilhelm Ritter (1847–1906), who was the first to demonstrate, in an 1883 article, how a modern suspension bridge could be both simply and correctly analyzed for static loads.[29] But Ritter's centrality to the future of structural art stemmed even more from his method of teaching, which put the completed works at the center of engineering education, and used scientific analyses merely as a means to the end of designing structures. He impressed upon his students the meaning of good design by using specific examples, and he did not hesitate to express his dislike of those designs he found aesthetically inferior. Ritter emphasized the simplicity of analysis, the centrality of full-scale experience, and the importance of aesthetic excellence. He disagreed in print with the German engineers over their reliance on mathematical analysis,[30] and he wrote research papers that were primarily aimed not at other researchers but at practicing designers. Ammann reflected these same ideals throughout his career, and he left a series of works, mostly around New York harbor, that express Ritter's aesthetic vision of engineering art at the far limits of structure.

Ammann was born in Schaffhausen on the Rhine in 1879. He graduated from the Federal Technical Institute in 1902 and came to the United States two years later. From 1912 to 1923 he worked for Lindenthal, serving as his assistant chief engineer for both the Hell Gate and Sciotoville bridges.[31] His paper on the Hell Gate is in its own way as monumental and as useful as the bridge it described. For it he won the same high award from the American Society of Civil Engineers as Lindenthal won for his Monongahela and Sciotoville bridge papers.

In 1923, Ammann left Lindenthal. He submitted his own design for the Hudson River crossing to the newly formed Port of New York Authority, which accepted it and, in 1924, appointed the 45-year-old Swiss to be their chief bridge engineer. Between 1924 and 1931, Ammann designed the most remarkable set of bridges ever completed by one man in such a short time. The two cantilever trusses over the Kill van Kull—the Goethals Bridge and the Outerbridge Crossing—would have been major works for any engineer, but while designing them, Ammann also carried to completion the George Washington suspension bridge and the Bayonne arch bridge, each of which became the longest span bridge of its type.

Mere size, however, is secondary to our narrative on structural art. The primary fact about Ammann is his aesthetic motivation; for Ammann, design meant the aesthetic choice of form. Moreover, this motivation was combined with a superb training. When he moved out on his own in 1923, Ammann had already two decades of direct experience with the design and construction of steel bridges. With Lindenthal, he had gotten the chance to direct design work on the world's largest arch, on the world's largest continuous truss, and on the world's largest (though unbuilt) suspension bridge. No engineer was ever better prepared.

The George Washington Bridge

The last illustration in Wilhelm Ritter's 1895 book on American bridges shows Lindenthal's 1888 proposal for the Hudson River bridge;[32] thus Ammann knew about the project as a student in Zurich. He thought deeply about it while with Lindenthal. When he eventually developed his own approach, it reflected the basic shift in transportation that occurred in the twenties: the heavy locomotive was giving way to the light automobile. For the great bridge project this meant two fundamental changes: first, it could be located away from the existing terminals, far uptown where the approaches would be less expensive; second, it would have a much lighter live loading. Ammann's proposal of 1923 shows therefore a lighter form in a location where rock banks make anchorage places more accessible. However, faced with the visual consequences of an unprecedented scale, Ammann wavered and finally decided that some "architecture" was necessary. He sketched immense stone towers to overcome his feeling that the bridge looked too light.[33]

At this time, the Brooklyn Bridge was being discovered by painters, poets, and critics, who were impressed by the visually powerful contrast between the massive stone towers and the thin metal spans.[34] Moreover, as Ammann later wrote, "whatever influence these various considerations may have had on the general conception of the design, the writer has admittedly been influenced by his personal conceptions and taste. He has always been an admirer of the early English suspension bridges with their general simple appearance, their flat catenary, light, graceful, suspended structure, and their plain massive and, therefore monumental towers."[35] There is no doubt, therefore, that Ammann's primary design motive for the George Washington Bridge was aesthetic and derived from the type of form best illustrated by Telford's Menai. In one respect, however, the direct influence of Lindenthal perhaps outweighed that of Telford or Roebling. For Lindenthal, the

FIGURE 8.4

The George Washington Bridge over the Hudson River between New Jersey and New York, 1931, by Othmar Ammann. Ammann's first bridge design, twice the span of any previous suspension bridge, featured a thin deck and massive steel towers covered with concrete and granite. The tower covering has never been added but the thin deck has been deepened by the addition of a second deck for the increased traffic.

stone towers at Hell Gate had been solely for appearance, whereas for Telford at Menai and for Roebling in the Brooklyn Bridge stone towers were structure; for the masonry pushed down the caissons during construction and it held up the cables when in service. Roebling did mold the towers slightly but their basic form is for use.

In any event, whereas aesthetic criticism in 1883 had condemned the towers of the Brooklyn Bridge as being inexpressive and dull, the critics in the 1920s saw the old stone towers as handsome and fitting when contrasted to the metal webbed spans. It was specifically in this context that Ammann could not bring himself to face the reality of metal towers; he wrote that "no matter how well designed such slender steel towers may be . . . they cannot compare in their monumental effect upon the entire structure with the massive towers so admirably exemplified in the Brooklyn Bridge and in many of the older suspension bridges."[36] Ammann, therefore, designed the towers to be steel, covered with reinforced concrete to strengthen the structure, and then faced in stone for appearance. The novel combination of steel and concrete where both participate in carrying load would have led to less steel than in a purely steel tower, but Ammann felt in the end that it would be unwise to use such a new idea on such a huge work, and therefore designed the steel tower to carry all the concrete and granite in addition to the loads of the steel tower and the suspended spans. But the economic constraints of the 1929 crash and the Depression helped to decide the Port Authority against adding the concrete and granite, so that the bare steel towers were left uncovered and have remained that way ever since (figure 8.4). The strange, densely trussed towers of the George Washington Bridge thus express not an intended impression of structure but the accidental view of a heavy skeleton designed to carry stone. Many writers agree with Condit that the effect is appropriate,[37] and even Ammann admitted that the uncovered towers looked better than he had anticipated. However, no one since has ever designed towers that even closely resemble these; and Ammann's own later towers, in their contrast, provide perhaps the sternest criticism of those over the Hudson River.

Unlike the towers, the steel suspension spans of the George Washington Bridge were planned without ornamentation, but its design was equally the result of aesthetic choice. Ammann reacted to several previous proposals for the bridge which had, as he put it, "clumsy stiffening trusses."[38] He knew well the existing examples of such graceless spans as the East River Williamsburg Bridge, whose ugly metal towers were matched by its heavy and clumsy stiffening trusses. Ammann decided, therefore, to design a "very shallow and flexible truss, which not only resulted in far-reaching economy, but also effected a light and graceful appearance."[39] He was quite explicit about this basic aesthetic idea and again identified it with the early English bridges. Like all the great structural artists, Ammann was designing unprecedented structures, and found inspiration from those who had done so before. But, unlike earlier structural artists, Ammann worked in an age captivated by the idea of mathematical science as a prerequisite to engineering practice. The creation of new designs based upon earlier experience seemed to become less useful once people began to believe that new works would come from new research, that scientific discoveries would produce technological breakthroughs. The unstiffened deck of the George Washington Bridge, and of other bridges of the time, provides a stunning example of how such an idea could not only mislead the entire profession but also lead directly to the most dramatic structural collapse of the twentieth century.

Science and Structure

In the nineteenth century, as we saw earlier, Eiffel had emphasized the importance of mathematical theory to design. Eiffel could call for theory because he had such an intimate association with the realities of construction. For the practical builder, theory gave a new precision and hence a fresh economy. But the 1920s were a different time than the 1880s. The men who gained prominence after World War I had been trained after the great works of the 1880s had been built. Within that forty-year span, the Industrial Revolution's second period began and developed at such a rapid pace that the history of modern engineering seemed irrelevant. A science-based future overwhelmed the earlier reliance upon the careful study of previous experience. During the 1920s people were blocked off from their traditions by faith in the new ideology of scientific method. Science now had an enormous prestige. Einstein became famous when Eddington's 1919 solar eclipse test proved the generalized theory of relativity to be correct. Yet, at the same time, it must be noted, the new science was obscure and incomprehensible to nearly everyone; Einstein's tensor calculus was miraculous but mysterious.[40]

To the prestige of science was added the discovery, by the General Electric Company, that prize-winning science could lead directly to huge industrial profits. Nobel laureate Irving Langmuir's argon lamp was big business. During the 1920s, 1,200 industrial laboratories came into being following the General Electric success, while in education the idea of the teacher-scholar became important.[41] No longer was the engineering teacher to write about things that had been built; instead, he was to develop general theories and teach methods of mathematical analysis. Designers of large-scale structures worried about the accuracy of their old, simplified calculations, and they looked more and more to researchers for guidance.

In 1909, for the Manhattan Bridge, Leon Moisseiff (1872–1943), a European-trained engineer, introduced the use of deflection theory in calculating how the horizontal deck and the curved cables worked together to carry loads. This theory, first published in 1888 by the Austrian academic, Josef Melan (1854–1941), showed how the deck and cables deflect together under gravity loads. The mathematical computations were well beyond the capability of most American-trained engineers of the time. They were not, however, beyond David Steinman, who translated Melan's theory into English in 1913 and began using it himself in the 1920s.[42] When Ammann set out to study his Hudson River bridge he recognized, as did those other two engineers, that this new general theory gave some remarkable new insights into suspension bridge performance. It showed, for example, that as the spans got longer and the suspended structure heavier, the required stiffness of that deck actually decreased. Indeed, Ammann finally concluded that for his 3,500-feet span, no stiffness was needed in the deck at all.[43] Thus, this technological breakthrough, following from Melan's theory, was accepted by each of these leading designers.

As has been indicated, not only did this new theory stimulate designers to build very thin decks, but it blocked them from looking back to the experience of Telford, Ellet, and Roebling. Whereas Baker, a man of the 1880s, evaluated the Britannia Bridge by going back to the basic writings of Stephenson, Ammann, in the 1920s, evaluated the Menai by admiring its aesthetics without going back to basic documents of the time. Just as it would have been foolish for Langmuir to have studied in detail the incandescent bulb of Edison, so it seemed to nearly all engineers that there was no technical value in studying the past. As the president of the Massachusetts Institute of Technology was to say at its 1965 centennial, "M.I.T. [is] a university that never looks back as a conserver of the past but always forward as a maker of the future."

The deflection theory sanctioned the George Washington Bridge design in which, before the second deck was added (because of increased traffic) in 1962, the vertical depth of the deck was about 1/350 of the span, compared to values of about 1/60 for the longest spans completed before Ammann's design. The technical success of this immense bridge seemed to confirm the theory, and a series of major bridges appeared in the 1930s with very slender decks. As Ammann himself wrote years later, "encouraged by this example [of the George Washington Bridge] engineers were led to the adoption of a progressively greater degree of flexibility of stiffening girders."[44]

Then, in 1939, Leon Moisseiff designed a 2,800-foot span with an 8-foot-deep deck girder for the first Tacoma Narrows suspension bridge in the state of Washington. In November 1940, just four months after completion, the bridge collapsed in a moderately strong storm, forcing structural engineers to reevaluate their reliance on deflection theory, and prompting some of them to return to the basic documents of the nineteenth-century bridge designers. There they found that published records described nineteenth-century failures that were amazingly similar to what they saw in the motion pictures of the Tacoma collapse. Further research revealed that the designers who understood the problem best were Telford and Roebling, just the two whose aesthetic motivations had also been the strongest. We have already referred to Telford's worries over Menai. Roebling described the same problem in his 1848 proposal for an Ohio River bridge, and explained "the necessity of a stiff floor, which of itself will prevent short undulations."[45]

The connection between aesthetic motivation and the clear perception of performance is not accidental because it is only from technical clarity that structural art can flower. When Ammann gave up on masonry facades, his tower design began to express a new elegance; and, when he recognized the need for deck stiffness, his bridge spans, while retaining the thinness that his aesthetic sensitivity demanded, became technically sounder. For example, the ratio of stiffening-member depth to span is 1/168 for the Golden Gate Bridge, compared to 1/180 for Ammann's Verrazano. The Golden Gate, which was built in the 1930s, had not enough deck stiffness, has since been stiffened, and still has problems. But Ammann, designing the Verrazano Bridge in the light of the Tacoma collapse, was able to create his even thinner stiffening member by developing "the tubular framework [which] may have been his most important contribution to bridge design."[46] His urge for a slender appearance, already made explicit in the George Washington Bridge, drove him to find a better technical solution in his later works.

Thus, Ammann did not give up his basic bridge design vision of a "flat, catenary, light, graceful, suspended structure, and plain massive and, therefore monumental towers." Rather, he found a way to achieve that vision and still create technically fine bridges. To see how that same vision appeared in an arch design, we turn next to Ammann's immense Bayonne Bridge, completed at the same time as the George Washington Bridge.

Hell Gate and Bayonne

In 1931, three structures gave New York dominance in scale to match its population, port, and financial power. These structures were the George Washington Bridge, the Bayonne Bridge, and the Empire State Building—each larger than any comparable work in the world. Both of the 1931 bridges were designed by Ammann. By this time, he had replaced Lindenthal as America's leading bridge engineer, and, indeed, a comparison of his arch bridge over the Kill van Kull between Bayonne, New Jersey, and Staten Island with Lindenthal's Hell Gate Bridge demonstrates the higher level of structural art that Ammann had achieved (figure 8.5). Even though Ammann's arch form, similar to that of the Hell Gate, is 70 percent longer in span, his design is significantly lighter than Lindenthal's: at Bayonne the main span required only 37,000,000 pounds of steel compared to 87,800,000 pounds in the much shorter Hell Gate.[47] Part of this decrease is, of course, due directly to the lower live loads. At Bayonne the car loading was taken as 7,000 pounds per foot of bridge length, whereas at Hell Gate the train loading was 24,000 pounds per foot. But the decrease is without doubt also attributable to Ammann's desire for the "general, graceful form of this type of arch." He believed that the arch would be cheaper than a suspension span, but in recommending against the competitive bidding of two designs to test that belief, he clearly wanted not only to avoid delay, but also to design a long-span arch like Hell Gate, and not merely another, very much shorter, George Washington Bridge. The great stimulant was the idea of carrying the arch form to limits comparable to those to which he was carrying the suspension form over the Hudson River.

Moreover, Ammann was quite explicit about the visual form of his arch, stating that "the general outline of the arch with height decreasing from the center toward the ends was preserved principally for its pleasing appearance."[48] By this he meant that the distance between the top and bottom chords (the longitudinal curved members) of the trussed arch was chosen to be smaller at the center than at the ends. The forces in the top chord are far less at the ends than at the center, and therefore it would have been logical to have decreased the chord distances from center to ends. Like Hell Gate, Bayonne is a two-hinged arch and so, as at Hell Gate, "in the first tentative design the two-hinged arch of the so-called crescent shape was selected." Eiffel's Garabit was in his mind, but Ammann's aesthetic ideas were different, for, as he said, "the end hinges would offer considerable difficulties, and also the shape of the arch did not seem to satisfy entirely on account of its greater height at the center compared with the ends."[49] His main motive was to create the same general form as at Hell Gate, because this form gave him a feeling of stability that the Eiffel form did not. This feeling led Ammann to provide, "for the sake of appearance, massive-looking granite faced concrete abutments," even though, as he explained, "these are but hollow structures with a steel framework carrying the floor above."[50] In other words, he was perfectly aware that only the concrete below the bottom chord—the arch proper—was needed, and that the rest was mere show.

As with the George Washington towers, the granite-covered concrete facades for the Bayonne abutments were never added. The result at Bayonne is much worse than at the George Washington Bridge because even the layman can see that the tangle of very light metal pieces in which the spreading arch chords end do not support the arch at all. This accidental result remains as a symbol of how structural art is impaired by ornament. Essentially, Ammann's impressive structural imagination relaxed into imitation when he chose an arch form that necessitated a facade to make it appear acceptable. As we shall see in the next chapter, his compatriot Maillart did much the same thing in his concrete arches of the mid 1920s, and for the same basic reason: the image of appropriate arch form was still conditioned by the two-thousand-year-old masonry tradition in which arches got heavier toward their ends and abutments needed mass to hold the arches in place. Eiffel in his last few bridges was able to overcome that outdated vision, but neither Ammann nor Maillart reached that point in their careers until

FIGURE 8.5
The Bayonne Bridge over the Kill van Kull, between Bayonne and Staten Island, 1931, by Othmar Ammann. This 1,652-foot-span steel arch bridge was the world's longest arch when finished. Ammann followed the main features of the Hell Gate design, except that his arch is lighter and the masonry abutments he designed (they were never built) were much less visually prominent.

after the 1920s. Moreover, the wide discussion of bridge aesthetics during this decade was, with one notable exception, still rooted in a masonry vision. The high point of twentieth-century structural art was fast approaching, but it would not arrive until the 1930s.

But the Bayonne Bridge, which opened officially in November 1931, was, in spite of its visual weaknesses, a major work of structural art, because Ammann expressed visually a new lightness in arch form at a new limit in scale. The lack of stone abutment blocks is actually a virtue at the distance of the most usual view from the New Jersey Turnpike for there the whole work exhibits a lacework lightness unequaled by any urban arch built before the Second World War.

Two Visions: Ammann and Steinman

Ammann's growing reputation after the 1931 completion of his two giant interstate bridges was paralleled by that of David Steinman. Like Amman, Steinman had worked for Lindenthal, who had put him in charge of Hell Gate and Sciotoville when Ammann was called home to Switzerland at the outbreak of World War I. Just as there had been an intense rivalry between Stephenson and Brunel, the two New York based designers Ammann and Steinman competed hard for major designs up to Steinman's death in 1960. Unlike their earlier counterparts, however, they did not stay on good terms personally. The competitiveness of twentieth-century America was not conducive to the spirit of cooperation that had characterized those two great Victorians. However, the intensity of bridge rivalry between Ammann and Steinman has a distinct virtue historically: both engineers were so intent on expressing their own personal ideas of design that we can see perhaps more clearly than in nineteenth-century examples how different personalities convert the same state of scientific knowledge and the same social setting into bridges of vastly different appearance. Each, at his best, was a fine structural artist, and each created unique works expressing an individual style. Each was conscious of being an artist and wrote explicitly about his structures as works of art. Each valued lightness and safety, economy and permanence, as well as aesthetic appeal. That these basic ideals led to different forms shows that there can be no optimum in structures, but only many reasonable choices, allowing the individual designer the freedom to express his own ideas.

Steinman was born in New York City in 1887, graduated from City College of New York in 1906, and from Columbia with a civil engineer's degree in 1909 and a Ph.D. in 1910. While at Columbia he produced a translation of Melan's book on bridges which was published in 1913 as the *Theory of Arches and Suspension Bridges*. Between 1910 and 1914 he taught civil engineering at the University of Idaho; from 1914 to 1917 he worked for Lindenthal. When Lindenthal's big bridge work stopped, Steinman served as associate professor at City College's newly formed engineering school and also worked with another well-known bridge designer, J. A. L. Waddell. In 1920, he was approached by Holton Robinson (1863–1945), already an experienced designer of suspension bridges, and they formed a partnership which lasted until Robinson's death.

By 1936, Robinson and Steinman had designed a series of major bridges which rivaled Ammann's work while showing Steinman's very different style. We shall illustrate the differences in style by making three comparisons: between two very long span designs, between two metal towers, and between two designs of 1939 completed just prior to the Tacoma collapse.

In 1929, Steinman concluded an address at the annual convention of the American Institute of Steel Construction by describing his design for a "Liberty Bridge" across the New York Narrows (eventually designed by Ammann and called the Verrazano Narrows Bridge). In the published paper, renderings of the Liberty Bridge and the George Washington Bridge (then under construction) appear on the same page.[51] Two things are remarkable about Steinman's proposal: first, the horizontal deck appears even thinner than the Ammann design (which, however, is shown in a rendering with the second deck in place) and, second, the towers are exposed steel but highly ornamental.

Without doubt, Steinman aims his remarks about the towers at Ammann. "I want to preach the gospel of *Beauty in Steel*," he wrote, with the bias of his audience clearly in view. "I want to drive home the truth that we have, in steel, a material that possesses the highest potentialities for expressing the harmonious union of beauty and strength." He noted that although earlier it was necessary to build lofty towers of masonry, it had since become possible to realize the "true artistic potentialities of steel . . . not by ornamentations, but by the development of structural forms that will be inherently beautiful in their simplicity." He then went right for his rival. "Some designers . . . are resorting to the dubious architectural expedient of building huge bridge towers of steel for strength and then masking them with concrete and stone for appearance." He can only be referring to the Hudson River bridge here, and especially to Ammann's 1928 article vigorously defending his choice of steel towers encased in concrete and covered with granite.[52] Steinman continued, "To me, such treatment of the problem is a subterfuge and evasion. To me, the fundamental requisite for the beauty is honesty and sincerity." The facing page showed Steinman's decorated 800-foot-high tower topped with a Gothic flèche and braced with Gothic cathedral-like arcades. Although Ammann's stone facades are certainly not honest, Steinman's design is filled with decorative forms which can in no way be called "inherently beautiful in their simplicity."

The debate between Steinman and Ammann of which this is part springs from personal animosity beginning during completion of the Hell Gate Bridge[53] and is unimportant to our present discussion except insofar as it impelled these two great figures to react strongly to each other's designs and hence accentuate their independent visions. Each sought artistic solutions to nearly identical problems and those solutions were always quite different.

It is ironic that, for all their differences, Steinman and Ammann were agreed on the significance of the deflection theory and its sanction of very slender deck structures. Steinman had already shown his approval in the Liberty Bridge proposal, and such slenderness reached its peak in 1939 with the completion of his Deer Isle Bridge. This 1,080-foot-span bridge only 25 feet wide, with a ratio of deck girder

FIGURE 8.6
The Bronx-Whitestone Bridge over the East River, New York, 1939, by Othmar Ammann. This slender-decked 2,300-foot-span suspension bridge shows Ammann's aesthetic desire for thin decks and solid-looking towers with only a single but relatively deep cross-frame at the top.

depth to span of 1/166, was just about as flexible as the Tacoma Narrows.[54] Ammann's slender Bronx–Whitestone Bridge, also completed in 1939, had a ratio of 1/210 and proved also to be disturbingly flexible in wind. Thus the very low deck stiffness was accepted by both Ammann and Steinman up to the end of the 1930s.[55]

While both slender, the Bronx–Whitestone and Deer Isle bridges show a decided difference in tower design. Where Ammann has a simple, "honest" design with one curved-bottom cross-brace at the top of the tower, Steinman has a complex system of four cross-members of lacework, with light verticals in between the main outer tower verticals on which the cables rest. For Steinman, beauty in steel is an expression of patterns with many relatively light members; for Ammann, hand-

144

some form comes from an austere simplicity with few relatively heavy members.

Ammann's solid-looking steel towers are hollow but visually that is not expressed. He never gave up on his desire for a contrast between light decks and solid-looking towers, even though after the George Washington and Bayonne bridges he never again proposed stone coverings. Steinman, on the other hand, preferred lighter and more intricate tower designs. We can see this difference in tower design clearly by comparing Ammann's plain Bronx–Whitestone towers (figure 8.6) with the romantic needle-topped Gothic arches in the towers of Steinman's 1931 St. Johns Bridge (figure 8.7). However dated those towers may appear today, they reflect Steinman's desire to create "a symphony in stone and steel" and "to secure a beautiful public structure."[56]

Because both designers were structural artists, striving for efficiency, economy, and elegance, both Steinnam's flamboyant works and Ammann's more austere structures could be carried through for low costs.[57] Ammann's designs, however, show more clearly a consistent

FIGURE 8.7
The St. Johns Bridge over the Willamette River, near Portland, Oregon, 1931, by David Steinman. Steinman designed his towers with many elements, as contrasted to Ammann's designs. The main span is 1207 feet.

personal style that reflects simplicity and clarity of form. Steinman, as we see, for example, in the St. Johns Tower, tended to create more complex forms embellished with decorative features. These light economical structures, consciously designed for artistic merit, helped make public the new idea of engineering as an art form. It was just at this same period, during the 1920s, that some artists and architects began to proclaim technology as somehow the new fact with which they must cope. To understand better the correctness of their insight, we must turn to the one new material of the twentieth century, reinforced concrete, which along with structural steel was beginning to bring forth new forms that put in question traditional views on art and engineering.

146

CHAPTER 9

ROBERT MAILLART

AND NEW FORMS IN

REINFORCED

CONCRETE

Prototypical Twentieth-Century Material

Just as the nineteenth century was an age of iron, so the twentieth has been an age of concrete. In both cases, the aesthetic potential for structural art appeared first in the relative wilderness, as old ideas on urban beauty kept the new forms out of the most prominent cities. Louis Sullivan was prophetic in his Wainwright Building, both in contorting the structure into a fake facade where every other column was unused, and in liberally ornamenting the detail to express a classical column.

But in fairness to the other side of the argument, it must be noted that the age of iron had produced many ugly buildings and bridges, designed without any sense of style whatsoever. More worrisome to critics were the thousands of industrial structures whose formless utility suggested both the creeping mechanization of life and the emergence of those iron cities that drove architects like Ralph Adams Cram back to the thirteenth century or engineers like Ammann to argue in favor of masonry facades. While critics and theorists praised the pseudostructure of Hell Gate but despaired of finding classical formulas in which to contain pure metal forms, there arrived at the turn of the century a completely new material further to confuse both Beaux arts and avant-garde. This material was concrete reinforced with iron.

The Romans had regularly mixed cement powder, sand, stones, and water to make an artificial stone called concrete; the dome of the Pantheon stands today as a high monument to Roman concrete. As already noted, iron was also used in earliest antiquity. What was completely new was the combination of the two ancient, artificially produced materials to make a material with extraordinary new properties. As with iron, the leading pioneers in reinforced concrete were also the most aesthetically conscious structural artists. Telford, Roebling, and Eiffel found counterparts a century later in Robert Maillart (1872–1940), Eduardo Torroja (1899–1961), and Pier Luigi Nervi (1891–1979).

German Science versus French Business

Reinforced concrete had three main sources in the late nineteenth century. In 1867, a French gardener, Joseph Monier (1823–1906), patented the idea of strengthening thin concrete vessels by embedding iron wire mesh in the concrete.[1] He later went on to apply his ideas to buildings and bridges. In 1879, another Frenchman, François Hennebique (1843–1921), set out to fireproof a private metal-frame house he was building in Belgium.[2] His decision to cover the iron beams with concrete led directly to the development of a structural system wherein the metal carried tension and the concrete compression. Hennebique made metal structures permanent by concrete cover. Finally, bridge designers in the latter part of the nineteenth century were finding that it was more economical to produce artificial stones by casting concrete than it was to quarry natural stones.[3] They tried to imitate stone structures and facades using the more labor-saving concrete.

Monier's ideas were taken to Germany by a trained engineer, G. A. Wayss (1851–1917), who directed the firm of Wayss and Freytag, the major German promoter of reinforced concrete until World War I. In the hands of Wayss and his colleagues, reinforced concrete became a standard building material whose properties were well tested and whose structures could be mathematically calculated. But Wayss did not see engineering works as aesthetic; in Germany the trend was increasingly to consider the aesthetic questions of bridges and buildings as the province of the architect, not the engineer. By the time Wayss and Freytag celebrated their fiftieth anniversary in 1925, the thinness of the early Monier works was lost and the bridge forms advertised by the firm showed the heavy-handed aesthetic of stone-minded architects.[4]

In direct competition with Wayss, the Frenchman Hennebique had established an international business in 1892. His business grew with such extraordinary rapidity that from 6 completed projects in 1892, his volume rose to 1,229 in the year 1900 alone. By 1902 he had completed a total of 7,026 structures: bridges, factories, city buildings of all kinds, water towers, industrial structures, and so forth.[5] Hennebique learned building, as had Telford, by starting as an apprentice to a stonemason. In 1867 he had established himself as a building contractor. Following his 1879 concrete and iron house, he constructed a small number of such works over the next twelve years while continuing to build conventional works. In 1892 he took out patents on the "System Hennebique," retired from building, and settled in Paris where he established a vast network of concessionaires throughout Europe. Hennebique never quite escaped his artisan background, and his work shows characteristics similar to Telford's: a drive for lightness, a distaste for calculations, and a growing self-confidence as his experience widened. Unlike Telford, however, Hennebique did not personally stay close to his proliferating designs. He became "le bon père Hennebique," directing a commercial empire from headquarters in Paris. He guaranteed all his works even though by the turn of the century more and more of them were being designed abroad.

FIGURE 9.1
Vienne River Bridge, Châtellerault, France, 1899, by François Hennebique. The longest-spanning reinforced concrete bridge of the nineteenth century, the central fixed arch spans 50 meters.

It is not easy to determine out of the thousands of Hennebique structures just what he designed himself. His three best documented bridges—at Châtellerault (1899) (figure 9.1), Liège (1905), and Rome (1910)—are all visually and technically different.[6] It appears that the Roman design was in fact made in the office of G. A. Porcheddu from Turin.[7] The Hennebique name did help local engineers get established in the face of public officials skeptical of the new material, but it is not possible to attribute designs, especially those outside of France, to the design imagination of François Hennebique himself. In a similar way, the many works of Wayss and Freytag cannot be attributed to a single designer. Both competing firms had so many engineers and did such a variety of structures that we cannot place their works in the mainstream of structural art.[8] We can, however, identify contrasting general approaches to design and thus be prepared to recognize the major structural art that would soon emerge from a synthesis of the best parts of each approach.

Whereas Hennebique relied on his own successful field experience, Wayss stimulated public tests, and wrote in 1887 perhaps the first textbook on reinforced concrete designs. Hennebique worked through financially independent licensees while retaining much central design authority whereas Wayss worked through financially dependent branch offices to whom he gave design authority. Hennebique was a commercial king ruling his centralized bureaucracy by divine right of personal experience; Wayss colonized Central Europe and justified his rule by public scientific calculations.

The German emphasis on calculations was a double-edged sword; it forced designers to think rationally but it also drew them away from forms for which they had no calculations, and thus narrowed the range of structural possibilities. This narrowness reflected an underlying faith in technology as an applied science, where applications must proceed from the "science" defined by mathematical formulations. Over against this faith stood the monolithic Hennebique network, sustained not by calculations but rather by successful structures. The one saw structure as elements fit together by mathematical formulas; the other took structure whole as derived from previous forms behaving successfully.

The lightness in the early Monier forms had not sprung from calculations, but because mathematical formulas could not define all factors in those early forms, Wayss had changed the forms to fit the formulas. Hennebique and his colleagues, on the other hand, did not feel bound by formulas; as forms proved successful they experimented further, and faced with economic competition tried lighter and lighter forms. That made commercial sense but was somewhat problematic as there were no regulations controlling such reductions in materials. Wayss's firm stolidly marched into the twentieth century, his carefully detailed designs making up in permanence what they lacked in elegance. Hennebique's designs began, in places, to come apart even though their daring lightness stimulated other designers. The Wayss organization still stands today; the Hennebique empire as such did not outlive its founder.[9]

The Swiss Synthesis

German science and French daring find their natural synthesis in Switzerland, the one place in Europe where both cultures meet without competing as nationalities. In Switzerland, then, one can be fluent in French and German without feeling obliged to take sides; there it becomes possible to pick the best of each side. This possibility has been a reality of Swiss structural engineering ever since its formal beginnings in 1855, when the newly reformed confederation established as one of its major national acts a Federal Technological Institute in Zurich, the only educational institution not run by the cantons or the cities.[10] Their first civil engineering appointment, Carl Culmann, in himself synthesized the French and German ideals of structure. He was a German, trained in the Technological Institute at Karlsruhe and experienced in German construction of railroad structures. But he had also studied at Metz in France, and was impressed by the French visual tradition of structural analysis pioneered in the eighteenth century by the great mathematician, Gaspard Monge. Culmann brought his German training and taste for calculations to Zurich along with his French ideal of visual studies. His great educational synthesis, *Graphic Statics*, which appeared in 1866, formed the basis of Swiss structural education for the next half century.[11]

Culmann was still more German than French, and his writing and teaching was, for all its visual intentions, imbued with a Germanic science of calculation. It took a native Swiss—Culmann's successor and favorite student, Wilhelm Ritter (1847–1906)—to make complete the peculiar Swiss synthesis that Culmann had envisioned. There could be no more ideal teacher for structural artists than Wilhelm Ritter, whose logical mind and strong aesthetic sensitivity stimulated the two greatest bridge designers of the twentieth century: Robert Maillart (1872–1940) and Othmar Ammann (1879–1965).[12]

Ritter rewrote Culmann's *Graphic Statics* into four short, clear books, and he produced a series of articles which, in contrast to much technical writing since, are of permanent technical value. Above all, Ritter taught the value of both experience and calculations: his lectures were animated by continual reference to full-scale, completed designs, and he unceasingly confronted his students with the fact that the creation of structures is both an aesthetic and a scientific enterprise. He put into the heads of his students images of structure while he was putting into their hands the means of computation. He never separated the two goals and his students thereby went into practice with visual experience and scientific confidence. Not only was Ritter's teaching ideally suited to the new material of reinforced concrete, but his attitude toward design itself helped shape the career of Maillart, for whose early designs Ritter served as the owner's consultant.

Ritter espoused three principles of design. The first principle pertained to the importance of calculations, and had as its objective the justification of more efficient forms by means of simple analyses. In one of his major articles from 1883, Ritter showed how the complex structure of a deck-stiffened arch could be analyzed with astonishing simplicity because the horizontal roadway deck was chosen to be much stiffer than the curved arch below it.[13] This idea came from Ritter's deep understanding of physical behavior, yet for many other academic engineers, such a simplification would have been inadmissable because it did not follow from a general mathematical theory. Ritter knew the general theory as well as anyone alive, but, since his goal was design rather than analysis, he directed the results of his research outward to the design profession rather than inward to the research community. Thus design for Ritter determined the type of mathematical calculations required. Structural function follows from the choice of form.

This principle would be dangerous if it did not go together with a second principle: that the designer's responsibility should include detailed considerations of the construction process as well as of the completed product. In an 1899 series of papers on reinforced concrete, Ritter directly attacked the Hennebique system of local concessionaires working from a centralized guarantee.[14] He argued the need for local engineering supervision of construction to avoid detailed defects and even general collapses. His published warnings became fulfilled prophesy when a Hennebique design of 1901 in Basel collapsed during construction with loss of life and with repercussions throughout Europe that effectively ended Hennebique's early dominance.[15] This highly publicized collapse, reported by a commission of three consultants including Ritter, established the significance of this principle of responsibility and led to the creation of Europe's first national code of practice.[16]

Ritter's third principle connects the calculation accuracy to the construction quality by full-scale load tests. The ultimate measure of structural success is the performance of the completed object in its natural environment. Both the French and the Germans made load tests but neither emphasized them the way the Swiss did. When Hennebique sought to prove the validity of his system, he relied largely on the published results of Swiss full-scale tests in the 1890s. In writing up some of these tests, the Hennebique people were careful to emphasize that Wilhelm Ritter had been present and hence, by implication, had approved.[17] Some Germans tended to rely much more on calculations and hence saw full-scale tests as a waste of time and money. General mathematical calculations, they argued, were much more efficient than individual physical test results. In 1892, Ritter defended the full-scale load test against the strong objection of one of Germany's leading academics, Franz Engesser (1847–1931), then professor at Karlsruhe.[18] Ritter's argument was characteristically Swiss; it assessed the value in practical terms and avoided sweeping generalizations. His central point was the importance of the physical insight gained by the engineer from seeing the structure in its actual setting. This idea includes the purely quantitative goal of checking measured deflections and strain against calculated ones, but also transcends that goal, for seeing the structure itself is profoundly an aesthetic experience. In structural art, the aesthetic experience is therefore made up of both technical correctness and visual surprise, not one or the other but both together. The test of technical correctness comes only after the work is in service. Calculations are indispensable but their value depends exclusively on the extent to which they predict correctly the full-scale behavior. Hennebique was right in emphasizing his broad experience, but wrong in leaving it largely unquantified before 1901. Wayss was right in promoting scientific model testing and standardized formulas, but Engesser was wrong in deemphasizing full-scale loading of specific objects. Ritter synthesized the two approaches, and by so doing prepared the way for the greatest designs in structural art of the twentieth century.

Robert Maillart

Between 1900 and 1940 Robert Maillart effected a revolution in structural art, the significance of which is only now becoming evident to engineers and the general public. He was the first twentieth-century designer to break completely with the masonry past and put concrete into forms technically appropriate to its properties and yet visually surprising.

Maillart was born in Bern on February 6, 1872, of a Swiss-German mother and a Belgian father whose parents had settled in Geneva shortly after the revolutions of 1848. In 1890, Maillart entered the Federal Technical Institute of Zurich, where he came under the influence of Ritter, who taught him graphic statics, structural design, and bridges. After graduation in 1894, Maillart worked first on railway design for a Bernese engineering firm, then on road and bridge design for the public works department of the city of Zurich, and finally on the design and construction of bridges and buildings for a designer-builder in Zurich.[19] In early 1902, he founded in Zurich the firm of Maillart & Company, designers and builders of reinforced concrete structures.

Within the next decade, his firm grew to international proportions, establishing offices in Spain and Russia. In 1914, while Maillart, his wife, and their three children were summering in Riga, they were cut off from home by the war and decided to remain in Russia, where they lived until late 1918. There Maillart built a number of large works, until the revolution ended his business and, in fact, nearly cost him his life. He returned to Switzerland in early 1919 in debt, without a home, a widower (his wife having died in 1916), and with no business. Between 1920 and 1940 Maillart reestablished himself as a designer (but not a builder) with offices in Geneva, Bern, and Zurich. Living mostly alone and, for the last decade of his life, in his office, Maillart created the major designs for which he is known today. Of his forty-seven major bridges all but three are still in active service, many after seventy-five years of continuous use. Nearly all his major buildings are also intact, his two greatest thin shells—the St. Gallen Gasholders and the Zurich Cement Hall—being exceptions.[20] In addition, he left a large body of writing, mostly published in the *Swiss Building Journal (Schweizerische Bauzeitung)*, which expresses his ideas on structural art.

Photographs and models of his structures have appeared in numerous art museum exhibitions since the pioneering one man show at the New York Museum of Modern Art in 1947. It was largely through Maillart's work that the twentieth-century modern art movement formed its ideas about engineering as art. He confronted the art world, for the first time, with a body of twentieth-century work that is acknowledged to be art but that came completely from the imagination of an engineer. The idea that there is an independent art form of engineering structure has its origin in studies of Maillart's work. Because concrete images must precede abstract formulations, we need to look closely at a few of Maillart's typical designs in order to understand the way he combined technical correctness with visual surprise in structure.

New Bridge Forms

Maillart had recognized by 1900 that concrete design allowed forms not previously possible with stone or metal.[21] In his 1901 Zuoz Bridge, he designed the curved arch and the flat roadway deck to be connected by longitudinal walls which turned the complete structure into a hollow box girder. Although this idea is the same as Stephenson's tubular bridge and Maillart used it for the first time in reinforced concrete, he did not get the idea from the earlier metal bridges. Rather the idea came to him visually from the image of the 1899 Stauffacher Bridge which he had designed two years earlier for the city of Zurich (figure 9.2). There, the curved arch was heavy and hidden behind a stone facade forming the longitudinal walls. The roadway deck load was carried to the arch by concrete cross walls.

Maillart copied the visual form of Stauffacher but for its useless stone facade walls substituted at Zuoz structural concrete longitudinal walls (figure 9.3). It was the visual suggestion of form that stimulated him to recognize how decoration could be turned into utility. Of course, he knew, through Ritter, all about metal bridge forms including hollow boxes in iron and steel. But that did not begin his design thinking; it only confirmed an idea gotten from thinking about his own

FIGURE 9.2
The Stauffacher Bridge over the Sihl River, Zurich, Switzerland, 1899, by Robert Maillart. The three-hinged concrete arch of 39.6-meter span is hidden behind a masonry facade designed by City Architect Gustav Gull.

FIGURE 9.3
The Zuoz Bridge over the Inn River, Zuoz, Switzerland, 1901, by Robert Maillart. In this 38.3-meter-span bridge, Maillart turned the decorative masonry walls at Stauffacher into structural walls forming the first hollow-box bridge ever built in reinforced concrete.

first-hand experience. The aesthetic idea preceded and controlled the technical one.

Both at Stauffacher and Zuoz, Ritter was the consultant for the owner (the city of Zurich and canton of Graubunden), and without Ritter's support Maillart would not have designed the Stauffacher nor built the Zuoz design. There was no mathematical theory for analyzing the concrete hollow box for Zuoz, and Ritter admitted to the canton that he had difficulty figuring out how to justify the design by calculation. In many countries that difficulty would have led to an official disapproval, but here it meant only that Ritter had to think harder about the idea and to design a careful full-scale load test to insure its validity.

Ritter's consulting report on the Zuoz load test is a model for bridge design, particularly as care in understanding physical reality is given precedence over concern for accuracy from mathematical approximations. The test did reveal minor cracking and thus instructed both Ritter and Maillart (who was there for the entire three-day test program) but overall the results permitted Ritter to endorse the design and to comment favorably on its new aesthetic.[22]

Maillart was to learn even more from the permanent laboratory at Zuoz. Two years later he returned, at the request of the authorities, to advise them on the new longitudinal-wall cracks which had appeared near the abutments. The overall work was unimpaired, but Maillart again had learned an invaluable lesson. In his 1904 bridge design, for a crossing of the Vorder Rhine River at Tavanasa, he removed that part of the wall which had cracked at Zuoz. The result was a new form with unprecedented visual power, increased material efficiency, and decreased cost for construction and maintenance—in short, a better bridge. Tavanasa (figure 9.4) was Maillart's first masterpiece, but the conventional taste of prewar Europe disregarded the bridge. A quarter of a century was to pass before Maillart could build such a form again.

Tavanasa, like Zuoz and Stauffacher, was a three-hinged arch. The concrete arches were made up of two identical halves and connected to both abutments and to each other at the crown by hinges which literally permit free rotation at those three points. These hinges allow the arch to rise freely without internal stress when the temperature rises, and to drop when it goes down. In Hennebique's 1899 Vienne River bridge at Châtellerault, the arches had no hinges and cracked badly at the abutments and at the crown. Hennebique never drew any

FIGURE 9.4

The Tavanasa Bridge over the Vorder Rhine River, at Tavanasa, Switzerland, 1905, by Robert Maillart. Here, Maillart removed those parts of the walls that had cracked at Zuoz and achieved his first bridge masterpiece in which the three-hinged arch form is expressed visually. The 51-meter bridge was the longest-spanning reinforced concrete arch bridge in Switzerland and the third longest in the world when completed.

conclusions from this full-scale fact and even ridiculed Maillart for his use of hinges at Zuoz.[23]

Maillart's famous bridges of the 1930s derived from the Tavanasa form. In 1927, an avalanche destroyed the Tavanasa Bridge and stimulated Maillart the next year to design, nearby, a bridge over the Salginatobel (figure 9.5) with the same form. For this 1930 bridge Maillart dispensed with stone abutments and created a form with no visual reference at all to other materials. The Salginatobel bridge marked the beginning of Maillart's last and most fruitful decade. Like Zuoz and Tavanasa, the Salginatobel came to Maillart because of a design-construction competition, in which his was the least costly solution. Those and later works, therefore, satisfy as well as any other twentieth-century design the criteria for structural art: minimum materials, minimum cost, and maximum aesthetic expression.

FIGURE 9.5

The Salginatobel Bridge near Schiers, Switzerland, 1930, by Robert Maillart. Maillart won the design-construction contract by submitting (with the builder Florian Prader) the lowest bid out of eighteen other designs. The 90-meter span was the longest of Maillart's career, and its spectacular setting has made it his most famous work. It is a hollow-box, three-hinged arch.

Throughout his many designs, Maillart kept learning from load tests, and from their results kept refining his mathematical calculations. His learning led to new forms and his refining to simpler formulas. Meanwhile, in Zurich during the 1920s, with Wilhelm Ritter dead, the German scientific influence had increased, and Maillart's ideas began to be attacked by a new generation of academics, whose research was directed more and more to other researchers and whose teaching was based less and less on the exemplary structures recently built.[24] This attack came most heavily against Maillart's second new bridge form: the deck-stiffened arch. Here again Maillart had gotten his ideas partly from field observations, and partly with the help of Ritter. The field observations came from a new arch bridge Maillart had completed in 1913. This bridge, at Aarburg over the Aare River, was neither hinged nor a hollow box. Instead, the arch carried all the load as at Stauffacher, and got no help from walls or deck as at Zuoz. In other words, Maillart made the arch relatively heavy, with the deck relatively light and the connecting columns very light. A rather deep concrete parapet, not part of the structure, gave the deck the appearance of a stiffness that it did not possess. Again, and as at Zuoz, cracks were observed several years after completion. Two things were apparent: first, the structurally light deck, where the cracks were substantial, was deflecting together with the arch, contradicting the standard assumptions of the time that a deck was rigidly supported on an unyielding arch; second, the visually heavy parapet suggested a means of stiffening the weak deck, much as the visually heavy and structurally useless masonry wall at Stauffacher had suggested a means for stiffening the thin arch at Zuoz.

Upon reestablishing himself after his return from Russia in 1919, Maillart began once again his search for thinner, more elegant forms, now in the light of his experience with the Aarburg bridge. In 1923 he designed a small bridge in the Wäggital over the Flienglibach, where, based on the Aarburg cracking, he designed the parapet to be part of the greatly stiffened deck. In effect he went back to Ritter's 1883 idea of a thin arch supporting a stiff deck. The resulting form used less materials, cost less, and was the first step in Maillart's search for a second new form type which culminated in 1926 with the Valtschielbach Bridge. From then until 1934, he designed a series of deck-stiffened arch bridges, successively refining both the form and the

FIGURE 9.6

The Schwandbach Bridge near Hinterfultigen, Switzerland, 1933, by Robert Maillart. With a span of 37.4 meters, this is the best known of Maillart's deck-stiffened arch bridges. Its very thin arch is stiffened by the horizontally curved roadway, and the two parts are integrated by vertical trapezoidal cross walls.

means of calculation until in the end he arrived at the masterpieces of Schwandbach and Töss. Maillart designed his bridge over the Schwandbach (figure 9.6) by removing entirely the heavy and unnecessary stone abutments, by replacing the heavy deck parapet with a lighter curb beam and metal railing, and by smoothly integrating the horizontally curved roadway with the vertically curved arch. At Schwandbach the full integration of form permits a new thinness and eliminates any superficial harmony in stone. The bridge is strikingly thin, fully integrated, and contrasts vigorously with the setting. It is undeniably a work of man not of nature. It springs not from any organic, natural forms (forms found in nature) but from the imagination of an engineer. It expresses the ideal of minimum waste in materials and monies as well as the unique personality of Maillart. No one else ever before or since has designed a work quite like it. It stretches the artificial stone to its limits just as Eiffel stretched iron at Garabit and the

Champs de Mars. But it is, for all its thinness, even more permanent than those works of iron. As with all those works of the highest art, there seems to be no way to improve on the Schwandbach Bridge.

At the same time, "scientific" researchers in engineering schools found more complex ways of analyzing deck-stiffened arches, and were thereby led away from the possibilities for new forms. A major national report published in the United States in 1935 addressed this same design form; because analysis coming from general theory was so complex, the committee did not see how a simple theory could be sound, and it never recognized Maillart's works or his ideas. The result was an arrested growth in structural art for American concrete bridges. Even in Switzerland, researchers carried out major studies during this period and completely neglected Maillart's designs, not because they were unaware of them but because they were overwhelmed by the complexities of general theory. An exception was a detailed Swiss report published by Mirko Roš, which fully discussed Maillart's designs by documenting a series of major full-scale load tests. This report provides a firm basis for stating that Maillart's highly simplified calculations more accurately predicted bridge performance than the complex computations publicized by the academic researchers. Maillart's aesthetic goal of a more beautiful form combined with his extensive field observations led him to develop a more rational procedure for calculations.

New Building Forms

As we saw in our discussion of the Chicago school, the structure is only one part of the city office building and, so long as the building scale is small, that structure can easily be considered after the overall design is set. Thus, apart from industrial works nearly all of the early concrete buildings did not reflect structure visually and many hid it completely. To find structural art we must look to buildings where the structure is the primary function and where, in Condit's phrase, the structure and the form are indissoluably one. Maillart invented new forms for three major types of building in which the structure and form are one: the column-supported floor, the beam-supported roof, and the thin-shell vault. In each case, he created works of art; each type, serving quite different purposes, led to a very different visual form.

In 1908, Maillart designed and tested a new type of column-supported floor system, primarily for warehouses. On this system the concrete slab rests directly on columns with exposed capitals. He eliminated all beams under the floor, thereby increasing the usable space and allowing the mechanical and electrical services to be run under the slab. Visually, Maillart designed the capitals to make a smooth transition both into the column below and into the slab above. At the same time, from among the many possible choices, he picked the one that appealed most to his aesthetic sense. In this way, he combined in one form "the most rational and the most beautiful." But we cannot accept that aphorism of Maillart's without discussion, because of the confusion that often arises with the term "rational."

For Maillart, the most rational form meant that form which transfers the forces from slab to column by a hyperbolic profile (in the engineer's language: the profile that coincides with the diagram of shear forces). But the forces are uncertain, and the structural difference between the hyperbola and, for example, the parabola are insignificant at the scale of Maillart's capitals. Therefore, Maillart had a wide choice of form (indeed, competing European designers in the 1920s and American designers before World War I used a wide variety of capital forms) and he chose that one which appealed most to him visually, the one where the transition was the smoothest.

Looking more carefully at Maillart's form (figure 9.7), we see that the transition is smooth overall, but broken in detail by his use of flat wooden boards for the concrete formwork. His rational smoothness was compromised by his need to build the form competitively. Many other designers used capital forms derived from various imitations of Greek columns. When done simply these forms were also competitive and transferred the loads satisfactorily, but they do not rise to structural art any more than does Sullivan's Wainwright facade. Maillart's capital form is structural art because it expresses the structure in a pure and new way, and with a simplicity that was inexpensive to build. Another solution to the problem of designing heavily loaded floors was invented, for example, by the Italian engineer, Pier Luigi Nervi, who designed and built flat slabs made with two sets of intersecting ribs (figure 9.8); these forms are no less rational but they express a different aesthetic, which we shall discuss in the next chapter.

FIGURE 9.7
The Mushroom Floor for the Giesshübel warehouse, Zurich, 1910, by Robert Maillart. The floor loads are transferred to columns directly from the beamless concrete slab through column capitals, shaped to provide a smooth flow of forces for both efficiency and elegance.

FIGURE 9.8

The Gatti Wool Factory, Rome, 1951, by Pier Luigi Nervi. Here Nervi has designed a flat-slab industrial floor supported by columns with capitals. Unlike Maillart, Nervi visualized structure as patterns of two-way ribs. In Italy, he was able to build such systems competitively. Comparison with Maillart's design shows how two structural artists can create visually different solutions to the same problem without either one being technically or economically superior in general.

If Maillart's deck-stiffened arches express his aesthetic idea of thinness, then his warehouse floors express the idea of integration. The problems of the second building type—beam-supported roofs—are more directly like those encountered in bridges, for there the need is for long spans to carry relatively light live loading. In 1924, Maillart designed a roof for the outdoor shed of a warehouse in Chiasso (figure 9.9). The building is only a roof; the form is pure structure and for that prototypical engineering problem Maillart found a solution inspired by bridge design. The long spans are made up of trussed beams in which the top part is the light concrete slab roof and the bottom part is essentially a group of steel bars minimally covered with concrete. This lower thinness is integrated to the solid slab by thin vertical struts, and to the column supports by a lateral widening. The overall effect is one of startling lightness and originality. Shortly after completion it was criticized for being forced and arbitrary, that is, not rational; but a recent detailed engineering analysis has shown it to be as fully rational as the column capitals Maillart designed for his warehouses.[25]

One reason for the criticism of the Chiasso, and for the fact that many critics who admire Maillart's bridges do not care for his roofs, lies in the difficulty of seeing certain types of buildings as structural

---

FIGURE 9.9

The Magazzini Generali Warehouse Shed, Chiasso, Switzerland, 1924, by Robert Maillart. The form of this truss-like roof frame deepens at midspan where the forces are greatest. Careful engineering studies have shown the form to be highly efficient; it is also original with Maillart.

FIGURE 9.10

The Cement Hall for the National Exhibition in Zurich, 1939, by Robert Maillart. The thinness of this pure structure is visible over the entire profile. The roof and walls are one, and the main vertical load is carried by four central columns tapered from arch ribs down to hingelike supports.

art rather than as architectural art. This difficulty applies as well to Maillart's third major new form, a thin-shell vault for the Cement Hall (figure 9.10), designed as part of the Swiss National Exhibition of 1939 in Zurich. Sadly, this thin shell concrete structure was demolished after the fair, although its behavior was minutely detailed in good Swiss fashion during a load test to destruction.[26] Again, the form is the structure, Maillart having expressed a surpassing thinness and integration by designing one continuous surface whose edges were fully exposed to view. Its remarkable strength is clearly documented in the load test report.

In what sense are these two roofs structural rather than architectural art? The answer lies in the distinctions of scale, use, and form. The scale is large enough so that the supporting structure requires engineering design. The use is simple enough so that the structure and form can functionally coincide. And the form itself is designed to control forces rather than to create spaces.

But, in both cases, the scale is small enough so that, for different uses, the form could be hidden or contorted. The Chiasso shed could be the roof of a one-story office building, in which case the walls and the interior complexity of uses would render the visible structure of secondary importance. Even the Cement Hall is not so large that it could not be a small office or large home, in which case *its* structure might be reasonably contorted to satisfy nonstructural functions. In short, the more the spaces become primarily intended for human living, the more the building becomes a means to the end of space, and hence architectural art. But in the warehouse, the shed, the exhibition piece, the structure creates space only secondarily. In the floor, it primarily creates a capacity for storage of heavy materials; in the shed roof, it provides the means for protecting materials from the weather by shedding rain and carrying snow; and in the exhibition piece, it served to express the potentials of concrete as structure—it was an advertisement for the new material and a stimulant to a new art form.

Judging by architectural ideas, many critics would argue that these structures cannot compete with, for example, the flat plate floor designs in Maison Domino, the intensely shaped roofs at Chandrigar, and the thin shell concrete roof for the Phillips Pavilion at the Brussels Fair of 1938. All of these Le Corbusier buildings have been heralded as exemplifying the finest of architectural art. It is not our goal here to criticize that judgment, but it is important to point out that those architectural works have very little to do with structural art. They follow quite different ideals and could never be judged by the standards of minimum materials, minimum cost, and expression of structure as structure.

A contrast between, for example, the Phillips Pavilion and the Cement Hall shows this difference immediately. The Le Corbusier building, small as it is, could not be understood as structure. The reason is simple; the building is more a work of sculpture. Le Corbusier's form did not spring from structural imagination, and even some of the finest thin shell concrete engineers in the world could not clearly explain its behavior.[27] Maillart, on the other hand, designed his form so simply that any engineer can see how he visualized the behavior which the load test confirmed.

The thinness of his pure roof structure is visible over the entire profile of the building, the roof and walls are one, and the main vertical load is carried by four central columns tapered from arch ribs down to hingelike supports. Thin slabs provide horizontal restraint at the shell edges, and the two arch ribs stiffen the parabolic shell. The primary function was to express structure, and this stimulated Maillart to invent a form that was thin, integrated, and contrasted strongly with its setting. Engineering imagination is partly undermined by the attempt to make the structure harmonize visually with its surroundings.

This difference in viewpoint explains why it was that many of the most prominent thin shell concrete structures designed during the 1950s by architects generally were not thin, far overran cost estimates, and often performed badly to the point of collapse: the Berlin Congress Hall, the Sydney Opera House, the Kresge Auditorium, the New York TWA Terminal—all proclaimed during this period as precursors of a new architecture.[28]

As we shall see, a few designers, including at least one architect, did understand Maillart's shell and even his aesthetic well enough to create, during this same post–World War II period, roof structures of great beauty that do reflect the criteria of structural art.

CHAPTER 10

ROOF VAULTS AND

NATIONAL STYLES

Engineering Imagination and Local Vision

When Sigfried Giedion (1888–1968) made the third revision of his classic *Space, Time and Architecture* in 1954 he added an afterword to the chapter on Maillart, stimulated largely by the Zurich Cement Hall.[1] There he spoke of the great future for thin shell roofs, and in a revised introduction to the book itself he called shells "the starting point for the specific solution of the vaulting problem for our period."[2] Giedion had discovered Maillart for the world of modern art even before most of his greatest works had been designed. The Swiss art historian saw in Maillart's bridges and flat slabs of the 1920s how pure engineering works could be works of art. But, although he could see that the 1939 Cement Hall, "in the hands of a great engineer. . . became at once a work of art,"[3] Giedion's evaluation of works built after World

171

War II was less incisive. In extolling such vault designs as the exorbitantly expensive Sydney Opera House, he missed the deeper implications of Maillart's works and, in more general terms, the separate tradition of structural art. Giedion came as close as anyone to appreciating the art of the engineer in his perceptive essays on Eiffel, Maillart, and others; but, with regard to vaults, Giedion did not follow the development of structural forms that had arisen after World War I. These vaulting forms arose from the engineering imagination which took off from simple ideas grounded in the laws of nature. For example, gravity dictates the shape taken by a suspension bridge cable under load. Imagine the cable frozen and turned upside down; the result is an arch, and a series of such arches can form a dome surface.

Yet the history of twentieth-century structural engineering does not follow a linear progression, mainly because the laws of nature must interact with—locally based—aesthetics. It is not a question of one development leading directly to another and so on, but rather of parallel ideas arising in different societies and then flowering in ways that reflect the particular patterns of those societies as well as the general laws of nature. In spite of serious efforts to share information and ideas internationally during the past century—indeed, since the first great World's Fair of 1851—local vision still strongly influences structural technology.[4] The importance of local biases was already made evident in our last chapter. And it was local biases, far more than any general theories or scientific discoveries, which set the direction of thin shell roof design following World War I.

We can identify at least three distinct, independent, and nearly simultaneous lines of development, each associated with a different cultural tradition. In Germany that tradition was mathematical and scientific, in Italy it was historical and artistic, and in Spain it was rooted in an artisan building tradition. All three lines of development were aimed at the goal of covering large areas with curved concrete surfaces, and of creating strong structures with thin, curved slabs rather than with thick, flat ones. (This is the principle behind corrugated metal and Gothic vaulting.) The Germans tended to work with surfaces that they could study mathematically, like spherical domes and circular cylinders, and they made visually separate systems of beams, walls, and arches to support those surfaces. The Italian, Nervi, by contrast, designed ribbed surfaces that were reinterpretations of earlier masonry ribbed vaults in Italy and elsewhere, and he sought to integrate visually the ribbed surface and the supporting structure. The Spanish designers, meanwhile, stimulated by a local artisan tradition of laminated tile vaults, used reinforced concrete to create smooth ribless surfaces, which they also tried to integrate smoothly with the support structure. Each of the three lines developed between the wars, but did not reach its full potential until the 1950s.

Dischinger, Finsterwalder, and the German School

When Wilhelm Ritter defended load tests against the arguments advanced by Franz Engesser, he was putting the Swiss concern with physical observation above the German concern with mathematical calculation. Thirty years later, one of Engesser's star pupils, Franz Dischinger (1887–1953), from that mathematical bias began a German development in shell roof design that has continued to the present. In 1913, Dischinger went to work for the German building firm of Dyckerhoff and Widmann A. G., which by then was already established, along with Wayss and Freytag, as Germany's leading designer–builders of reinforced concrete structures. In 1922, Walter Bauersfeld (1879–1959) of the Zeiss Optical firm, in collaboration with Dischinger, designed a thin shell hemispherical dome roof for a planetarium in Munich. Together Bauersfeld and Dischinger took out patents on what came to be called the Zeiss–Dywidag system of thin shell concrete roof structures.[5] They then sought more general applications for their system, and began to design factory roofs and market halls. But, being Germans in a scientific tradition, they felt uncomfortable with any structural form that they could not analyze mathematically, and hence immediately set out to find a mathematical formulation for domes. In 1928, Dischinger was able to present a full mathematical treatise on domes and to show numerous designs, either built by then or under construction, that were based upon these formulations.[6]

More important than the mathematics itself, however, is the way in which Dischinger used the formulas to make the forms. His starting points, as a designer, were physical images developed from mathematical formulas. Because the formulas assumed axial symmetry (a surface of rotation formed geometrically by rotating a curve about a vertical axis), the plan form had to be close to a circle. Because the designers assumed roof loads to be carried to columns by separate structural systems, either beams or arches, they expressed the supports between columns by such systems.[7]

None of these limitations prevented Dyckerhoff and Widmann from building shells; indeed, the confidence inspired by the mathematical theory encouraged them to explore other forms. Dischinger tried to find ways to apply his thin shell ideas not only to domes but also to buildings rectangular in plan. For such plans, he tried to devise shell forms by stretching domes in one direction so that he could use some variant of his axisymmetrical thin shell theory. He tried to make form follow formula. This attempt did not work; Dischinger needed another approach. He knew that a simple barrel shell form (a slab curved to a circular arc) would be easy to build, but he could not find a satisfactory mathematical theory for it. However, a younger colleague took up that challenge and soon had a formulation. That colleague was Ulrich Finsterwalder (b. 1897), who would become the most versatile designer of reinforced concrete structures of his generation.

Finsterwalder inherited the German scientific tradition directly from his father, a professor of mathematics in Munich and a pioneer in photogrammetry and the theory of glacial movements. During World War I, as a prisoner of the French, the young Finsterwalder studied mathematics, and, after his release, completed the course in civil engineering at the Munich Institute of Technology. He graduated in 1922 and immediately joined Dyckerhoff and Widmann, with whom he remained for his entire career.[8] Starting with his diploma project at Munich, Finsterwalder worked on the mathematical theory of barrel shells until he published the first workable formulations in 1933.[9] Again the form came from the formulas.

Finsterwalder's first mathematical theory (which is technically called the membrane theory and considers the shell to have no resistance to bending) showed that unless the edge slope was purely vertical, the longitudinal edges of the barrel needed tangential supports. Therefore, he designed an elliptical cross-section to create a vertical edge. When this vertical wall-like edge proved difficult to build, he tried another form suggested by his more general theory of 1933. This form had a circular cross-section with longitudinal edge beams. But even this theory was restricted by the mathematical requirement that the barrel be supported vertically along its entire arc length at each end. This requirement from the mathematical theory led Finsterwalder to design a thin vertical wall at each end to give the calculated support.

The theory—and, for the Germans, therefore the designed form—was restricted to circular barrels with longitudinal edge beams and transverse wall supports. This new form was economically competitive, and showed how concrete shells could be substantially lighter than other types of concrete roof forms. Dischinger showed, for example, that each of his Leipzig shell domes of 1929 (figure 10.1) was only one-third as heavy as the 1913 Breslau arch-ring dome (also built by Dyckerhoff and Widmann), even though the Leipzig structures each covered an area about 30 percent greater than that covered by the pre-war dome.[10]

These domes and barrels did not show visually their thinness, however, and they appeared more to be made up of separately functioning elements than to be a single integrated form. But, even if these German forms did not achieve the highest qualities of structural art, they at least proved convincingly that thin surfaces in artificial stone could be economically built and would safely stand. This was a major achievement in structural engineering, and it encouraged subsequent developments elsewhere, though others did not take up these specifically German forms.

FIGURE 10.1

The Market Hall, Leipzig, Germany, 1929, by Franz Dischinger. Each of these 76-meter-span polygonal domes was only one-third the weight of the 67-meter-span Breslau dome of 1913, then the longest-spanning concrete dome. The lightness was possible because these Leipzig domes were designed as thin-shell surfaces.

Nervi and the Italian Tradition

Turning from the Germans to the Italian Pier Luigi Nervi (1891–1979), we come to an engineer who centered his entire career on aesthetics. There is no doubt whatsoever that Nervi saw himself as an artist whose mission was to create beautiful objects. Beginning to design on his own at the time Maillart's greatest works were appearing, Nervi saw that structure could be art when it arose out of correct form, careful construction practice, and a conscious aesthetic intention. During the 1930s, Nervi was designing and building large concrete structures, mostly as a result of winning cost competitions, although his intellectual bent was for reflection and for aesthetics. Whereas Dischinger and Finsterwalder were writing about domes and barrels designed on the basis of the theories they had developed, Nervi was writing such articles as "The Art and Technique of Building," "Thoughts on Engineering," "Problems of Architectural Achievement," and "Technology and the New Aesthetic Direction."[11] He wrote no treatises on scientific analyses. Indeed, even a more technical paper written in 1939, "Considerations on the Cracks in the Dome of Sta. Maria del Fiore and on Their Probable Cause," serves to indicate something of the role that the ancient Italian monuments played for Nervi. His first book appeared in 1945 with the title *Is Building an Art or a Science?*[12] By this title he meant to imply, as he stated in his next book *Structures* (1955, English edition 1956), that structures "can be solved correctly only through a superior and purely intuitive re-elaboration of the mathematical results."[13] To illustrate this intuitive approach, he told of his teacher at Bologna who in 1913 read his students "the alarmed letters of his German colleagues, who proved mathematically that the Risorgimento Bridge in Rome was in immediate danger of failing—and in fact should have failed already—although the bridge had been built and was then in full use."[14] In fact, the bridge still stood, and Nervi's point was that the designer, François Hennebique, had not needed a complicated mathematical theory to create a beautiful and safe bridge.

Nervi began practicing after graduation from Bologna in civil engineering in 1913, but it was not until 1932, at the age of forty-one, that he completed a major structure on his own. During those nearly twenty years of practice, however, he gained design and field experience

FIGURE 10.2
The Pantheon, Rome, 124 A.D. This Roman design in unreinforced concrete spans 43.5 meters and remained the widest-spanning concrete dome until surpassed in 1913 by the Breslau dome.

with reinforced concrete, so that when he first began to design and build his own works they were the product of considerable maturity. The most spectacular of these are certainly the domes and barrel shells he built between 1935 and 1959. These are also the works that best illustrate Nervi's preoccupation with very simple overall shapes made up of an interplay of individual elements. In his domes, these elements are ribs which make the overall dome both stable and light. This is precisely the tradition that one sees in earlier Italian domes. The two earliest shells of great size that still stand are the Pantheon (figure 10.2) and part of the Basilica of Constantine. In both cases, the heavy masonry surface is lightened by a coffering, which results in an interior structure of two-way ribs, the type of system used by Nervi in his Little Sports Palace (see figure 10.3, p.181).[15] Moreover, the two great domes of the Italian Renaissance, although differently made, are both ribbed. St. Peter's has meridional ribs outside and decorations inside that resemble coffering. The Brunelleschi dome in Florence has, between inner and outer shells, two-way ribs which cannot be seen but which are evident in the well-known drawings of the construction. Significant dome ribbing also characterizes the works of the Turin designer Guarini (1624–1683), whose crossways ribbing for St. Lorenzo in Turin appear as small-scale precursors to Nervi's modern works. Some of Nervi's most spectacular early works were in fact in Turin.

With this historical background, Nervi approached reinforced concrete in just the way Maillart had: both as a builder of competitive structures and as a designer of new forms. As Nervi put it, his early experiences "had formed in me a habit of searching for solutions that were intrinsically and constructionally the most economic, a habit which the many succeeding competition tenders (almost the totality of my projects) have only succeeded in strengthening."[16] Nervi's whole outlook was, therefore, influenced by the search for economy. He would have had almost no chance to build had his designs not been the cheapest. At the same time, this economy was, for Nervi, intimately connected with finding "the method of bringing dead and live loads down to the foundations . . . with the minimum use of materials." Economy of cost and efficiency of materials were, however, never enough, for as he continued, "I still remember the long and patient work to find an agreement between the static necessities . . . and the desire to obtain something which for me would have a satisfying appearance." Nervi continually emphasized that although in structural design the study of external loads and internal resisting forces (the statics) "offers a definite direction, . . . the detailing of forms and their interrelationship is a personal choice."[17]

Nervi also realized clearly that his own vision had been formed in his native Italy and could only with great difficulty be transferred to another country. "Many times," he wrote, "I have refused to accept commissions . . . in countries with whose possibilities for building [large structures] I was not familiar in order to avoid running the risk of designing shapes and structures which might prove impossible to build."[18] Once world famous, Nervi did accept a few prestigious commissions abroad, the best known being the UNESCO center in Paris and the Port Authority bus terminal in New York near the George Washington Bridge. However, these do not reflect Nervi's greatness as a structural artist, even though the UNESCO buildings are good examples of fruitful collaboration with architects. It is to his Italian works that we must look for an understanding of Nervi's art.

Nervi completed a series of eight aircraft hangars between 1936 and 1939, which are essentially barrel shells 131 feet wide and 328 feet long. For the first two, chosen after a cost competition and built in 1936, Nervi designed, as he called it, "a unified structural system . . . in a vaulted form." But because the supports were unsymmetrical, he chose a system of cast-in-place, two-way ribs covered with tiles rather than a thin-shell surface. While removing the scaffold, Nervi meticulously measured the deformations of the roof to check its safety and to learn more about the performance of his novel structure. As Maillart had done with his early bridges, Nervi learned from full-scale behavior and was thus stimulated to develop new forms. When the roof tiles on the 1936 hangars began breaking away and falling from the ribs, he realized that these two parts—tile covering and rib structure—moved differently with temperature changes.[19] He was able to correct that defect on the built hangars and then, when the Italian air force asked for bids on a new series of six new hangars in 1939, he, recalling the experience years later, "began to study the problem trying to make use both of the positive and negative experiences of 1936."[20] The most significant change was Nervi's idea of saving materials by precasting the ribs as concrete trusses and by making the supports symmetrical so that the analysis was easier and the results more predictable.

He made detailed small-scale model studies, and again he measured deformations over the entire surface as the scaffold was lowered. Nervi always considered "these structures . . . the most interesting . . . I have studied in my long career as designer and contractor." Moreover, he stressed, "I saw again how a purely technical process also brought aesthetic results and suggested promising architectural directions."[21] His new cross-wise lacework ribbings clearly satisfied him, and they were to become more and more the mark of his personal style.

In his next major work, the 1948 Agnelli Exhibition Hall in Turin, he again used open, light precast ribs, this time for a barrel span of 262 feet over a 328-foot-long rectangular room. At one end, the room ended with a 197-foot-diameter semicircular apse or half-dome, for which Nervi devised a new system of precasting, developed during the winter of 1944 when he had closed the office so as "not to collaborate with the Nazi occupation forces."[22] The system consisted of precasting small diamond-shaped pans in smooth metal molds, placing these pieces side by side on the scaffold, and then casting a thin layer of concrete over top and in between the pans. The result is a monolithic thin shell dome with ribs exposed on the ceiling. As Nervi noted, "the process [is] effective from a technical and economic point of view and resulted in a great plastic richness."[23] By technical, he meant that the system carries loads easily with little material, and by plastic richness, he of course referred to the elegant diamond patterns formed by these diagonal ribs. He achieved the same richness in his ribbed flat slabs for the Gatti Wool Factory of 1951 (see figure 9.8, p. 166.).

In the final and greatest masterpiece of this diagonally ribbed style, Nervi's 1957 design for the Little Sports Palace in Rome, the double rib system creates a decorative pattern out of a technically superior design idea. (figure 10.3)[24] That idea is related to the major technical problem in thin shell domes—buckling. It is possible to construct immense ribless domes of exceptional thinness in which under gravity the internal compression stresses are small. But even small stresses can cause deformations, which in a very thin surface can change the geometry enough to buckle the shell and result in collapse. The problem is, in principle, the same as in the compression of a very thin rod of steel. If the rod is long, and if I push on its ends, it will buckle sideways even when its stresses are very small. Buckling is combated by stiffness and not by mass. The thin rod can be made, for example, into a system

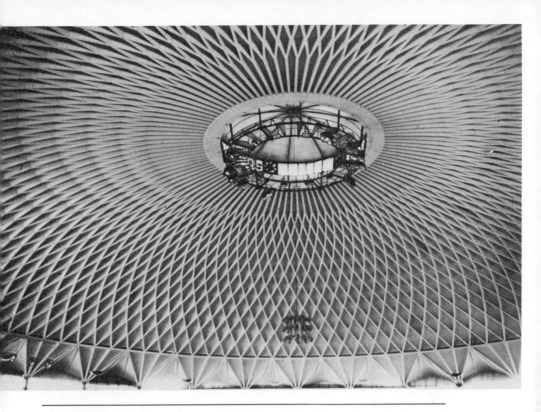

FIGURE 10.3

The Little Sports Palace, Rome, 1957, by Pier Luigi Nervi. Nervi designed and built this 197-foot-span with two sets of ribs which intersect to form an elegant pattern roof. At the same time the ribs allow the structure to be both stiffer and lighter than a solid-surface dome, the same principle followed by the designer of the Pantheon.

of four rods laced together—as in each leg of the Eiffel Tower—without adding material (the sum of the four rods could in fact be made less than the one rod they replace). In the same way, Nervi has made his Little Sports Palace dome much stiffer by adding the ribs but with no more material because of the coffers. The ribs brace the shell just as Eiffel's four rods brace each other. Material is not added but merely redistributed, and that redistribution can be done in many ways, which opens up the possibility for personal aesthetic style. By 1948, Nervi had found this method of enhancing the safety of domes without increasing mass; his system in Italy was economical, and it liberated his imagination to express a variety of spectacular forms. With the Little Sports Palace, Nervi achieved a high point in the structural art of building in concrete, and he achieved it on his own by learning from his past works and by striving always for beauty and economy.

THE NEW AGE OF STEEL AND CONCRETE

In many of Nervi's buildings there is a collaborating architect, but the constant development in style is entirely Nervi's. Just as Eiffel had excellent collaborating chief engineers, so Nervi frequently worked with sensitive architects, but the structural design for his Italian works was always his own. Nervi's works are the greatest when the architectural requirements converge most closely with pure structural ones. Where there is a complexity of functions, such as that which we saw in the Chicago sixteen-story buildings, then Nervi's art is compromised. For example, the Little Sports Palace is almost pure structure, and it shows that purity both from within and from without. By contrast, the Large Sports Palace (figure 10.4), which Nervi designed for the 1960

FIGURE 10.4

The Large Sports Palace, Rome, 1960, by Pier Luigi Nervi. Designed and built by Nervi for the 1960 Olympic games, this 330-foot-span dome has a different two-way rib system, showing how Nervi put variety into his designs without compromising his technical or aesthetic quality.

Olympics, is so large that its auxiliary functions produced a surrounding building complex that destroys the exterior structural expression, and partly disrupts the visual logic of the interior structure as well. The main domed space is spectacular but the approach view is more like that of some giant water tank than of a buttressed Nervi dome.

By 1948 Nervi had already fulfilled Giedion's prophecy that the shell roofs would be the "solution of the vaulting problem for our period." What is essential to see now is that Nervi's direction was not the only one. As Nervi himself continually stressed, structural art stimulates many possible solutions to the same technical problem. To see this diversity of solutions we shall turn next to other designers who were at the same time studying other ways to achieve technical excellence, extreme economy, and visual richness. Along with Nervi and Maillart, it was the designers from Spain who led the way before World War II.

The Spanish School: Gaudí, Torroja, and Candela

Modern vault designers in Spain differed sharply from those in Germany and Italy by expressing visually the structural ideal of thinness, by emphasizing smooth, ribless surfaces, and by searching more widely for forms never used before in large buildings. The long tradition of Catalan vaulting made from laminated tiles provided a ready-made technique for this development, and the spirit of rationality popularized by Viollet-le-Duc gave it a theoretical justification. The three designers who best characterize this modern Spanish school are Antonio Gaudí (1852–1926), Eduardo Torroja (1899–1961), and Felix Candela (b. 1910). Gaudí, a Catalan architect, reacted against nineteenth-century historical facade making, and attempted in his mature works to find new forms which would coincide with rational structures. "For Gaudí, form did not *follow* structure and construction. It was identical with them."[25] Torroja, an engineering professor and designer, showed how the identity of form and structure achieved by Gaudí in masonry could be realized with thin vaults of concrete. Candela, trained in Madrid as an architect but skilled in mathematical analysis, followed Gaudí in his search for new forms and Torroja in his belief in new materials. Candela, like Maillart, succeeded in creating a new style out of forms appropriate to concrete.

Gaudí was born in Reus, near Barcelona, on June 25, 1852. He studied architecture at the Escuela de Arquitectura of Barcelona between 1874 and 1878, during which time he also worked for various practicing architects and with an engineer. Between 1878 and 1885, he designed a variety of buildings, including a machinery shed—a work of almost pure structure, made of parabolic wooden arches. In 1884, he began work on the Expiatory Church of the Holy Family in Barcelona (Sagrada Familia). Initially, the church had been begun in 1875, planned by other architects as a neo-Gothic design. Gaudí explored vaulting forms for the nave, and, in 1891, completed the crypt which had been begun in 1882. Work continued under Gaudí's direction until the end of his life and has proceeded sporadically since. Because of its grandiose design and a consequent shortage of funds, the church remains very far from completion.

In the early 1880s Gaudí had begun to do work for the Güell family, who became his patrons for many years. Beginning in 1898, Gaudí worked on the chapel for the Colonia Güell, a workers' settlement for the Güells' textile factories just west of Barcelona. He based his design for the high chapel roof on the rational idea of a string model which he loaded with weights to form a series of intersecting curves. Gaudí draped cloth about the model, photographed it, and turned the photoprint upside down to provide himself with the basis for a new vaulted form.

In 1900 he began to design for Eusebio Güell a suburban-garden housing development on the slopes of the Monte Carmelo overlooking Barcelona. As an overall plan it was unsuccessful, and at the death of Eusebio Güell the park was turned over to the city for which it has served as a very successful municipal public park. Gaudí himself lived there from 1906 until just before his death in 1926 in one of the only three houses built. Here, probably for the first time, Gaudí used hyperbolic paraboloid roofs for two of the houses. This new form, which closely resembles a saddle in shape, held a great fascination for Gaudí, partly because the visible form was the load-carrying structure and partly because this doubly curved form was "of a higher order and greater complexity than the [usual forms] of the middle ages which were being revived at that time."[26] Those older Gothic forms, based on circular curves, were essentially what Dischinger and Nervi both had used, although certainly not in the sense of Gothic revival. The saddle forms of Gaudí had three advantages over those more traditional shapes. First, a saddle shape has opposite curvatures, a downward arch in one direction (following the rider's legs) and an upward arch in the other (following the horse's back). A saddle-shaped roof surface is therefore much stiffer. Such a shape has less tendency to buckle and therefore can be thinner than a comparably large dome or barrel roof. Second, this thin form lends itself to construction by Catalan tile vaulting because the laminated tiles are able to carry both compression (the downward arch) and tension (the upward arch). As America's leading Gaudí scholar has observed, "Gaudí was . . . updating—by means of modern materials, in particular superior mortars—an ancient Mediterranean tradition of vaulted masonry in which the Spanish and French Catalans had always been leaders. [It] consisted of . . . a repertory of vaulting types, most famous of which is the boveda tabicada, a thin vault of laminated tiles that operated to all intents and purposes like a [curved] plywood board."[27] Third, and finally, those saddle shapes had the virtue of containing within their surfaces straight lines, something impossible with a spherical surface. Certain imaginary planes, passed through these surfaces, will intersect them in straight lines. This curious property of saddle shells makes them easier to construct, especially in concrete as Candela would demonstrate later. For Gaudí, this geometric property actually had a deep religious meaning as well, which confirmed his sense of the naturalness of the form. He took this form to be "a miracle of mathematics" and "attributed holy properties to the *trinity* of straight lines which determine any such surface."[28] This combination of passion and discipline, so similar to Maillart's drive for thinness, reappeared a half-century later in the similar straight-line form devotion of Candela.

For the development of new vaulting, Gaudí's most significant structure is the roof of the 1909 school (figure 10.5), which was built alongside the Sagrada Familia. Its form is conoidal—also saddle-like, and having the same advantages as the hyperbolic paraboloid.[29] Using Catalan vaulting, Gaudí for the first time directly expressed the structure by overhanging it from the walls so that we may clearly see its thinness and its smooth ribless curvature.

When first confronted with Gaudí's work, the observer is struck

FIGURE 10.5

The School Roof alongside of the Church of the Sagrada Família, Barcelona, 1909, by Antonio Gaudí. Probably the earliest large-scale, saddle-shaped roof in which the shape is fully visible and the thinness expressed, it is made of laminated tile.

by its fantasy and its exuberance. However, as we have seen, an essential basis for his designs was structural rationality; and for that reason his works and ideas were a powerful stimulus to structural artists, especially his fellow Spaniards, Torroja and Candela. It was Eduardo Torroja who explored smooth vaulting of double curvature using the material of reinforced concrete.

Torroja began designing concrete structures in the late 1920s, and created three major works in the mid 1930s which characterize his vision. The first of these works was a cantilevered hyperboloid shell to cover the stands of a race track in Madrid called the Zarzuela Hippodrome (figure 10.6). In his autobiographical book Torroja described the way in which he arrived at the form and emphasized that its design was neither purely rational nor purely imaginative, "but rather both together. The imagination alone could not have reached such a deci-

FIGURE 10.6

The Zarzuela Hippodrome Roof near Madrid, 1935, by Eduardo Torroja. The 42-foot cantilevered thin shell formed by segments of hyperboloids of revolution shows Torroja's style that emphasizes smooth ribless surfaces, the thinness of which are clearly visible.

sion unaided by reason, nor could a process of deduction, advancing by successive cycles of refinement, have been so logical and determinate as to lead inevitably to it."[30] This design process led Torroja to choose finally a doubly curved surface with a hyperbolic form not unlike Gaudí's. Again, it is a structure without ribs. This roof cantilevers out 42 feet from the main support and goes 23 feet back in the other direction. At about 15 feet back a vertical tie keeps the cantilever from falling over. The shell is only 2 inches thick at its free edge, and thus has an extraordinarily light appearance. The thickness increases to 5.5 inches at the crown over the line of main supports, which are separated laterally by 16 1/2 feet. The shell is very strong, however; when the builder made a full-scale model of one section of the roof, it carried three times its design load. As further evidence of strength, the roof withstood substantial bombardment during the Spanish Civil War when 26 holes were blown into it; these were covered over with concrete, and the roof remained intact.

Torroja's second major work of this period was the Fronton Recoletos of 1935, a singly curved barrel shell which sadly was destroyed in the Spanish Civil War. Not having the stiffening effects either of a double curvature or of a rib system, this vault was weaker than the hippodrome roof. Indeed, Torroja admitted later that some ribs on the outside of this shell would probably have saved it and yet "would not have affected its aesthetic aspect nor the total cost."[31]

The third major work, the Market Hall at Algeciras, is a domed roof with a radius of curvature of 145 feet and with a diameter of its covered area of 156 feet.[32] Torroja was a specialist in stress analysis as well as a designer, and he wrote a highly regarded book on the mathematical theory of elasticity.[33] This special interest led him to see a connection at Algeciras between the stresses in a shell and the reinforcement to be placed in it, but not to express those stresses in terms of visually evident ribs. We can contrast Torroja's Algeciras dome with Nervi's Little Sports Palace, two structures of about the same dimensions. Although the Algeciras dome is somewhat smaller, the two structures are similar. The major differences are two: first, whereas Nervi sees shells as ribbed Torroja sees them as ribless, hence at Algeciras the dome is smoothly curved inside and out; second, since domes tend to spread horizontally, Nervi designed exterior ribbed buttresses as the shell supports, whereas Torroja avoids buttresses by connecting vertical supporting columns with a polygonal ring of horizontal ties. Torroja's ties are prestressed to counteract dead load and to lift the shell slightly off its scaffold; this is probably the first application of prestressing to a doubly curved shell. In the Nervi dome a similar principle is applied; the buttresses are supported below ground on a ring which carries the horizontal thrust and which transmits the vertical weight to the ground. Nervi's solution requires a larger foundation, and hence more material, but the material cost for the foundations is the least expensive part of the structure. It would be difficult to say that one solution was less expensive than the other. Both are excellent engineering solutions, and the difference lies in the aesthetic preferences of each designer. Nervi chose to express ribs and buttresses, Torroja to express the smooth surface. As we have seen, these choices are related to the local traditions in Italy and Spain.

The third figure in this Spanish school is Felix Candela. Born on January 27, 1910, in Madrid, Candela became the Spanish national champion skier in 1932, and in 1934 he led his rugby team to the Spanish national championship.[34] He graduated from the Escuola Superior de Arquitectura in Madrid in 1935, and the following year won the traveling fellowship of the Fine Arts Academy of San Fernando with a proposal to study shells in Germany and to meet Finsterwalder and Dischinger. Candela had shown a talent for mathematics in school and had likewise developed a fascination for thin shells. However, the outbreak of the Spanish Civil War prevented his leaving for Germany. He fought with the republican army, was promoted to captain of engineers, and with the Franco victory was forced to flee from Spain. In 1939, he was interned in a concentration camp at Perpignan, France, and under the auspices of the Society of Friends he sailed to Mexico, landing at Vera Cruz in June 1939. From 1939 to 1951, Candela worked sometimes on his own, or with his brother Antonio, or for Jesús Marti in his large architectural firm in Mexico City. This period, in Candela's words, "served to finish my apprenticeship." Toward the end, he returned to his earlier interest in shells, and began to collect articles on recent works and to develop an attitude toward design that was strongly influenced by the works and writings of Robert Maillart, especially in the sense of relying more on his experience as a builder than on mathematical theories of structural behavior.[35] In the summer of 1949 he built some funicular vaults, and by 1951 he had built seven shells.

The 1951 Cosmic Rays Pavilion, built in Mexico City, was Candela's first major structure. Since the shell roof of this laboratory had to be thin to prevent blocking the rays, he took the design architect's cylindrical shell and gave it a double curvature, making a thinner shell possible. With this design, he won the building contract. It was his first hyperbolic paraboloid, a saddle shell of 1.5 centimeters in thickness (0.59 inches) on a span of 10.75 meters (35.4 feet). This shell brought Candela immediately to the attention of the building world. Awarded a number of contracts between 1951 and 1953, he was able to try various other types of vaulting and he gained invaluable experience in design and construction. In 1954, he was invited to the Massachusetts Institute of Technology to give two talks at the first United States conference on thin shells, about which he said, "having arrived with a complex about the prestige of the place and the numerous experts gathered there, I suddenly found that I was somewhat ahead of the experts myself."[36]

In 1955, he completed the Iglesia de la Virgen Milagrosa (Church of Our Miraculous Lady) in Narvarte, Mexico, in which the hyperbolic paraboloids form the entire structure, walls, and roof. The church committee had wanted a traditional Gothic-type design, but what they got was a new form which, nevertheless, like Maillart's broken-arch bridges, reminds one of the Gothic although its origin is in modern ideas about structure. Having for twenty years been fascinated with thin concrete shells, Candela was able to produce the design quickly; it "was made in an afternoon, drawn up in a week, and calculated during construction."[37] Like Maillart, Candela created new forms out of long experience with construction and used calculations as a guide and check; and also like Maillart, Candela's first great works, because they were built by him, served as full-scale models for his own future development.[38]

Beginning in 1954, Candela's business became highly successful, largely because of his umbrella shells which he was able to build for only 50 cents per square foot in industrial construction. This low cost partly reflects low labor rates, but it also reflects the rapidity of construction with reusable forms as well as the small amount of materials required. The umbrella shell is supported on one central column and looks mainly like an umbrella blown upward (inside out). With a few exceptions, mostly small buildings, all of Candela's umbrellas appear in Mexico.

Candela and the Discipline of Thinness

Candela broke the stranglehold of academic science on thin shells, and showed how beauty and utility could combine and open up limitless new possibilities for form. The basis for Candela's art was a vibrant imagination liberated by the discipline of structure. After some early explorations, he settled on one type of form, the hyperbolic paraboloid, and by necessity he was restricted to his adopted Mexico;[39] these restrictions freed his imagination so that he was able to conceive of new solutions to old problems, ranging from industrial roofs to free standing sculpture.

As with all structural artists, Candela had difficulties with some of his works from which he learned and improved. But his overall success as a designer came primarily from his central aesthetic motive and his recognition that proper predictions of thin-shell behavior could only come from observations of full-scale structures in service. For Candela, thin-shell design was not stimulated by thin-shell theory. He used only

FIGURE 10.7

Xochimilco Restaurant Roof near Mexico City, 1958, by Felix Candela. The extreme thinness of 1 5/8 inches is clearly expressed in this 140-foot ground-plan-diameter roof made of eight hyperbolic paraboloidal vaults. Candela shows here the remarkable lightness possible in thin-shell concrete structures. No ribs are needed.

the simplest type of mathematical theory, called the membrane theory. At the request of some American engineers, Candela published a series of articles on that theory, but even those articles merely obscure the source of Candela's design ideas;[40] and in any event the membrane theory proved to be an unreliable basis for the study of some types of hyperbolic paraboloids.

Candela was a builder as well as an engineer and architect, and the main basis for his business was the industrial shell roof which he could build only because of its remarkable economy. The surfaces of these inverted umbrella shells, merging into vertical columns, are the lightly loaded, roof-structure analogues of Maillart's flat slab and column capital designs for heavily loaded floor structures:[41] for Candela, as for Maillart, these industrial structures provided a continual source of income.

Candela, above all, carried the Spanish tradition of smooth surfaces and visually expressed thinness to new limits with new forms. Two of Candela's numerous Mexican thin shells serve to illustrate how his desire for thinness and his mature experience with full-scale structures and competitive contracting led him to new and original forms. The first of the two shells is Candela's 1958 restaurant roof at Xochimilco (figure 10.7). This roof is made up of eight hyperbolic paraboloidal vaults arranged on a circular ground plan of about 140 feet in diameter.[42] Apart from deeply recessed glass walls, the paper-thin (1 5/8 inches) roof is the entire structure. Structure and form are one, and the thinness is expressed so powerfully that it is hard to believe the building is concrete. It is emphatically not a natural form; rather, it is artificial and the product of a disciplined mind. Yet it is starkly original and obviously a work of joy. There are no ribs and no discontinuities; it is thin, integrated, and contrasting. Candela made no concessions to the wooded surroundings. He considers Xochimilco his most significant work. Its influence on the next generation of structural artists has been profound; as we shall see, it stimulated the Swiss Heinz Isler in his own search for new forms.

The second illustration of Candela's rich imagination is the 1960 Bacardi rum factory structure north of Mexico City. Here, in a three-unit groined-vault hyperbolic paraboloid, Candela shows openly his love of surprise and of challenging existing ideas. At the 1954 MIT conference on thin shells he had learned of the collaboration between the engineer Anton Tedesko and the architect Minoru Yamasaki on the St. Louis airport terminal three-unit groined vault. This traditional circular vaulted roof had been stiffened by cross arches and thickened at the edges by ribs.[43] Candela took that idea of a groined vault, and designed a roof of almost exactly the same overall dimensions (100 feet square in plan) as the St. Louis terminal but without any cross arches or edge ribs.[44] He used the twentieth-century form of hyperbolic paraboloidal vaults rather than the pre–Industrial Revolution form of the circular cylinder. Candela's form became an integral shell rather than a complex of separate elements delineated by ribs. Candela was thus stimulated by a major, highly publicized new shell structure to create his own counter-structure. The result shows how much more successful is a structure designed directly as structural art than one begun as architectural art and modified by structural ideas. Candela could design his vaults in Mexico, in part, thanks to a lack of restrictive building regulations, relatively low labor costs, and a rapid industrial growth following World War II. He was in the right place at the right time, and he even had the luck of financial backing from his brother, who had won a large lottery prize. But he had prepared himself by studying thin-shell publications in all languages, and most importantly he had brought with him to Mexico his Spanish heritage, which included the tradition of their doubly curved surfaces begun by Gaudí. Through his hyperbolic paraboloids Candela had found one "solution of the vaulting problem of our period," and had thus helped to fulfill Giedion's prophecy for thin shells. But when he first wrote about concrete vaults in 1929, Giedion had in mind the works of another structural artist, Eugène Freyssinet, to whom we now turn.

CHAPTER 11

THE DIRECTING IDEA
OF EUGENE FREYSSINET

A New Material

In 1949, Eugène Freyssinet (1879–1962) wrote, "in itself the idea of prestressing is neither complicated nor mysterious; it is even remarkably simple, but it does belong to a universe unknown to classical structural materials and the difficulty for those first coming to the idea of prestressing is to adapt themselves to this new universe."[1] Even Hennebique had not claimed so much for reinforced concrete, although its properties could have rightly been called unknown to the universe of stone, wood, and iron structures. Yet both Frenchmen proclaimed a new era in building based on the union of metal and concrete, and both sought what Maillart had called the lightness of metal and the permanence of stone.

Maillart himself had achieved this by integrating previously disconnected elements and by creating forms that carried loads more by shape than by mass. A parabolic arch carries uniform loads by a pure axial compression, which arises only when the abutments are firm. Thus vertical loads from the dead weight of the bridge (dead load) and the traffic or snow (live load) can be resisted by a stone arch bridge only because the abutments prevent the motions of both vertical settlement and horizontal sliding. Vertical and horizontal reactions prevent those motions and cause the arch to be under compression; that is why unmortared stones (whose joints have no resistance to tension) can carry vertical loads without pulling apart and collapsing.

Concrete is like stone: it is strong in compression and weak in tension. Thus, the horizontal reactions put into the arch a compression that overcomes the tendency of the concrete to pull apart in tension and crack. If the curved arch were replaced by a straight beam, no such horizontal reaction can occur. The arch tries to spread to flatten out, and this motion causes the horizontal reaction, whereas the beam merely sits on top of the abutments, which serve only to prevent vertical motion. The thin arch, properly supported, can carry uniform loads in pure compression, but a beam can only carry such loads by bending, with its top half in compression and its bottom half in tension. Stone or concrete requires a great mass of material to resist tension. The arch carries by geometry or shaping, whereas the beam carries by mass. Geometry makes forms lighter and, hence, loads smaller, whereas mass makes forms heavy and increases loads. The former tends toward a minimum, the latter toward a maximum.

With stone it is only possible to use a beam for very short spans. Light stone arches open up spans whereas heavy stone beams close in building forms. This is, of course, the classical contrast between Greek and Roman, between Parthenon and Pantheon. It is, again, the difference between that optical elegance of the Greek so prized by architects, whether beaux-arts or modernist, and that utilitarian power of the Romans so basic to the engineer's ideal of structural expression.

It was Hennebique who showed how concrete together with metal could make a beam without the heaviness and the close column spacing required in stone. But Hennebique's beams required substantial metal reinforcement, and even then, in their bottom parts where bending caused tension, they had small cracks, not harmful, but reminders that much of the concrete was used only to protect the metal from corrosion rather than to carry load.

Freyssinet showed how such cracking could be eliminated, as it had been in arches, by a horizontal compression force. Here, however, that compression did not come from the abutment reactions resisting the tendency for the arch to flatten and spread, but rather, from forces put in artificially either by jacking directly against the structure or more commonly by high strength steel cables. A concrete beam is cast with a hole from end to end shaped into a curved profile; a cable, fitted into the hole, is stretched and anchored at either end. This cable under high tension pulls the two anchored ends together, and the concrete beam is thereby put under high compression. In addition, the curved cable pushes the beam upward. The designer can make that upward pushing equal to the downward pushing expected from the dead and live loads. Thus, prestressing can put the tension-weak concrete all into compression and can bend the structure in a direction opposite to that caused by its dead and live loads.

Because of this control of tension and compression forces, it became possible to use very high strength steel, five times as strong as that used in ordinary reinforced concrete. In a reinforced concrete beam, the steel is bonded to the concrete, and therefore the larger the steel stresses are, and thus the more the steel gives, the larger the cracks in the concrete will be. In a prestressed concrete beam, on the other hand, with the anchored steel cable always putting the beam under compression, the steel stresses can be very high so that the cable gives a good deal without affecting the concrete and causing it to crack. Using high strength steel meant that the amount of steel could be reduced drastically, which in turn meant reductions in the amount of concrete needed for corrosion protection. With less concrete, the beam became lighter, and with less steel it became cheaper.[2] The materials combined now in a way that stretched both components to new limits: smaller amounts both of high strength concrete and of high strength steel. No wonder Freyssinet claimed for his invention "a new universe." Even so, he unconsciously misrepresented the idea.[3]

Freyssinet rigidly separated reinforced concrete from prestressed concrete by insisting that once prestressing is used in a beam, then all of the load must be resisted by the prestressing. He argued his viewpoint so persuasively that nearly all textbooks and building codes written after World War II followed his lead. But a few engineers recognized that many structures could be better designed by carrying loads partly with prestressing and partly with reinforcement. Gradually this practice has gained favor although even today it is followed far less than it could be. The Austrian, Paul Abeles (1897–1977), had proposed the idea as early as 1941. Finsterwalder was using it in bridges by 1952, and Christian Menn (b. 1927) has used it extensively in Switzerland for over two decades. Freyssinet's passion for proclaiming a revolution in structures prevented him from seeing this wider potential for prestressing that others more rationally recognized.

Here we meet an example of the deep interplay between the rational and the emotional bases for structural engineering. Its history cannot be understood without recognizing the centrality of this emotional–rational balance. Although this seems so obvious, if only because the history revolves around people, yet it needs continual restatement in an age which has been so imbued with the rational so-called scientific basis of engineering that it cannot easily see the equally powerful emotional basis.

To understand better Freyssinet's emotional heritage, and how it conditioned his ideas and led him to misrepresent prestressing, we shall briefly sketch his background and its interplay with the evolution of prestressed concrete. Between Freyssinet and other engineers who at the same time or even earlier had the idea of prestressing, there is a major difference which can only be called a difference in personality. Many of the others were as well trained, had field experience, and thought clearly about structures. But none had the same emotional drive as Freyssinet. As he put it himself in 1949, "When by chance, they approached this domain, the absence of a directing idea prevented the drawing of conclusions that were of any practical consequence."[4] Freyssinet's directing idea of prestressing necessarily narrowed his vision as it intensified his focus on concrete as a material that had to be in compression. Freyssinet always believed that he had the clearest picture of how compressed concrete really performed and that this picture was absolutely essential to his directing idea—which, as we shall see, was an aesthetic one.

Eugène Freyssinet

Because Freyssinet lived beyond the divide of World War II, and thus into the vast postwar building boom, he became much more famous than contemporaries such as Robert Maillart, who died before the end of that war. Freyssinet lived to become something of a legendary figure in his own lifetime; and he was prevailed upon, much as was Telford, to write autobiographically. In two writings in particular—a retrospective paper in 1949 and a lecture published in 1954—Freyssinet spoke about his past.[5]

Freyssinet was born in 1879 in the Corrèze plateau east of Bordeaux. For Freyssinet, this land was an important part of his heritage: "for many centuries, my ancestors lived clinging to the flanks of the steep gorges through which rush the torrents of the Corrèze plateau." This land, characterized by its "impenetrable thickets with a harsh climate and a poor soil," had "throughout the ages, been the refuge of the unsubdued and the rebel." It instilled Freyssinet with a feeling of independence which he carried with him to the end of his life. When his family moved to the French capital in the mid–1880s, he was deeply unhappy with what he called that "abominable Paris." He thought always of his native region, whose wilderness had "formed a tough, violent and unsociable race, very poor and proud, little inclined to beg assistance, and which has wrenched from its arid soil, all it needed to live."

From this contrast came Freyssinet's reaction to the massive, wasteful pomp of Paris before the First World War. He did not see Paris as a seething, stimulating center for the avant-garde to debate in ever more abstract terms the ideals of analytic cubism or symbolist poetry. As he himself put it, his own people were not artists, in that sense of art for art's sake, but rather they were "universal artisans." He summarized their ideals, which were his own, and in fact those of all structural artists, in saying that, "these men have created for themselves a civilization the main characteristic of which is an extreme concern for the simplification of forms and economy of means." This was the context for the directing idea of Eugène Freyssinet which he followed passionately throughout his long life in structural art, because, as he put it, "I loved this art of building which I conceived in the same way as my artisan ancestors, as a means of reducing to the extreme, the human toil necessary to attain a useful goal."[6] Freyssinet's parents soon discovered that it was necessary to send their strange introverted son back to his ancestral wilderness for long periods if he was to tolerate life in Paris at all.

In 1898, the Ecole Polytechnique rejected Freyssinet as they had Eiffel a half-century earlier, but unlike Eiffel, the younger man tried again and was admitted the following year "with a not very brilliant position of 161st." However, he graduated 19th and was then accepted by the Ecole des Ponts et Chaussées. Here, for the first time, Freyssinet's artisan love of building coincided with the ideals of his teachers, who were themselves "great artisans with an enthusiasm for their work: Résal, Séjourné and Rabut." And it was here, during the 1903–04 lectures of Charles Rabut that the idea of prestressing—the idea which was to direct his work from then on—first came to Freyssinet.

The Wilderness Origins of Prestressing

Just as with Eiffel, Freyssinet's early works were in the wilderness of south central France, where he was forced by local conditions to seek the simplification of forms and economy of means. Employed as an engineer with the highway department, he began, as had Maillart, with a series of small bridges which, as he wrote in 1949, "made me perfectly happy because the joy a work gives to its creator does not depend upon its size but upon the love which he brings to it and those things would stay with me to old age." It was a great satisfaction for him to find a solution for a problem under stringent constraints. All of Freyssinet's inventiveness came directly out of conditions that required "naturally the least cost because we [the provincial highway department] were very poor."[7]

He spoke about the formative experiences in that poor region, and especially about his 1907 bridge design at Le Veurdre. Three old suspension bridges over the Allier River needed replacement, and the highway department had already made a stone bridge design for the one at Le Veurdre, estimated to cost 630,000 francs. This high price would have made it impossible to build the other two nearby bridges. Freyssinet, therefore, after careful study proposed that he be allowed to build all three bridges to his own designs, and stated that he would do them all for the money that had been allocated for the one. The result was extraordinary, as Freyssinet recalled it in 1949, "an official letter put me in charge of supervising . . . the execution of these bridges whose designer I was, for which I was to be the contractor and the plans of which had never been submitted for anyone's approval. . . . [My superior granted] me unlimited credit out of his funds but without giving me a single man, tool or piece of advice. Never was a builder given such freedom. I was absolute master, receiving orders and advice from no one."[8] Freyssinet eventually was able to build Le Veurdre for about 210,000 francs or approximately $2 per square foot of roadway surface, compared to $3.12 per square foot for Hennebique's 1899 bridge at Châtellerault where the spans were only about two-thirds those at Le Veurdre. Maillart's 1901 Zuoz Bridge cost about $2.28 per square foot. Each of Freyssinet's three span bridges was to have one span of 72.5 meters (238 feet), which in 1907 when they were designed would have made them the world's longest spanning bridges in reinforced concrete.[9] Freyssinet was both exhilarated and apprehensive. With no clear precedent for such structures, he decided that in spite of the extreme economy necessary he had to build a full-scale test arch to study the behavior of concrete at such a scale. For this 50-meter (164 feet)-span arch, he designed steel tie bars running horizontally from one abutment to the other, anchored into one arch end, pulled at the other and then anchored. In this way, the two arch ends (resting on abutments which could provide no horizontal reaction) moved together, putting the arch into permanent compression. This test span was, in effect, Freyssinet's first prestressed structure. The arch moved too much under the prestressing, and in a way that the 1906 French code for concrete did not predict; but this 1908 experiment did teach Freyssinet about concrete creep, the continual contraction of the compressed material even when the compression load does not change. "This was a fearsome unknown," he wrote, which was "energetically denied by official science,"[10] and he did not forget that increased movement when building Le Veurdre.

FIGURE 11.1

Le Veurdre Bridge over the Allier River, near Vichy, France, 1911, by Eugène Freyssinet. It is one of three shallow arch bridges designed by Freyssinet. Here he introduced for the first time jacks into the crown of the arches to apply artificial forces that raised the bridge. Thus began Freyssinet's patient development of the idea of prestressing. When designed in 1907 these 72.5-meter spans were the longest-spanning arch bridges in the world.

After the 1910 completion of the Le Veurdre bridge (figure 11.1), Freyssinet continued to observe carefully its performance, and, in early 1911, he began to see the bridge moving downward at an alarming rate because of concrete creep. This primarily visual experience impelled Freyssinet into action:

> Returning to Moulins in the night, I jumped onto my bicycle and rode to Veurdre to wake up Biguet and three reliable men. The five of us then re-inserted the decentering jacks—I had always kept this possibility in reserve—and as soon as there was enough daylight to use the level and staffs, we began to raise the three arches simultaneously. It was market day and every few minutes we had to interrupt the operation to allow a few vehicles to pass. However, all ended well and once more aligned, cured of the illness that had almost killed it, the Veurdre bridge behaved perfectly until its destruction in the war in 1940.[11]

Freyssinet had left at the center or crown of the arch an opening into which he put jacks; these pushed the two sinking arch halves apart, thus raising the arch. When filled with concrete, the opening became a solid part of the arch, which was permanently fixed in its new and higher location. In introducing an artificial force which caused compression in the arch and which moved it in the direction opposite to which gravity pulled, Freyssinet successfully completed his first major prestressed concrete structure. For Freyssinet this had been an exhilarating experience, and thereafter he considered Le Veurdre his finest bridge, not just for the rational reasons of its performance, but also because in it he had stretched the limits of structure so far that only by invoking a completely new idea could he save it from destruction. The lightness of the bridge is striking but its history of near failure is even more remarkable. Only outside the normal French bureaucracy could such a wild scheme have been carried off. Only where economy was the discipline could such lightness arise. Le Veurdre is Freyssinet's Tavanasa, a form wrought from field failure, and like Maillart's slightly older work, it is through no fault of the design that it no longer exists.

In 1914, Freyssinet left the highway department and joined the building firm of Claude Limousin, where he stayed until 1929. During this period, he designed and built a series of spectacular works which gained him international fame. First came the 96.25-meter-span (315 feet) two-ribbed arch bridge at Villeneuve-sur-Lot, begun in 1914 but not completed until 1919. The hingeless concrete arch supports an arcaded viaduct faced in brick. During World War I, he designed a number of industrial structures with barrel-shell-like roofs, and between 1921 and 1923 he built two immense parabolic-arched dirigible hangars at Orly with spans of 86 meters (282 feet) and a clear height of 50 meters (164 feet) at midspan. The arches were thin hollow sections connected laterally by thin slabs giving a corrugated overall appearance.

In 1921, Freyssinet began seriously to develop his ideas on prestressing, completing the 64-meter-span two-hinged arch railroad bridge over the Sambre, the Candelier Bridge. In this bridge, he introduced concrete hinges at the supports and he jacked apart the arch at the crown to lift it off the centering. Here he incorporated the lesson from Le Veurdre into the construction plan for the bridge; soon he was to use the same ideas in a much larger work. In 1919, he had won the competition for the crossing of the River Seine at Saint Pierre du Vauvray. The 131.8-meter (435 feet)-span hollow arches, completed in 1923, were the longest-spanning concrete arches in the world. They rose 25 meters (82 feet) at midspan and the deck was suspended below. Destroyed in 1940, this bridge was rebuilt in 1946 in the same form.

Between 1924 and 1928, Freyssinet built a small suspension bridge at Laon (1926), completed the conoidal thin shell roof sheds for railway repair shops at Bagneux (1927), and, most importantly, worked on his largest arch bridge, the three-span crossing of the Elorn estuary near Brest by the town of Plougastel. This bridge (figure 11.2) was completed in 1930. Each arch is a hollow box, 180 meters (592 feet) in span, 27.5 meters (90.5 feet) in rise, with a midspan section

FIGURE 11.2

The Plougastel Bridge over the Elorn Estuary near Brest, France, 1930, by Eugène Freyssinet. For each of these three openings Freyssinet designed 180-meter-span, hollow-box reinforced concrete arches, then the longest concrete spans in the world. The elegance of his construction procedures both visually and in concept made Freyssinet world-famous both to engineers and to architects.

4.5 meters (14.7 feet) high and 9.5 meters (31.2 feet) wide. Because of the great scale, Freyssinet studied in detail the creep of concrete, and it was out of this study that he evolved his more general idea for prestressing. After patenting his idea in October 1928, with his friend J. C. Séailles, he left Limousin and in 1929 set up a business at Montargis to produce factory-made prestressed concrete electrification poles. The business did not succeed, but Freyssinet was able to demonstrate the potential of prestressing by saving the sinking marine terminal at Le Havre in 1935. That same year he joined the building firm of Campenon–Bernard, where he designed and built numerous prestressed structures before, during, and after World War II.

Freyssinet's major prestressing works after 1945 were the 1946 Marne River Bridge of a 55-meter span at Luzancy begun in 1941 (fig-

FIGURE 11.3

The Luzancy Bridge over the Marne River, France, 1946, by Eugène Freyssinet. Freyssinet's first major prestressed concrete bridge spans 55 meters and dramatically portrayed the possible lightness of concrete-beam bridges when compressed by large forces induced by high-strength steel cables within the structure.

ure 11.3); five other Marne bridges, completed between 1947 and 1951; three 150-meter-span arch bridges near Caracas, Venezuela, between 1951 and 1953; the Basilica at Lourdes of 1956–58; the Orly Bridge of 1958; and the Saint Michel Bridge in Toulouse, completed in 1962 just three months before his death. But even if Freyssinet had never pursued the idea of prestressing, there were so many other significant structures to his credit that he would still have been regarded along with Robert Maillart as the greatest engineer in reinforced concrete in the first half of the twentieth century.[12]

Le Veurdre and Arch Aesthetics

To understand Freyssinet as an artist demands, as a start, a more careful discussion of his views on Le Veurdre, because, as he wrote, "I have always loved it more than any other of my bridges; and of all that the War has destroyed, it is the only one whose ruin has caused me real grief." Why did Freyssinet prefer Le Veurdre to all his later works? The answer comes from his 1949 comparison between Le Veurdre and its companion bridge, Boutiron (another of the original three that Freyssinet designed while he was with the highway department). With Le Veurdre destroyed in the war, Boutiron remained as a replica in all but one central way. "The piers and arches at Boutiron are the same as at Le Veurdre and the construction quality was even better than at Le Veurdre; but Boutiron is much less beautiful than its older brother [Le Veurdre]." The aesthetic difference is what counts most in the end, and Freyssinet goes on to describe why Le Veurdre was such a fine work. For him the contrasts of the pointed piers with the flat water surface, and the strong abutments leaning back against the hills with the lightness of the long-span arches, gave the bridge its character and value. "The beauty of a bridge is only made by the delicate harmonies between its parts and its site; it is only necessary to change things a very little in order to spoil a handsome appearance."[13]

This notion of aesthetics has nothing to do with rules of proportion or with ideas about decoration; it has to do with contrast and lightness. Moreover, Freyssinet is not trying to instruct anyone in aesthetic principles; he is invoking appearance to explain why Le Veurdre was his favorite bridge. (And it is typical that after describing its aesthetic value he immediately refers to the great visual defect of large noticeable deformations which nearly ruined it in 1911.) The experience of the completed work is primarily visual, both as a tranquil object in nature and as a working structure under load. Freyssinet liked to quote the great French poet Mistral by way of expressing his feelings about Le Veurdre:

> C'est mon coeur et mon âme
> C'est la fleur de mes ans.
> [It is my heart and my soul
> It is the flower of my years.]

And for him this work informed his entire career because it gave everything he did "that style which . . . marks all my works and allows them to be recognized at the very first glimpse and which is the style of the artisans of my race."[14] The driving force for that style was Freyssinet's love of the art of building, which appears not just in his bridges but also in his thin-shell roof structures.

Thin-Shell Vaulting: Orly and Bagneux

Because of restrictions on steel during World War I, Freyssinet designed a number of industrial barrel shell roofs. Unlike Finsterwalder's later barrels, those of Freyssinet come from arch rather than dome forms. His French barrels have horizontal steel bars tying the shell edges together transversely, much as he tied his test arch together in 1908. With such ties and because of their relatively small span, these shell-like forms did not call for any special thin-shell ideas and they did not attract any international engineering interest. In contrast, his two Orly hangars (figure 11.4) became world famous immediately. Perhaps for the first time artists and architects began to sense that something totally new was emerging in concrete. These immense arches seem to rise directly out of the ground.[15] There is great visual power in the overall sight of these objects but as load-carrying elements any expression of forces is missing. They are more than giant Quonset huts but they are less than aesthetic masterpieces. Each hangar consists of a series of single arches side by side. Each arch, like a bridge, carries its load directly into the ground. In Nervi's 1949 Turin exhibition hall, by contrast, the same barrel vault problem is solved in an entirely different visual way. Nervi has chosen to channel the forces from several arches through ribs merging into a single buttress. Nervi's decision to make such ribs and buttresses is aesthetic; he could have done it otherwise, as for example in the much less expressive form he gave his field house at Dartmouth College. For Freyssinet, however, these great Orly hangars reflect much more the regular and brilliant scheme of construction.

In Freyssinet's second-most-famous building of the 1920s, the 1927 railway repair shop at Bagneux just south of Paris, we find a series of small identical shells used to cover a great floor area (figure 11.5).[16] These are north light shells formed as conoids such that over one pair of columns the arc is high while over the next pair that same surface changes to a much flatter arc. In this way, over each column pair one surface begins in a high arc and the adjacent surface ends in a flat arc. Between those two arcs is a nearly vertical crescent of glass admitting the north light. Viewing these shells in the direction of increasing arc, we see the structure nearly disappear in light. This striking view contrasts strangely with the dull, repetitive slant-barrel look from without.

FIGURE 11.4

The Orly Dirigible Hangars near Paris, 1921, by Eugène Freyssinet. Freyssinet designed these 86-meter-span, 50-meter-high arches as thin hollow sections connected laterally by thin slabs, giving a corrugated overall appearance.

As in all of Freyssinet's shed roof shells, these north lights are supported vertically on thin columns and restrained horizontally with thin ties which themselves are supported by two vertical suspenders from the shells. Again, there are horizontal ties also midway between columns. The result is a disquieting maze of thin linear elements hovering beneath the smooth surfaces of shell and glass. These works are remarkable for their thinness but not for their integration of form. The ties and suspenders, in Giedion's photos, have the look almost of a separate structural system added to support interior services, rather than seeming what they actually are: parts of the shell roof designed to enforce an arch-like behavior. In comparable German shells, such ties are absent because of the different way in which the designers visualized the

FIGURE 11.5

The Railway Repair Shop Roofs at Bagneux, near Paris, 1927, by Eugène Freyssinet. Freyssinet designed these northlight shells in the form of conoids such that the structure becomes nearly transparent when viewed toward the north from within. Thin horizontal ties connect the column tops together.

action of the structure. Freyssinet's ties show him to have concerned himself with the behavior of shells less as surfaces and more as arches.

When we compare these sheds to similar ones of Candela twenty years later, it is clear that the younger man's surfaces are both thin and integrated: there is no longer a second visually separated system of structure hanging below the shells. Candela's inverted umbrella shells built in differing heights admit light in a manner similar to Freyssinet's conoidal roof sheds. The differences are, however, central to ideas on structural art. Candela saw these shells as expressions of thinness and of a pure integrated form. Freyssinet's shells also express thinness but the system of ties breaks the integration of form and distracts from the visual power of the shell surface. The "ties" needed in Candela's hyperbolic paraboloids are there as the integral reinforced straight-line edges of each unit.

Freyssinet's shell forms anticipated later works and his designs had more visual power than most of the German shells of the twenties, but he did not reflect on his work the way Nervi and Candela did. Part of the reason lies in his independent vision, which seemed not to be affected by developments outside of France, and part lies in his overriding concern for prestressing, which dominated his thoughts even before Plougastel was completed. Freyssinet's inventiveness led him away from structural art just as he was completing his most mature reinforced concrete forms. Had he pursued hangars and sheds in the 1930s, and had he interested himself in the works of Maillart, Nervi, Torroja, and the Germans, perhaps his later designs would have taken on a new strength and beauty.

Freyssinet and Maillart

"At the age of 50 I was abandoning a life that was already mapped out in order to throw myself into one that was full of uncertainties and perils," wrote Freyssinet about his turn to prestressing by 1930.[17] By contrast, Maillart wrote in 1931, "I have bought no books and read no journals in this specialty [reinforced concrete] for 10 years. And even so 'the soup' succeeds just about always."[18]

Freyssinet was turning from his own established world of large-scale reinforced concrete arches to a new universe for the creation of which he would need strong support from others. Maillart, by contrast, had turned inward and was drawing on his own inner resources, built up piece by piece through thirty-seven years of experience with reinforced concrete. Freyssinet saw the future as a new material, Maillart saw it as new forms. Freyssinet proclaimed a revolution and propagated a new faith; the break with the past must be complete. Between reinforced concrete and prestressed concrete he perceived an unbridgeable chasm and, in the latter, a new universe in which he would be the prophet. Maillart, at the same time, began living alone in his Geneva office, writing and designing alone on the train between his other offices in Bern and Zurich, and restricting his contacts to old friends and close family. As Freyssinet became more and more prophetic, Maillart became more and more monastic.

This contrast in direction after 1930 went together with a contrast in business life. Freyssinet, for the first time in his life was establishing a business venture; and that venture would prove his only major failure. By 1935 he had become once again the chief engineer for a skilled builder, Edmé Campénon. Maillart, on the other hand, ran his own business from 1902 to the end of his life. He did require financial backing from others, but they took no role in running the firm or making decisions about design or construction. Freyssinet spoke about his heritage of independence and self-sufficiency; but in a business and managerial sense, he was dependent upon others. Thus, in the 1920s Freyssinet had worked successfully for the firm of Claude Limousin: Freyssinet had the ideas; Limousin was the entrepreneur. In this respect, Freyssinet was most like the Germans Dischinger and Finsterwalder, working always for a big design–construction company. On the other hand, Maillart was more like Nervi and Candela, himself in charge of the entire operation.

It appears at first sight to be a paradox that Maillart, under the pressures of running his own business, designed with a greater originality of form than Freyssinet for whom such pressures were missing. Yet the other great artists—Telford, Roebling, Eiffel, Nervi, and Candela—were all in full charge of their works, and even those who worked only as designers—Brunel, Lindenthal, Steinman, and Ammann (after World War II)—were all in charge of their businesses as well as their designs. If economic competition is important to structural art, so is independence of responsibility. Candela stated this idea when he said of both Maillart and himself that "the only way to be an artist in this difficult specialty of building is to be your own contractor."[19] There is a deep emotional drive in all of the arts to transform ideals into realities, to place an artist's realized conceptions in the hands of the public.

All the great structural engineers combined aesthetic motivation with an inventive flair. New forms played both with and against new techniques, sometimes reinforcing each other and sometimes competing for the attention of their creator. Maillart, Freyssinet, and the others could not but see new ways to achieve new forms and even new ways required by those new forms: new tools, construction procedures, and methods of analysis. But when any of those ways became dominant in the artist's mind, then the will to form seemed to weaken. This was the case with Freyssinet, and not just after his 1928 prestressing patent.

Throughout Freyssinet's career, it was the means of construction—rather than the end of form—that dominated his imagination. In the history of structural engineering, Freyssinet's place is secure. Modern prestressing starts with him, and he led the way to large-scale concrete arches. But he belongs, nonetheless, to that small group whose importance rests more with the pioneering of new ways of building than with the forms they created: his arches, vaults, and prestressed structures are analagous to Hennebique's frameworks in monolithic reinforced concrete and Dischinger's Zeiss-Dywidog roof methods. Of these, Freyssinet's means were the greatest because his new idea had the broadest range of use. Yet, like the others, he had patented a system and to some extent became trapped in this system, and less willing to explore other ideas and other forms.

Looking through a recent compilation of Freyssinet's works, I am struck by the beauty of the construction photographs.[20] Comparing the best of these construction photographs with the best photographs of the completed works, I am driven to the surprising conclusion that the construction pictures are the more beautiful. In this conclusion, I am not alone. The best set of pictures of Freyssinet's greatest arch bridge, the Plougastel, appeared in *L'Architecture Vivante,* and nearly all are of its construction.[21] They show dazzling views of the great arch scaffold, itself a thin elegant wooden arch of unprecedented span, floating on the Elorn estuary, and visually working with completed arches and the wide waterway to create unforgettable images that exist only because of this man-made process. Freyssinet had a way with scaffolding and with temporary cables that reminds us of Eiffel. The completed Plougastel, as impressive as it is, is not an integrated work in the sense of Maillart's designs or even of comparably long span arches. Plougastel has heavy piers at either end of the three-arch span and its lightly trussed deck seems designed by a different hand than its solid arched support.

Both Freyssinet's greatest arch bridge and Maillart's Salginatobel were completed in 1930, and both have become famous. But a wide audience has made very different judgments about the two bridges. In book after book on bridges or on modern art or architecture, the works by Maillart are displayed and praised whereas the Freyssinet works, if shown at all, are noted for their size, the novel construction techniques employed, or their role in the origins of prestressing. In short the judgments always came down to aesthetics. Maillart's works are smaller, they are more out of the way, and they do not seem so novel constructionally; yet, in an age that has idolized size, quantity, novelty, and radically new ideas, Maillart is nonetheless receiving increasing recognition.

These observations are all external and circumstantial; they must go together with internal and psychological analyses to which we shall refer at the end of this book. To Freyssinet's biographer, Fernandez Ordóñez, it appears wrong-headed that Maillart should be preferred to Freyssinet.[22] But the thesis of the present book is that the best engineers were precisely those who were the most aesthetically sensitive to the new forms arising out of the constraints of structural engineering. And, just as the general culture over time establishes the relative merits of different composers, painters, and poets, so it has been doing for structural engineers. Telford, Roebling, Eiffel, Nervi, Torroja, Candela, and Maillart have been all subjected to a growing body of writing and criticism. There has, in contrast, been far less interest in Rennie, Ellet, Dischinger, Lindenthal, or even Freyssinet.

It would be wrong, however, to conclude a chapter on Freyssinet on a negative note. If one unhesitatingly proclaims Bach greater than Handel, that does not call for any relegation of the *Messiah* or the *Water Music* to second-rate status. Both composers are great artists; it is only to underscore what characteristics make them great that one indulges in comparative criticism. Freyssinet was a great structural artist whose life and works should and will be studied historically and criticized sympathetically in much greater detail than heretofore. Many people will prefer his works to those of Maillart just as many prefer Handel to Bach or Brahms to Beethoven. Moreover, the writings and the exhibitions that will proceed from studies of Freyssinet will undoubtedly enrich the general culture and make it ever clearer how essential the ideas and examples of artists like Freyssinet and Maillart are to the future structuring of society.

CHAPTER 12

DISCIPLINE AND PLAY: NEW VAULTS IN CONCRETE

The obvious success of technology following World War I together with the growing prestige of science seemed to indicate that in the union of the two lay the key to peace and prosperity.[1] Einstein's general theory proved, in the 1919 solar eclipse experiment, the power of expressing truth by formula; and the rapid rise of the electrical and chemical industries, following the prewar model of German research and development, confirmed the general idea that science was the key to the future. Everything from factory management to the unconscious sex drive was thought to be amenable to scientific analysis. The truths of life were bound up in formulas which great minds, in academic settings, were carefully setting about to refine and solve.

Form and Formula

In structural engineering, this faith in formula led to an emphasis on mathematical analysis which, particularly for vaults, seemed to require that designers justify their works by sophisticated calculation. As we have already observed, the leading structural artists resisted that trend and sought rather to base design on simplified calculations and on observations of physical behavior. This contrast of viewpoints between analyst and designer, although existing since Telford, became particularly apparent for thin shells with the studies of cylindrical water tanks undertaken early in the twentieth century.

In 1902 Maillart designed and built his first project as an independent designer-builder, two gasholders in St. Gallen, which remained for some years the largest reinforced concrete water vessels in the world. Maillart gave his tanks an unprecedented form and, following the ideas of Wilhelm Ritter, devised a graphical method of analysis on which to base dimensioning. In 1907, a German engineer, Hans Reissner, developed a mathematical formulation for this same vertical cylinder problem and published formulas with charts for use by designers. A general formulation would have been so complex that Reissner was forced to simplify it radically to get solutions which were thus restricted to only two shapes of tank walls: constant thickness or linearly varying thickness. Maillart's method, by contrast, was specific to cylinders and simple to begin with and fully general in its results; any shape of wall could be used.[2]

In the most comprehensive early publication on reinforced concrete, Fritz von Emperger's *Handbuch*,[3] Maillart's method was fully explained in the first (1907) (where it was the only method given) and second (1910) editions (where Reissner's theory was also given); but by the third (1923) edition Maillart's method disappeared and Reissner's dominated. Thus, as the 1920s wore on, science-based formulas gained prestige. The major results of these formulas were to create a scientific discipline of analysis isolated from design, to set up standard methods of analysis which would come to have quasi-legal status in codes of practice, and, finally, to turn some designers away from the physical and visual methods which they had integrated into their design procedures. This was not a question of intuition versus rigor, or of approximate and uncertain estimates versus precise and scientific predictions: the primary uncertainties in reinforced concrete behavior have never been removed by mathematical analysis, however rigorously consistent. Rather, it was a conflict of emphasis. Would the designer's time and thought have to go into ever more complex attempts to remove analytic uncertainties or could it focus on physical behavior and on the choice of form? It was this conflict that would engage Maillart over his entire career, and the power of his designs both scientifically and visually would grow as he went further and further from the mathematical tradition which was increasingly dominating the profession.

In concrete roof shells, a similar trend arose in the 1920s, as the Germans tended to develop ever more complex mathematical formulations while designing only very restricted forms—barrels and domes. Meanwhile, the ideas of Nervi, Torroja, and Maillart were in the 1930s to liberate thin shells from that dependence upon formulas.

After the Second World War, thin-shell vaults, as proclaimed by Giedion, began to appear throughout Europe and the United States. But a curious paradox became evident by the 1960s. Although more and more articles were being written on thin shell analysis, fewer and fewer thin-shell concrete roofs were being built.[4] The science began to overwhelm the structures. Some people thought that electronic computation would remove analytic difficulties and hence lead to a greater use of thin concrete shells. However, some leading designers disagreed. As the pioneer in American shell design, Anton Tedesko, stated in 1970, "I know that none of the great classic shells of the past would have become a better shell by the use of any one of the computer solutions available today." Tedesko had come to the United States in 1932 to propagate the ideas of Dischinger and Finsterwalder, and up to the late 1940s had been responsible for almost every thin shell concrete roof in the United States—scores of large-scale barrel shells and domes. When he spoke of classic shells, he meant not just his own designs but also those of Finsterwalder, Nervi, Torroja, Candela, and others. Tedesko did not mean that the computer is of no use; he always based design on careful analysis. Rather, he wished to emphasize the centrality of the design personality and to stress, as he put it, that "the purpose of calculations is not to keep us in trim intellectually. Their purpose is to build!"[5]

In structural design, computations can only be estimates, because of the fundamental uncertainties in materials and in costs. The designer certainly computes both stresses in materials and costs in labor, but these are estimates which serve as guides to design and not as determinants. Stresses in concrete (pounds per square inch of compression), for example, are mere guesses—even when computed following the most rigorous formulations of theoretical mechanics. After a half century of stress analysis, for example, the American Concrete Institute changed its building code (in 1963) to permit designs that did not even compute concrete stresses under design loads. But, even if stresses could be realistically computed, that would not help because costs can never be scientifically defined and are not tied to stresses by any higher law. The computer can produce a cost estimate for a large number of designs but someone has then still to pick one of the designs.

In the hands of mature designers, however, computer graphics does offer new possibilities. Here, the visual display of structures deforming under load, in the words of a leading authority, "returns us to a more traditional mode of engineering" where designers look at computational results, and then modify their designs to see how to make the structure more efficient. In this process "the machine takes on the tedious calculations, data manipulation, and figure drawing, while the person visually integrates and evaluates patterns of behavior and makes conceptual decisions."[6] These decisions can best be made by designers who have made such calculations manually and who understand materials and full-scale structural performance. The best designers have always sought ways to estimate structural behavior by very simple formulas and they would surely have delighted in the new interactive computer graphics. The great danger that engineers such as Maillart and Nervi saw in complex mathematical formulations is that they can lead inexperienced designers away from evaluation and conception, and into the labyrinths of complex numerical analysis. The most prolific shell designers between 1950 and 1980, Felix Candela and Heinz Isler, illustrate best the priority of conceptions over complexity.

Candela, Maillart, and the Aversion to Ugliness

Candela is the first structural artist we have considered here who was trained as an architect. But his talents and motivations seem always to have been directed toward structural engineering. As he wrote in an essay on Maillart's influence on his work, "since I never had a high opinion of myself as an artist, I was more interested in the technical part of the curriculum and began to read extensively about structures." Years later he found that this technical background "made me more knowledgeable on the matter [of structural analysis] than most practicing engineers."[7]

After his relocation to Mexico, Candela began to think again about thin shells. He discovered Maillart's work in Giedion's *Space, Time and Architecture,* and then in Max Bill's book *Robert Maillart,* where he read for the first time some of Maillart's writings. "I devoured his articles" wrote Candela, largely because they were "well provided with opinions, something I could rarely find in other engineering articles." Maillart had stressed the goals of thinness and of calculation simplicity, both of which appealed to Candela: "I found Maillart's thoughts delightfully sympathetic and encouraging," he wrote. Furthermore, he added, "If a rebel was able to produce such beautiful and sound structures, there could not be anything wrong with becoming also a rebel, which was besides, my only way to break the mystery surrounding shell analysis." Thus the beauty of Maillart's thin, sound structures provided Candela with the incentive to try new ideas. He welcomed "Maillart's advice that simpler calculations are more reliable than complex ones."[8]

Thus did Candela begin to design and build shells. He became a practicing structural engineer, however, largely because he was also a builder, as had Maillart. New ideas in structural art require careful attention to construction economy; in fact, they grow out of the search for that economy. Candela found that to become a master of thin shell design he had "to accept the whole responsibility for the good performance of the structure." Accepting this responsibility enabled him to learn, because, as he wrote, "I could control what was happening, check the results and confirm the accuracy of my judgment or correct any mistakes. In a way, I was working with full-scale models."[9]

As for Maillart and aesthetics, he wrote, "I like to think however, that Maillart did not judge himself an artist. . . . His main concerns must have been efficiency and economy of means . . . but an efficient and economical structure has not necessarily to be ugly." Then Candela, in describing how he imagined Maillart must have thought, and at the same time expressing his own design procedure, announced the central ideas of structural art: "Beauty has no price tag and there is never one single solution to an engineering problem. Therefore, it is always possible to modify the whole or the parts until the ugliness disappears."[10] Here is the aesthetic choice of the artist who makes a personal style without violating efficiency or economy. How different is this approach from that of some twentieth-century designers. We have only to read some discussions of modern architecture to see how, in some cases, Candela's ideas are misunderstood. Consider, for example, the following, from a biography of Le Corbusier: "Robert Maillart, Eugène Freyssinet and Pier Luigi Nervi . . . understood all the new structural techniques. . . . Still Le Corbusier, Mies van der Rohe and Wright will ultimately appear more important . . . because they were greater as artists—as poets of architecture. . . . Scientists, engineers, and businessmen are essential to the creation of a civilization but it always takes poets to point the way."[11]

Candela is expressing an artistic—poetic, if you like—vision of design, and he is clear in contrasting it to what he takes to be the posturing of famous architects. "This aversion to ugliness is quite the opposite of the task of the professional artist who has to produce beauty as an obligation or of today's star-architect who has to be original at any cost in each new project." What separates Maillart and Candela from Le Corbusier and others is their insistence on efficiency and economy as the intellectual setting for their art. One does not find much reference to such ideas in Le Corbusier. Le Corbusier is no less an artist than Candela or Maillart, but he practiced a different art. Architecture in its complexity is perhaps more like the art of prose; structure in its greater simplicity is perhaps more like poetry. Candela concluded his essay on Maillart with such intensity and clarity that it is best simply to quote this conclusion in full:

Maillart's works did not need to be beautiful. This word did not even exist in the practical world of the serious citizens who had to judge his competitive bids. He achieved a beauty without need or purpose; just for the pure joy of it. The kind of joy that you can feel also in the works of Haydn or Vivaldi. They were simply enjoying what they were doing, and so was obviously Maillart.

He did also possess that rare quality, source of artistic creation and of all invention, of being able to challenge the conventional wisdom and come up with the obvious solution, one, nevertheless, which nobody could think of before. I can imagine the fits of rage and jealousy of some of his contemporary colleagues at the sight of one of his bridges (Landquart or Schwandbach), in which the curved route is supported in a straight arched slab. The problem with this unusual combination—which, of course, looks perfectly logical after the fact—is that it was very difficult, if not impossible, to analyze with the methods available at that time. But Maillart would not take any unnecessary risk and first he tried the soundness of his approximated calculations in a small example (the Habkern Bridge) with a span of only fifteen meters. This was his testing model which gave him firm ground from which to extrapolate at the next opportunity.

I would like to insist at this moment on something that everybody knows but which is easily forgotten; that all calculations, no matter how sophisticated and complex, cannot be more than rough approximations of the natural phenomenon they try to represent by means of a mathematical model. The complexity, or even elegance, of such a model bears no relation at all with the degree of approximation. There is not such a thing as an exact method of structural analysis and, notwithstanding the popular belief in the letter of the codes, the accuracy of any calculation is still a question of personal judgement. This fortunate circumstance allows engineering to reach sometimes the highest category of art, to the despair of dull and inflexible technicians.[12]

This final paragraph on the accuracy of calculation summarizes the view of every great structural designer from Telford on. It is the credo of the structural artist, who must at every stage in the design be in full control of the design process. We shall see this process even more clearly when we turn later in this chapter to Candela's successor as the leading shell designer, Heinz Isler of Switzerland.

The New Swiss Synthesis

While the Salginatobel Bridge was under construction, a young mathematician teaching at Schiers just below the bridge site decided to turn from mathematics to structures. So it was that Pierre Lardy (1903–1958), already armed with a PhD. in mathematics, returned to Zurich in 1930 to study structural engineering. He received his second doctorate, and in 1945 was appointed professor of structures at the Federal Technical Institute, continuing in a direct line from Culmann and Ritter. Lardy's talents combined those of a mathematician with those of an artist; he was a gifted pianist. But, more than anything else, he had fallen in love with structural art, and his lecture on aesthetics impressed his students. He attracted a remarkable group of young engineering graduates, including Christian Menn (b. 1927) and Heinz Isler (b. 1926), who are among the top-ranking structural artists of the late twentieth century. Like Wilhelm Ritter a half century before, Lardy inspired his students with images of structural form while at the same time stressing careful mathematical analysis. Even more important was his emphasis on physical models and precision measurements of structural behavior.

Lardy was attracted to the ideas of the Spaniard Eduardo Torroja long before books on the aesthetics of his works had appeared.[13] Torroja emphasized that projects should begin with a model. In keeping with this idea, Lardy had one of his students (Hans Hauri, later to become president of the Federal Technical Institute) develop a laboratory for model making. Here students could see firsthand demonstrations not only of how the actual forms would look, but also of the detailed care essential to extract useful technical understanding from them. The laboratory was never a question of researchers using complex, extensive, and costly equipment to make new discoveries, but rather of engineers using the simplest means with great care to produce safe designs. In fact Lardy did very little research; his major contribution came through his influence on his students—through expressing his ideas to them and encouraging them in their design work.

Along with models, Lardy put emphasis on the importance of aesthetics for full-scale structural design. When Lardy approached the design of a structure, he always began with its appearance and he never shrank from critical judgments. Not being a designer, he had no special viewpoint or set of works to defend. His independent critical judgment left a lasting mark on his students.

There was something about Lardy's personality that encouraged his students to bring him their ideas. At one such time Isler brought up his idea that one should first see every structure as a whole and only afterward analyze it as parts. Lardy gave Isler his spontaneous and enthusiastic agreement.[14] The prevailing attitude toward the study of structures was then, and to a large extent remains now, analytic in the sense that a structure is separated into parts, which are then analyzed with highly mathematical means. Much academic teaching and research since World War II and even earlier has been devoted to refinement of analyses and to the mathematical and scientific description of structural form. This approach leads to an emphasis on those forms which can readily be analyzed, while ignoring those for which no mathematical analysis exists; it also omits aesthetic judgments, even on those analyzable forms. Lardy's teaching tended to reverse that analytical approach, and to describe overall form first before seeing it as parts or attempting to analyze it. One reason physical models appealed to Lardy was that they provided a means to study forms for which no mathematical analysis was available.

Thus, what Isler, Menn, and many others got from Lardy was a strong emphasis on models as a means of expanding design possibilities, on aesthetics as a primary design objective, and on overall form as having precedence over the analysis of parts. This type of teaching was directly in the spirit of Wilhelm Ritter and is very Swiss in its openness both to the German mathematical tradition and the French visual tradition. Lardy himself represented just that synthesis in his own heritage and personality. Born of a French Swiss family, he nevertheless studied in Zurich and was fluent in German.

Heinz Isler's Shells

Born in Zollikon, now part of Zurich, on July 26, 1926, Heinz Isler attended public primary school in Zurich, and entered the canton school (high school) in 1939. In 1944, at the urging of one of his teachers, the school held an exhibition of Isler's drawings and water colors, which reflected his love of the Swiss landscape. All through school he had the reputation of working alone and of doing his work in an unusual way. Following graduation in 1945, he spent nine months in compulsory military service, where he did outdoor construction work, which he enjoyed immensely. In November 1945, he entered the Federal Technical Institute in Zurich, and he graduated in 1950 with a degree in civil engineering. For his final-year design project, he chose to study thin shells; of the more than one hundred students in the class, he was the only one to choose that subject.

Following graduation, he accepted Lardy's offer of a position as assistant at the Federal Technical Institute. From January 1951 until May 1953, he helped Lardy with teaching, and also worked on the many cases of structural failure that Lardy had been asked to explain. When Isler left his position at the Federal Technical Institute, he considered the possibility of a career as a painter, but challenged by shell design problems that he encountered while doing free-lance engineering work, he settled on the career for which he was already trained. While still doing free-lance design in late 1954, he designed a pneumatic form, thin shell factory for the Trösch Company. It was the first work in which he set the form completely on his own. In 1955, at an international congress in Amsterdam, he presented publicly for the first time his new designs, thus confirming his independence from other designers.[15] Practical-minded Swiss businessmen quickly recognized the virtues of Isler's early designs, and he began to get numerous commissions. Two important events marked Isler's early period, prior to 1959. The first was his idea in 1956 to build 5-meter-diameter plastic skylights, which interested a manufacturer in Thun, to whom Isler sold the idea. This project financed his own model laboratory, from which new forms began to emerge. The second event was his collaboration with the building firm of Bösiger, near Burgdorf, whose personnel Isler instructed carefully in his methods for precise construction. Ever since, that firm has built almost all Isler's Swiss shells, and the association has assured him the quality control essential to structures that are both competitive and permanent.

In 1959, Isler created somewhat of a sensation with the paper he presented at the First Congress of the International Association for Shell Structures, held in Madrid under the direction of Eduardo Torroja. Torroja's goal for the congress had been to present new developments in thin shells rather than to summarize the major works completed since the 1920s.[16] As can be seen from the published proceedings, the first twenty-four papers were not unlike most such papers, presenting individual structures or groups of structures. Each paper elicited a few questions from the audience, with the longest discussion equaling two pages for a fourteen-page paper on Polish shell designs. Nothing preceding quite prepares the reader for paper twenty-five. It is entitled simply "New Shapes for Shells," and it contains a little over one page of text and nine illustrations.[17] In that text, Isler describes very briefly three ways to arrive at shell shapes: (1) the freely shaped hill, where, for instance, molded earth is the form; (2) the membrane under pressure, where an inflated rubber membrane gives the shape; and (3) the hanging cloth reversed, where a draped fabric defines surface shape just as a hanging cable defines a funicular line. His illustrations are of some models and a few completed concrete shells, and there is a full page showing thirty-nine possible shapes followed by the word "etc." The implication is of unlimited possibilities.

The paper had an immediate impact. It resulted in a rash of discussion, which in print is about five times as long as the paper's text. (The actual discussion was substantially longer than the printed version.) The quality of the discussants was as remarkable as its relative length; comments were dominated by the most distinguished designers present: Torroja himself, Nicholas Esquillan of France, and Ove Arup of Great Britain. The discussants took up three themes from Isler's brief presentation: first, that new shapes come from simple models; second, that these nongeometric shapes could be economically built; and, third, that the shapes were designed without reference to architecture.

Torroja concentrated on the question of models, worrying about the dangers of their being used without experience. He emphasized the risks involved in forming ideas based on visually stimulating models that are not related to actual full-scale structures. He also noted the problems of scaling in going from small models to full-scale designs. Esquillan, fresh from completing the world's longest spanning (206 meters) thin shell roof in Paris, disputed the economy of Isler's nonmathematically defined shell shapes: "I say that the cost of the scaffolding and formwork is at least 50 percent of the total construction cost of a thin shell. That is how it is!" Isler had claimed those costs were only 20 percent in his shells, in response to which Esquillan had asked, "Are the prices in Switzerland so different than in other countries?" Finally, Ove Arup, head of the largest firm of consulting engineers in Great Britain, spoke about the need for collaboration with architects and about buildings being "functionally right, architecturally right and aesthetically right, and it is not any great consolation that we get something else cheap." He discussed the problem of shape only in the context of architecture, in complete contrast to Isler. Undoubtedly, on Arup's mind was the Sydney Opera House, on which he was to struggle for years as structural engineer.

Isler's responses get at the heart of structural design, revealing the true function of basic research in design. Torroja's concern over models reflected his vast academic experience, which was based on the scientific analysis of structures. Isler's response met that concern directly by emphasizing that shaping (with models) comes first but is only "the first link in a whole chain of investigations; the other links are [small-scale] model tests and measuring the first structure, i.e., model tests at full scale as we have it out there; these are of primary importance." Isler noted that technical education in mathematics and geometry did not provide directly the means for studying new shapes. What is important, he stressed, are *physical analogies,* such as the inflated membrane or the draped cloth. But that was only a first part of the problem; a second part was the cost. To answer Esquillan, Isler stated that "we use a system which maybe has a few new ideas." These consisted of very carefully made glue-laminated wooden arch pieces put on light tubular scaffolding and supporting wooden boards, over which wood fiber insulation plates span as formwork. In short, Isler had used both new shapes and new construction methods together. When asked how he could build shells to accurate shapes when his design used such small models, Isler gave a typically Swiss response, "We measured the coordinates with very subtle, accurate instruments and then it [the shape] is drawn in a larger scale, and you get a series of curves. If there

is a little mistake, it is seen immediately and then you can correct it."
This is machine precision controlled by visual observation. With regard
to the question of architecture, Isler made no response at all. He merely
emphasized that finding good solutions to thin-shell shaping was an
engineering problem which could be solved only by imaginative shaping controlled by full-scale and small-scale measurements and by extreme economies resulting from careful construction procedures.

One day in the early 1960s while Isler was walking in Zurich, a
book cover in a shop window, showing a beautifully curved shell form,
caught his eye and helped set in motion a new emphasis on the visually
expressive potential for thinness—an emphasis for which Lardy's lectures on structures like Maillart's Tavanasa bridge had laid the ground-
work. The book cover showing the Xochimilco shell by Felix Candela,
himself deeply influenced by Maillart, stimulated Isler, who was now
in command of the technical discipline, to a fuller visual expression
of his own unique ideas.

Twenty years after that first Madrid congress, Isler was to return
to Madrid for a second congress at which he and Candela gave the
keynote addresses. Candela, by then no longer building shells, gave a
retrospective view which nicely complemented Isler's address. What
Isler demonstrated in 1979 at Madrid was that he, possibly more than
any other presently practicing structural designer, has found the limitless potentials for thin shells. Unlike numerous other designers who
have filled books and articles with elegant sketches and photographs
of seductive models, Isler almost never discusses abstract design ideas;
nearly everything he presents is already built. The staggering reality
of his Madrid presentation was not so much the richness of his visual
imagination but the cool practical fact that this richness is all built and
nearly all of it because of competitive economy.

Isler's work illustrates a deep understanding of the nature of concrete. Concrete as a material tends to crack. The thin shell solution
is a structure made as thin as is practical, which is at the same time
mainly in compression. The designer best satisfies this goal by making
a form that is doubly curved (a dome as opposed to a cylinder) and
that has a minimum of sharp changes in thickness, in curvature, or in
boundaries. This is best achieved when the roof, its edges, and its supports are fully integrated into a single form. This integration is missing,
for example, in the thin shell at Chamonix (figure 12.1), whose form

FIGURE 12.1

Roofs for a School, Chamonix, France, 1973, by Rogier Taillibert. These flat spherical segments required strong edge-ribs, and the resulting appearance is heavy. The shells meet in massive edge supports at the corner.

FIGURE 12.2

Roof for the Sicli Company Building, Geneva, 1969, by Heinz Isler. Isler designed this roof to be a single, integral, thin shell on seven supports. Because the form is structural no edge ribs are needed. The building required two roofs, which Isler smoothly integrated into a single form so that all massive edge supports could be eliminated.

was set by the architect Roger Taillibert, for reasons unrelated to structure. Because its flat spherical shape was structurally inappropriate, Isler, the engineering consultant for the project, was forced to make the edge ribs heavier just to carry the loads safely. When separate shells are connected at the corner, massive edge supports are required. Compare this to the Geneva shell roof for the Sicli Company, where Isler gave the form (figure 12.2). Here two shells are made into one by a simple form on seven supports with no ribs whatsoever and without heavy edge connections. In spite of the complicated ground plan, the entire shell is one single unit whose resistance comes entirely from its double curvature rather than partly from ribs.

In the early 1960s, Isler began to develop his ribless shells by using geometric forms, as in the garden center in Solothurn (figure 12.3). Here the difficult edge problem is resolved by a sharp discontinuity of curvature and by the use of steeply overhanging edge shells, which are not integrated smoothly into the main shell. In contrast, in Isler's more recent design for the same four-point support problem, the garden center in Camorino (figure 12.4), all edge stiffening is gone and there is no discontinuity. The entire shell is one slender form down to the light supporting points. Less material was needed to make this integrated structure and the stresses are still well below allowable limits; hence, the structure is still scientifically correct without requiring edge ribs.

Isler's forms are so carefully designed that there is no cracking of the concrete and hence no leaking, and, therefore, no roofing need be applied to the concrete. The competitive economy results from carefully training the builder, from designing the form-boards (planks of wood fiber board on which the concrete is cast) to serve as insulation, and from the frequent reuse of the expensive curved wooden ribs. Isler takes careful measurements of deflections; and, for some larger works, these deflections are measured long after completion to insure their stability. Although Isler always stresses the centrality of physical observations, today he also makes full use of the computer to analyze the shell forms he has already chosen. This use of computers has not changed his design approach.

Along with integration of elements and competitive costs, the symbolic or visual aesthetics of a structure are an essential part of Isler's designs, which are characterized by extreme thinness, bare texture, and vivid contrast to the setting. In his 1979 Heimberg indoor tennis center

FIGURE 12.3
Roof for the Wyss Garden Center, Solothurn, Switzerland, 1961, by Heinz Isler. The edges of this four-point, supported thin shell are stiffened by steeply overhanging edge shells.

FIGURE 12.4
Roof for the Bürgi Garden Center, Camorino, Switzerland, 1971, by Heinz Isler. All the loads on this four-point supported roof are carried by the thin shell entirely. No ribs are needed and the thinness of the 3-inch-thick shell is visually expressed everywhere in profile.

(figure 12.5), four similar units are built in the form of thin arched slabs separated by joints between edge curves which may appear, at first glance, to be ribs but which are only the shell turned up for stiffness. These strange shapes exhibit the thinness directly at their edges, the texture of concrete outside with the bare texture of the form-boards inside, and a form and texture that contrasts vividly with the surrounding countryside.

The same expressive features appear in the Geneva and the Camorino thin shells. The fact that these works result from a design process of experiment and precision, and a construction process of economy and control, is just what permits Isler to express his own personal vision of structural art. As he develops his forms, the ideals of integration and competition are always present, but above all the idea of aesthetics remains primary, as it did for his teacher Lardy, as it did for Maillart, and as it does for all structural artists.

FIGURE 12.5

Indoor Tennis Center, Heimberg, Switzerland, 1979, by Heinz Isler. Isler designed four similar units of thin-arched slabs spanning 60 meters and separated by joints between the edge curves; these appear to be ribs but are made of the shell, corrugated to give extra stiffness. Isler found this new, non-geometrical form by patient experimentation with models of the reversed hanging-membrane type.

Isler and Scientific Theory

As we have seen, the general mathematical theory of shells did little to stimulate design; rather, the construction of shells stimulated academics to study the theory. Isler found, as did Candela, that the theories were of little help; he had to turn to the physical world rather than the mathematical one. While use of the computer increased between 1955 and 1980, Isler found a method of physical analogies by which he could develop a scientific theory appropriate to structural art. His theory is as easy to state as it is difficult to practice: he found that the laws of nature could be put directly into the service of society by means of designs based upon the perhaps startling idea of play. His is a scientific theory of play, for all the laws of nature are obeyed. As rules, they are strict but they determine nothing; and it is through these rules, learned ever more thoroughly as he plays, that the player discovers moves that he never before dreamed of.

Isler stretches a cloth held at seven points, coats it with wet plastic, lets it sag, and when the plastic hardens there has solidified a new form, which when inverted makes a thin shell roof on seven supports. The form will satisfy all the laws of gravity and of concrete; that is, the inverted hanging form will put the concrete into compression where it belongs. The prime law of concrete is that it must be uncracked to be permanent; it is the same law that the Gothic masons had to follow.

Isler's game is not like chess, which the computer can handle, but rather a game of solitaire played on a board with no fixed boundaries: each game has new borders which shift with the play and no one else makes any moves. It is a lonely business, and when Isler is at work on a new design he is always alone, sometimes working through the night and for days on end until he has found the correct sequence of moves.

It is the most serious of games and mathematical analysis can add nothing to it. There is already a vocabulary for this scientific theory, even though written to a different goal. The Dutch cultural historian Johan Huizinga (1872–1944) argued in a full-length book that humanity goes by three names: Homo Faber, Homo Sapiens, and Homo Ludens (man the maker, man the knower, and man the player).[18] Huizinga centered his book on man the player, and he characterized play by its freedom, by its "stepping out of 'real' life into a temporary sphere of activity with a disposition all of its own," by "its limitedness. It is 'played out' within certain limits of time and place," and by its creation of order, "it *is* order." He notes then that "the profound affinity between play and order is perhaps the reason why play seems to be to such a large extent in the field of aesthetics. Play has a tendency to be beautiful."[19] I would not press this correspondence too far except that Huizinga himself does so. He really means to argue that play is central to civilization and that it is essential to an ordered society. He ends his book filled with images of a civilization crumbling under the playless, humorless, pseudo-order of a goose-stepping Germany. It is the fake order promised by making without playing that Huizinga saw as demonic, and that sensitive intellectuals fear in contemplating automation and the computer.

Isler's career stands, obscure as it currently is to the general public, for a full-scale rejection of dehumanized technology as the way to order. Nothing in building construction is as ordered as his roof structures. They stand in the harsh Swiss environment, thin sheets of stone exposed without any waterproofing, fully unprotected from the weather, and yet without cracks or leaks. Smooth as the cloth from which they were first envisioned, these stone surfaces cleanly define strange, unanticipated spaces. These are not the beaux-arts spaces of high architecture built in spite of cost and the nature of materials; rather, they are only built because they reorder materials in new ways and at low costs.

These shapes are free in the sense that the designer alone decides the form, but they are limited by the laws of nature (gravity) and the patterns of society (costs). It is these two disciplines that permit that freedom to play. In the Sydney Opera House, the so-called freely shaped shells acted as the most rigid prison for the architect, the engineers, and the owners. In the end the architect had to be fired, the engineers gave up on the analysis after untold man-years of labor, and the owners had to pay over twenty times the initial cost estimate for a scaled-down version of the initial plan.[20] The designer did not follow the rules of the original competition. As Huizinga puts it, "fair play is nothing less than good faith expressed in play terms. Hence the cheat or spoil-sport shatters civilization itself." The making of ostentatious objects without regard to public cost or to the right use of material shatters the basis of democratic civilization by tempting us all to worship golden calfs in a desert of limited resources. "To be a sound culture-creating force this play-element must be pure," Huizinga continues.[21] That is the purity of public service rather than propaganda of self-aggrandizement.[22]

The sense of play so dominates Isler's life that someone unaccustomed to the idea of the engineer as artist would think him slightly mad. His office roof is a swamp sprouting mosses, small trees, and shrubs; model trains run out from his office window and around hundreds of feet of twisting track through the jungled yard; in that yard may also be found weathered plastic shell models, balloon-formed concrete houses, and fruit-laden trees. But even more remarkable are the transformations that occur in winter near his Bernese-style farmhouse. There, as the Swiss air freezes, Isler can be found night after night spraying water on tent-like sheets of gardners' netting or inflated balloons or on shrubs and trees to create a world of ice forms—pure play out of nature's cool discipline. These temporary forms flow from Isler's exuberance and curiosity: not the scientist's curiosity to discover the laws of nature, but the engineer's urge to learn, make, and play all at the same time and by means of the same objects. This integration of man's deepest instincts is the ground for civilization and for civil works.

CHAPTER 13

NEW TOWERS,
NEW BRIDGES

Competition and Play

Both the Eiffel Tower and the Brooklyn Bridge emerged from the process of competitions. For without winning bridge competitions earlier in their careers, neither Eiffel nor Roebling could have dared project those final structures, so far beyond previous scales. Of course, for each of those structures, there was no longer any real competition because the two men had so surpassed any rivals. Still, the tower and the bridge stand for competition; and they also stand for play both because they show visually their designers' play with form and because they are technological parks designed for the direct pleasure of visitors.

Huizinga has made this connection between competition and play as follows: "The more play bears the character of competition the more fervent it will be." The fervency imparts to play "a certain ethical value insofar as it means a testing of the player's prowess: his courage, tenacity, resources, and . . . his spiritual powers—his 'fairness,' because, despite his ardent desire to win, he must still stick to the rules of the game."[1] Moreover, as Huizinga recalls, competition was central to the creation of such great structures in the past as Brunelleschi's Dome in Florence.[2] This same spirit helps explain the rise of so many immense cathedrals in the small towns of northern France during the twelfth and thirteenth centuries—a time of intense civic competition. All of these works combine competition and play, discipline and emotion, in design.

The mistaken idea that engineering is only a rational application of science not only leads us away from the reality of structural art but also seriously obscures the creative place of competition in the process of building. Two late-twentieth-century structures symbolize the ideas of competition and play in the same way as the Eiffel Tower and the Brooklyn Bridge. Each is the product of a structural artist whose career matured under the steady testing of competitions. One of these two structures is a tower in Chicago, designed by Fazlur Khan (1930–1982), and the other is a bridge in Switzerland, designed by Christian Menn (b. 1927). These structures carry forward the same basic ideals as their nineteenth-century predecessors, but they also symbolize a new set of ideals which address two major social issues of the late twentieth century: the decay of large cities and the destruction of the wilderness. Just as occurred with those earlier works, the new tower and the new bridge have been criticized as ugly, technological, and misplaced. Again art in new forms offends many people, but it is time now to recognize that structural art has a long history as well as a bright future in spite of attempts to retreat to facades, imitations, and the costly symbols of pomp and waste.

Fazlur Khan and the Second Chicago School

Fazlur Khan used to say that his Chicago firm would be hired when a company wanted an inexpensive, useful, and good-looking office building, but that when the same company wanted a prestigious corporate headquarters it would hire a New York star architect instead. He could compete with anything except the corporate urge toward high fashion. This contrast between Chicago and New York brings us back to the development of skyscrapers, and to the remarkable ideas of Khan that characterize the Second Chicago School.

Born in Dacca, East Pakistan (now Bangladesh), Khan graduated first in his class from Bengal Engineering College in 1950, worked for two years, and then came to the University of Illinois on a Fulbright and a Pakistani scholarship. He received a Ph.D. in structural engineering in 1955 and immediately began to work with Skidmore, Owings and Merrill, architects and engineers in Chicago. In 1957 he returned to East Pakistan, fulfilling the terms of his scholarship, but after three years he was back in Chicago; his Pakistani job had had great status but gave him little chance to design.[3]

From his return to Chicago until his death in 1982, Khan designed a series of buildings, including some of the tallest in the world, which together constitute a new approach to tall building design. As with the other great structural artists, Khan was technically a master of engineering. No one practicing structural engineering since World War II has better understood building structures. But that technical understanding was not his primary motivation. As he stated it, "the social and visual impact of buildings is really my motivation for searching for new structural systems," and to get the right visual impact, "a building's natural strength should be expressed."[4] With his rich imagination, Khan has created new forms for buildings, in a class with the new forms created by Maillart for bridges and by Nervi for vaults.

In the early 1970s he became the only engineering partner of his firm. His two largest designs—the John Hancock Center and the Sears Tower, both in steel and both in Chicago—made him internationally known. Just before his death, design began on the Onterie Center, his diagonally braced concrete skyscraper design in Chicago;[5] by 1968, he had already designed, in Houston, the world's tallest concrete skyscraper. He used both major building materials with equal mastery, and he even devised special ways to combine concrete with structural steel.[6]

Structural Expression in Tall Buildings

Perhaps Khan's most remarkable achievement is that he managed to design any tall building at all. Following Sullivan and the decline of the first Chicago school, tall building design came thoroughly into the hands of architects. The idea of structural expression almost disappeared. For example, although the gothic Woolworth Building in New York does emphasize vertical columns by cladding steel in vertical shafts of masonry, the Chrysler Building, the Empire State Building, and Rockefeller Center all emphasize walls and windows rather than ideas of structure. Following the war, the modern movement gained popularity with its emphasis on glass and on neat grids of metal. Some took this for an expression of structure, but more properly it was an expression of the metallic crispness of machine technology.

Structural expression in tall buildings can arise from any of a series of design problems which invoke the structural imagination: lateral loads (usually wind), the reduction in floor space as the building gets higher, the need to open up the ground floor plazas, and the uneven gravity load distribution on an exterior wall. There are other problems as well, but with just these we can amply illustrate how Khan found new solutions by insisting that the structure be expressed.

Merely showing structure is not the same as expressing it. The Britannia Bridge shows its girders but it does not express how they carry their loads because they are visually as heavy near their supports (where they could be much more slender) as they are at mid-span. Maillart's Chiasso roof, on the other hand, which may be thought of as a visible girder, expresses its carrying action through a changing distance between the lower chord and the roof—a maximum at mid-span and a minimum near the supports.

In the same way, the Hell Gate Bridge shows the structure of the arch but does not express the fact that the upper chord ends in thin air, while all the load passes into the foundations through the hinge in the lower chord. The Garabit Viaduct, by contrast, clearly expresses that same hinged action by bringing the upper and lower chords together at the foundations. Maillart expresses the same thing in the Salginatobel Bridge.

The expression of structure in tall buildings begins with the Eiffel

Tower and includes suspension bridge towers as well as high office buildings. The two basic actions typical of all high towers are the carrying, first, of vertical loads and, second, of horizontal loads. The Eiffel Tower, as described in chapter 6, expresses the second, while the suspension bridge tower expresses the first. In the bridge tower, the primary load comes from the vertical action of the cables at the tower top. This concentrated load creates large, constant, vertical forces throughout the tower height; the weight of the tower is less important. Thus we find Ammann creating towers that express nearly constant strength from top to bottom.

In office buildings, by contrast, the vertical load is zero at the very top, and increases gradually toward the base. This gradual change does not in itself give much scope for expression unless there is some discontinuity in the load, a condition, for example, that allowed Khan to display his talent with concrete towers.

Concrete Towers

For gravity loading, Khan designed an external and visible skeletal frame for the twenty-story Hartford Plaza in Chicago in 1961. A hidden interior core provides the lateral resistance, and the visible wall carries only vertical loads. This relatively low building shows the structure, but, as with works of the first Chicago school, the loading is too small and gradual to provide much scope for expression. In the thirty-eight-story Brunswick Building of 1965, the concrete skeleton again is fully shown. Here, however, Khan also faced the load-discontinuity problem of opening up a wide column-free plaza. He solved it by designing massive 24-feet-deep beams to carry the loads from closely spaced columns of the skeletal wall down to a few large widely spaced columns below. But this massive solution did not satisfy Khan, and several years later he devised a new structural form for a building in Rochester, in which wall column forces are transferred directly to widely spaced plaza columns. The heavy transfer girder is eliminated, and the result is a facade in which some of the vertical columns are thickened near the base to give an arch-like look and hence an arch action, transferring load to the large plaza columns in smooth and visually expressive pathways.[7]

The problem of lateral loads led Khan in 1963 to create a framed tube in which all the lateral rigidity is provided by exterior walls formed of a closely spaced grid of columns and beams. The DeWitt–Chestnut apartment building completed in 1965 first used this tube idea.[8] But the facade has a uniform look even though the skeletal structure gets thicker lower down the wall. Finally, in 1968, Khan succeeded in expressing the framed tube with a new visual interest, with his One Shell Plaza in Houston, where the floor slabs caused uneven loadings on the wall. The exterior wall received heavy loads just at points opposite to where the interior core ends. Here the exterior walls needed extra strength, which could have been provided within the columns by hidden steel reinforcement. Khan, however, seized the chance to work out a new form by making the more heavily loaded columns deeper and hence project outward from the wall. This slightly undulating exterior wall is, as Khan put it, "a direct expression of the structural behavior and load flow." But far more important to him, "the visual effect obviously breaks the monotony of the disciplined grid and creates an unusual and yet honest structural facade." The engineer could have strengthened this wall in other equally efficient and economical ways, which from the technical viewpoint would have also been honest. (The structure would still have been shown but the chance for expression would have been lost.) Khan uses "honest" to mean that the form and structure were conceived of together as one idea, and not, as he said, "because of an *a priori* architectural concept" in which the form obscures the structure.[9]

Khan's two final concrete tower designs are in Chicago. Both are multiuse structures just under sixty stories high. Both have a grid of columns and beams exposed on the exterior wall, but in one, the Onterie Center, Khan introduced diagonal bracing by making solid a series of windows running diagonally along the exterior to form a series of X-braces that resemble his John Hancock Tower in steel. Indeed, a concrete tower following Khan's design has just been completed in New York City, in which the diagonals are expressed on all four sides.[10] Khan had developed this idea ten years earlier while working with students at the Illinois Institute of Technology. In a 1972 article, he predicted that this system "will find its way to reality in the near future."[11]

These new forms in concrete would have easily been enough to mark off Khan as a front-rank structural artist, but they are equaled, and in fame surpassed, by his towers of steel.

Steel Towers

When the American Institute of Steel Construction summarized tall buildings in 1972, it showed the seven highest ones, it compared steel weights, and it raised a series of questions about the origins and future of these immense works.[12] Looking at those seven (figure 13.1), we can see right away the affinity between the Eiffel Tower and the John Hancock Center: both have a technological look and a tapering profile. The unsymmetrical Sears Tower expresses a new structural idea, but that idea needs explanation to be clear. The Chrysler and the Empire State are architectural compositions typical of the style in the twenties; the Standard Oil and World Trade Center are similarly typical of the postwar architectural style loosely called modernism. Of the American designs, Khan's are the only two that reflect structural ideas in the creation of form.

FIGURE 13.1

A Comparison of the World's Tallest Buildings, the Eiffel Tower, the Chrysler Building, the Standard Oil Building in Chicago, the John Hancock Center, the Empire State Building, the World Trade Center, and the Sears Tower. Along with the Eiffel Tower only the two designs by Fazlur Khan—the Hancock Center and the Sears Tower—reflect structural ideas in their creation of form.

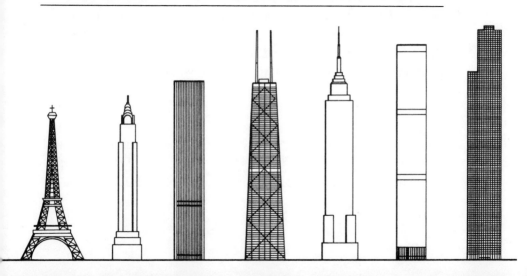

The Hancock tower project (figure 13.2) began as two separate buildings: one for offices and one for apartments. Because of the limited site, the project architect, Bruce Graham, suggested combining them into one, and Khan immediately proposed designing a diagonal-ly-braced tube for structure. He and his partner Myron Goldsmith had in 1964 jointly proposed the use of exterior diagonals to one of their students at Illinois Institute of Technology for a thesis project.[13] Khan never claimed to have invented the X-bracing, although he felt sure that he had designed the first tube building to be built (the De-Witt–Chestnut, completed in 1965). In the case of the Hancock tower, Khan proposed the design and saw it through all stages until it was opened for use in 1970.

The tube's efficiency derives from the fact that the external walls carry a major part of the vertical gravity loads and all of the lateral wind load. The form is especially efficient in the Hancock tower because the diagonals tie together the otherwise widely spaced columns, thus distributing the vertical forces evenly among them. As Khan said, "taking advantage of this bearing-wall characteristic of the system, all exterior columns on each face at any floor were made of the same size. . . . This resulted in a considerable reduction in construction fabrication and erection time as well as cost."[14]

By making a tube, Khan took maximum advantage of structural changes introduced in tall building construction over the preceding forty years—namely, larger column-free interiors (the Empire State is a forest of interior columns), lighter removable interior partitions, and more open exterior walls. His tube structure provides, with relatively little material, relatively high strength and stiffness.

The safety of the tower also derives from its tube form. Since the dead load in a tube form is carried primarily by the outermost columns, they are necessarily heavy enough to carry wind-load forces without significant overstress. Stiffened by the floors at every level, the tube form also provides safety against excessive vibrations. The endurance

FIGURE 13.2
The John Hancock Center, Chicago, 1970, by Skidmore, Owings, and Merrill, with Fazlur Khan as structural designer. Khan designed the X-bracing to create a rigid exterior structure and thus carry loads efficiently by an open tube.

of the tower is aided by having the exposed steel frame covered by a protected aluminum coating. Economy of construction was achieved by having the owner, developer, architect, engineer, and builder all working on the original plan during design.

By using a tubular structure made up of few columns with huge diagonals, Fazlur Khan was able to express visually an efficiency of structure that is probably more easily understood by the general public than has been the case for any other major skyscraper. That it was built economically in comparison with similar buildings lends further meaning to this highly visible and unique structural form. Moreover, the designers clearly saw themselves standing in the tradition of the first Chicago school during the time of Jenney and Root, for whom structural engineering had been a stimulus to tall building design. Thus, the idea of daring new forms that express structure might be said to come naturally to designers living and working in Chicago.

Before the Hancock opened, design work was already underway on an even higher tower, this one for the Sears Roebuck Company (figure 13.3). Here Khan pursued a different concept in which nine tubes make up the structure so that the building can get smaller toward the top without being tied to a given taper as in the Hancock. Two tubes stop at the 50th floor, two more at the 66th floor, and three more at the 90th. The last two go all the way to the 110th floor.[15] In this way each tube retains its integrity and hence its rigidity. Moreover, the building shows a different profile from each side.

Its 1,450-foot height makes the 1974 Sears Tower the highest office building in the world, just 100 feet higher than the twin towers of the New York's World Trade Center completed in 1972. Its visual interest is greater from a distance than from close up, where the great expanse of glass and metal wall has little differentiation. As a concept, the Sears Tower is brilliant, but it is not as visually powerful as the Hancock. Indeed, the earlier tower was Khan's favorite and the one for which he will always be best known.

FIGURE 13.3

The Sears Tower, Chicago, 1974, by Skidmore, Owings, and Merrill, with Fazlur Khan as structural designer. Khan designed nine tubes, each 75-foot square in plan. Each tube is structurally complete in itself so that the tubes can be stopped at different levels with no complex framing. The 1450-foot tower is the highest building in the world.

BRADNER
SMITH
COMPANY
PAPER

Chicago Loop

94 WEST

90 94 EAS

Khan and Collaboration

I have spoken of these buildings as if Khan were *the* designer just as Eiffel was for his tower. However, Khan's designs were collaborations between him and one of his architectural partners, usually Bruce Graham. Khan always emphasized his role as collaborator rather than as principal designer. He repeatedly urged that "the design process of any major building . . . must be multi-disciplinary in nature," by which he meant that "the idea of the architect drawing up a nice sketch representing his vision of a building may have some possible validity for a minor structure such as a residential building or for a small commercial project, but would result in an utter architectural disaster for any major building."[16] His argument for collaboration, in short, was a reaction against the idea of the architect alone producing the visual design and the engineer merely making the work safe and inexpensive. He exemplified in his own work the ideal of the engineer directly taking the lead in designing the visual form rather than merely following "a preconceived design by an architect where the engineer has to simply solve the problem given to him."[17] He made this clear in the posthumously published article on the design process for the Hancock Tower from which the preceding quotes were drawn. As he went on to say, "in looking back fifteen years, one can now objectively discuss and elaborate on the various aspects and nuances of the design process of this major building which, in fact, could not be done as openly at the time of the actual designing of the building."[18] He told of how he and his partner Myron Goldsmith while teaching in Chicago had developed the exterior diagonal idea and how he had proposed this idea to their architectural partner, Graham, once the design group had begun to consider a 100-story tower instead of two shorter buildings. Khan gave his collaborators "assurance . . . that the proper details can be developed to keep the unit price of steel the same as that of a traditional frame building, [and] that helped to make the historic decision to [build] a single tower." Then came the test: "The architectural team responding to the owner's concern, wanted to take the diagonals on the exterior of the building only up to the 90th floor. . . . It was vehemently argued by the architectural team that diagonals above that level [would spoil the view from within and] first renderings of the building were developed without showing the top ten floors having any diagonals." Here was a direct confrontation between architects and the structural engineer. In his article, Khan even admitted that "from a structural point of view, one could have designed a building without diagonals in the upper floors." That was not the point for him; a deeper issue was at stake, for as he continued, "from a philosophic point of view and from a structural visual continuity of the system itself, it would be a tragedy to terminate the diagonals abruptly on the 90th floor." Khan saw his visual design about to be crippled; he spoke then not as an engineering consultant but rather as a structural artist, and as such he brought all his passion to bear on saving his concept. Writing perhaps the last paragraphs of his life, he told how he had "made an impassioned argument that not having the diagonals on the upper ten floors would add tremendous amounts of additional steel. . . . the cost would skyrocket and it might, in fact, be too flexible, causing motion discomfort on those floors."[19] That "impassioned argument," it should be obvious, was not fully rational, especially as Khan has conceded earlier in the article that the diagonals could have been omitted above the ninetieth floor "from a structural point of view." Khan was arguing the way any front rank artist would at the attempts to truncate his central artistic idea.

Khan's conclusion was "that the structural-architectural concept, once developed, should be given its full visual expression without jeopardizing any integral visual part of the concept." But Khan was not just referring to concept in the sense of the overall form. Concept "also means," he continued, "that the structural details must be developed in close cooperation with the architectural team so that the meaning of every joint and intersection be well represented and expressed . . . it would be philosophically wrong to develop a cladding [to protect the steel structure from fire and weather] detail with stone or masonry." The entire visual expression, from overall form to every detail of exposed structure, all reflect "the real structure," and the engineer must not give way to any other arguments. Here Khan is following the long tradition of structural art from Telford on, and is especially close to Roebling in his Cincinnati report, wherein all details are thought about structurally and aesthetically. Like Roebling's 1867 report, Khan's 1982 article, recording events of 1967, was to be his last statement of ideals. As such, I quote his conclusion in its entirety:

The process of design for major architectural projects often does not take advantage of team effort, of all disciplines working together to create the most relevant engineering architectural solution. A-priori architectural facades un-related to natural and efficient structural systems are not only a wastage of natural resources, but will also have difficulty in standing the test of time. The author, in this particular case, has attempted to highlight the structural–architectural team interaction which has resulted in a significant architectural statement based on reason and the laws of nature in such a way that the resulting aesthetics may have a transcendental value and quality far beyond arbitrary forms and expressions that reflect the fashion of the time. Through the case study, the opportunity and responsibility of the engineer to actively participate in the architectural evolution of a building is demonstrated. It is hoped that engineers will not abrogate this sense of responsibility in the face of architectural movement of today commonly referred to as post-modernism.[20]

This is a statement of collaboration in which the ideals of structural art are paramount. Sometimes the architect is thought to be like the symphony conductor, directing all the instruments and shaping the results to his own vision. Khan, by that analogy, is like a great pianist, playing a concerto with his architectural partner conducting the orchestra. The concerto obviously makes no sense without the orchestra; but it only becomes transcendental when the soloist is a great artist.

The Highway Explosion

If the inner city towers seem to centralize, the inter city highways seem to disperse. The Hancock tower brings people back into the living city; turnpikes open up the whole country to anyone who can afford a car. The United States and Western Europe both began extensive highway programs within a decade of the war. This highway explosion has not been without its critics, of whom perhaps the most widely read has been Lewis Mumford (b. 1895). Mumford, for example, denounced the 1957 Highway Bill as reflecting the "current American way of life [which was] founded . . . on the religion of the motor car . . . [which]

appeared as a compensatory device for enlarging an ego . . . shrunken by our very success in mechanization." The permanent consequences of this new religion, as Mumford saw it, were the direct result of "the engineer [who] does not hesitate to lay waste to streams, parks, and human neighborhoods in order to carry his roads straight to their supposed destination."[21] No one would dispute the fact that roads change the landscape just as buildings change the city. But Mumford's criticism, portraying engineers as villains, springs from two basic ideals central to environmentalist ideology that he and other critics have never been able to reconcile: one artistic and one political.

Mumford stated the artistic ideal in his Bampton Lectures of 1951: "Art, in the only sense in which one can separate art from technics [engineering], is primarily the domain of the person; and the purpose of art . . . is to widen the province of personality." Art is what individual people do and it "arises out of man's need to create for himself, beyond any requirement for mere animal survival, a meaningful and valuable world." The contrast between art and mere utility is present throughout Mumford's writings. He is quite explicit about this distinction. "Man's technical contrivances have their parallel in organic activities exhibited by other living creatures."[22] His examples range from bees as structural engineers to eels as electrical ones. The meaningful and the valuable are, on the other hand, the province of art. This misleading dichotomy, once established, leads Mumford, first of all, to deny his own sensitive and prophetic instincts and, second, to propose for contemporary problems solutions that require authoritarian control and centralized bureaucracies.

In his early writings, Mumford had instinctively singled out bridges as works of art—long before they were recognized as such by most engineers and architects. His 1931 appreciation of Brooklyn Bridge ended with the clear insight that "the lesson of the Brooklyn Bridge has not altogether been lost: far from it. Dams, waterworks, locks, bridges, power plants, factories—we begin to recognize these as important parts of the human environment. They are good or bad, efficient or inefficient by something more than quantitative criteria. The Roeblings perhaps never used the word aesthetics in this relation; but it was their distinction to have made it visible."[23] As we have seen, John Roebling was in fact deeply conscious of aesthetics and wrote vigorously about appearance and artistic design by engineers.

Thus Mumford had initially perceived that structures could become art when their designers were artists. Yet by the 1950s he had lost faith in engineers and even in the inherent potential of engineering. He came to believe that pure engineering could not express personality and hence could not be art. One consequence of this belief was that perceptive critics like Mumford and Giedion ceased, after World War II, to encourage engineers and politicians to seek better solutions within technology. These influential critics seemed to despair of engineering and engineers. They preferred rather to see engineering only as mechanization and as a dehumanizing force. A potentially great stimulus to better engineering design was, therefore, dissipated in negation. Mumford's belief that engineering could not be art had the second consequence of encouraging many people to view engineering and engineers as the cause of society's sickness, "the engineer . . . does not hesitate to lay waste to woods, streams, parks, and human neighborhoods in order to carry his roads straight to their supposed destination." Engineering not only lost a teacher, it gained a detractor.

Mumford had developed the position that art and engineering were separate things and that "once we have achieved the right form for a type-object . . . a bridge, a chair or a pitcher . . . it should keep that form for the next generation or for the next thousand years."[24] As we shall see, the new bridges of Christian Menn fully disprove Mumford's idea of a type-object.

For Mumford, the problems raised by this separation can be resolved only by "a shift of values; a new philosophic framework; a fresh habit of life." He calls for a reintegration of "the sundered halves of the modern personality: the empiricist and the idealist, the scientist and the man of religion, the fact finder and the form maker; ironically, he is describing the structural artist without knowing it. Mumford's artistic ideal, as expressed in his later writings, entails "displacing the machine and restoring man to the very center of the Universe . . . as the creator of a significant and valuable life."[25] By relegating engineering to the animal he cannot find any way to do this displacing short of a radical political restructuring. But this separation of art and technology and the negation of the latter leads Mumford to advocate a massive, controlling bureaucracy: "Until," as he concludes *The Highway and the City*, "these necessary tools (city and regional planning . . . an adequate system of federated urban government on a regional scale) of control have been created most of our planning will be empirical and blundering."[26] Somehow the individual artist will flourish better, we are told, when there is more centralized planning and stronger political tools of control.

But as should by now be obvious, the solution to the highway and the city is in fact not control or centralization but rather discipline and play. And precisely at the time when Mumford was beginning his attacks on the highways, a young Swiss engineer, Christian Menn, was investigating a solution to the problem. Menn is in a sense a direct refutation of Mumford: his bridges express individuality and symbolize the integration of art and engineering within a political democracy that fosters openness and competition.

Christian Menn

Christian Menn was born in 1927 in Meiringen, Berneroberland. Because of his father's work, he lived in various parts of Switzerland, but his family was from the Graubünden, the largest and most sparsely settled Swiss canton. In 1946, he entered the Federal Technical Institute in Zurich, graduating with a degree in civil engineering in 1950. In 1951, he began theoretical studies in his doctoral work, and in 1953, became an assistant to Professor Pierre Lardy, from whom he had first learned in detail about the work of Maillart.

His father, Simon Menn (1891–1948), a distinguished civil engineer in his own right, had in the 1920s worked as chief engineer for the builders on Maillart's two largest bridge projects. Simon Menn and Maillart were good friends as well as engineering associates.

After receiving his doctorate in 1956, Menn worked in Paris on the UNESCO buildings whose structural designer was Nervi. He returned to Switzerland in 1957, and in June of that year he opened his own office in Chur. In the years that followed, he designed numerous bridges and buildings, mostly in the Graubünden, and he won first prize in many bridge competitions throughout Switzerland. In 1971 Menn was made professor of structural engineering at his old institute in Zurich and gave up the office in Chur. Since then he has been consultant on most of the large bridges in Switzerland, and since 1977 he has been president of the commission for the revision of the Swiss building code for reinforced and prestressed concrete.

Christian Menn's earliest bridges clearly reflect the influence of Robert Maillart, particularly of Maillart's bridges in the Graubünden.[27] Indeed, the Graubünden is where Maillart had made his first original design (in 1900, for the bridge over the River Inn at Zuoz), and in the early years of the century he had studied and was influenced by the stone bridges of that mountainous canton. Menn, too, has always been deeply affected by these structures, which include ancient bridges such as the one over the Hinterrhein, near the farm where he had stayed as a boy, and the spectacular curved Landwasser viaduct.

Menn's style evolved slowly from his early bridges as he faced the changing conditions of construction during the 1960s. Three significant factors influenced his ideas. First, the rapid increase in labor costs made uneconomical the closely spaced vertical supports in deck-stiffened arches. Menn responded by spacing the supports much more widely apart, as shown in his first 100-meter-span arch at Reichenau in 1964 (figure 13.4) and in his Viamala bridge of 1967. This wider spacing, which still permitted deck stiffening, was made economically attractive by the second major change, the introduction of prestressing. Thanks to prestressing, longer spans could be built of straight girders, as in Menn's 1962 bridge over the Rhine at Bad Ragaz. For such a low river crossing, it was relatively easy to build a scaffolding for the entire bridge. At this time, however, for longer spans and for higher crossings, Menn still used deck-stiffened arches, as in the Nanin and Cascella bridges of 1967 in the Mesocco valley in the Italian-speaking part of the Graubünden. The third factor to influence Menn's style was the increasing cost of scaffolding for very high works. Since the 1950s, ways had been sought to reduce the cost of arch bridges by simplifying the scaffolding. At Reichenau, the scaffolding was supported at a number of places directly in the river. In a 1970 competition for a very large viaduct north of Bern, over the Aare River at Felsenau, Menn submitted not an arch design, needing complicated scaffolding, but a plan for a fully prestressed cantilever bridge built entirely without ground scaffolding (figure 13.5).

FIGURE 13.4
The Reichenau Bridge over the Rhine River, Reichenau, Switzerland, 1964, by Christian Menn. Menn designed this 100-meter-span arch to be stiffened by the prestressed concrete hollow-box deck girder.

FIGURE 13.5
The Felsenau Bridge over the Aare River, Bern, Switzerland, 1974, by Christian Menn. Menn won the design competition for this bridge by designing a cantilever-constructed hollow-box, prestressed girder. The 156-meter span was the longest in Switzerland when built.

The type of bridge Menn proposed had been pioneered in Germany, by Ulrich Finsterwalder. Such a bridge is built out on itself: the forms for small sections are slid out horizontally from already built columns, and the sections are cast and allowed to harden, and are then prestressed by tendons, which tie the newly formed sections back into those previously cast. Three important features of Menn's bridge demonstrate how he impressed his own personality upon an accepted design idea and thus created a fresh work of art.

The first aspect is the curved roadway plan. For this, Menn provided a curved box girder supported in the main spans by two thin and narrow high concrete walls. This solution provides relatively long overall spans of 156 meters with a girder whose materials are based only on the 144-meter clear spans. Furthermore, in spite of very thin walls, the longitudinal stiffness is great because of the wide spacing (12 meters). The double narrow column solution is therefore efficient. It is economical as well, because the wide column spacing permits a very simple scaffolding for the girder sections over the columns and a long platform from which to launch the first cantilever scaffold from both sides at once. Finally, the double narrow column solution permits a more open structure visually. Earlier viaducts usually had two columns side by side, supporting a pair of box girders. Thus the views from beneath those bridges tended to present wide solid walls blocking out the landscape, especially as one set of columns merged with the next set from an angled view. With a curved bridge especially, this merging would have closed a striking view which Menn's solution opens up.

The second aspect arises from the profile of the roadway through a wide valley which is partly wooded and partly suburban. Here Menn designed relatively long spans out of guiders whose overall depth increases toward the supports, giving its longitudinal profile a slightly arched (or haunched) appearance. These haunched guiders are efficient because they require less material than a girder of constant depth. The haunching does, however, require an increase in field construction cost above that for a girder of constant depth. Clearly the cost saving gained by material efficiency is at least partly offset by the extra cost of field labor. This classic problem underlines the fact that each criterion—efficiency, economy, and aesthetics—is internally complex and also, to some extent, can compromise each of the others, which means that the best designs are those that satisfy all three reasonably well.

Although the haunching does not give a clear minimum of cost, it does provide a more striking visual form than would a prismatic girder.

The third unusual aspect of the Felsenau design is in its girder cross-section, characterized by the use of a single box for a wide roadway. In the past, the way to build prestressed segmental bridges was to use two boxes, one for each half of the bridge, and thus to build, in effect, two bridges side by side. The single box with wide cantilever slabs requires less material than would two boxes. The single box as compared to a double one also achieves greater economy by halving the forming operations and by allowing the cantilever slabs to be built later on very simple scaffolding supported from the completed box girder. Finally, the single box solution goes together with the narrow column walls to give a strikingly light appearance. Of equal importance is the way Menn has designed the transition between the box and the columns. The box not only changes depth longitudinally, but it changes width as well, getting narrower as it gets deeper near the supports. Menn achieved this narrowing by tapering the box so that its top width remained constant while its bottom width decreased as the box depth increases. This smooth transition at the support is aesthetically superior to a transition in which the bottom box width is greater than the column transverse dimension. It would have been somewhat less costly to provide vertical web walls, but the resulting appearance would have been substantially heavier. As it is difficult to know if the overall costs would have been influenced in even a minor way, Menn did not hesitate to design the more handsome form. His competition entry was judged one of the least costly overall. As long as the overall concept (performance and construction procedure) is sound, minor changes in form will not appreciably change cost.

From Felsenau to Ganter

As the Felsenau was nearing completion in the spring of 1974, Menn was consulted by the canton engineer of the Valais, who asked him for advice about a new bridge on the Simplon Road. The canton had proposed to avoid the bad foundation conditions in the Ganter Valley above Brig by building a tunnel whose costs were estimated in the range of 50 million Swiss francs. Worried about this high cost, the canton engineer had asked advice from the federal highway department in Bern, which in turn suggested that the canton consult with Menn.

After inspecting the site and the foundation conditions, Menn developed a proposal for a bridge which he estimated would cost about half of the tunnel estimate. He drew up preliminary plans and had a model made. Normally, on such a major project there would have been a design competition, but the canton of the Valais was so taken with Menn's ideas that, fearing that a jury might select another design, they simply commissioned Menn to proceed with final plans. This example does illustrate the notion of the conservative jury: because the Ganter bridge form appears to have no direct precedent, it is likely that, in comparison with the Felsenau, it would have had substantially more difficulty in winning a competition. Nevertheless, its form comes from Menn's thinking about that earlier work. A brief consideration of his development of this form helps to show how the soundest innovations arise directly from experience with full-scale structures.

At Felsenau, Menn has purposely created long spans (the longest then in Switzerland) to avoid piers in the waterway and to achieve a lighter looking structure in the heavily traveled Aare Valley. In the Ganter Valley, his starting point was also the support conditions. He began by locating the tallest pier at the base of the solid rock on the north side, the next pier high up at the existing road level, with the other main span pier positioned so that the bridge main spans would be symmetrical.

With these preliminary ideas, Menn then began to think about the superstructure in detail. At Felsenau he had been struck by the immensity of the forces in the main girders. Menn felt that the larger forces arising from a 174-meter-span Ganter required a fresh approach. His solution was to bring the 87-meter cantilevers on that main span back down to about the same dimensions as the shorter spans by providing an intermediate support through cable stays.

For the high pillars, two separated thin walls as at Felsenau would have required much heavier sections because of the greatly increased height leading to higher lateral bending. Therefore, Menn used single hollow boxes which, for the 150-meter-high pillar, have flanges that increase in longitudinal width from 6.5 meters at the top to 10 meters at the base. Just as at Felsenau, the roadway girder and the pillars are designed as rigid frames, so that in the main spans there are no joints or bearings (except at the bases of three shorter pillars to separate the structure from the creeping valley).

Ganter Bridge Design

These comparisons between Felsenau and Ganter show how Menn modified his earlier experience for a newer and larger work. To see his ideas more clearly, it is essential to analyze the Ganter Bridge (figure 13.6) because it represents one of those rare events where a new form arises. As before, we consider separately the plan, profile, and section, and for each the questions of efficiency, economy, and aesthetics.

In plan, the roadway curves away from the north bank, has a straight section over the valley, and curves back to meet the existing road going up the south bank to the Simplon Pass. Menn initially positioned the supports on the basis of foundation conditions, but adjusted them with two other criteria in mind: symmetry and uniformity. The choice of single hollow box pillars of about the same width as the two-lane roadway leads to visually strong supports which, compared to the great valley width, still give an overall appearance of openness because of the wide spans. The single hollow-box pillars are, therefore, efficient forms for resisting the heavy lateral bending, mostly from design wind speeds of 150 kilometers per hour (94 mph). They are economically positioned to permit substantial deck girder form reuse, as well as shaped and spaced to give a striking and open overall structure.

In profile, the Ganter Bridge shows most clearly its new form, owing to Menn's decision to avoid deep girders at the supports. He has, rather, introduced cable stays which provide a total structural depth of 16 meters at the supports while reducing the 87-meter cantilevers to spans of only 36 meters. However, because the stays extend well into the 127-meter curved side spans, they must be encased in concrete walls to permit them to follow the plan curvature. These walls then become prestressed by the stays, a new procedure which brings three advantages: first, the cables are protected from corrosion; second, there is no fatigue danger since the cables, being bonded to the concrete walls, experience only about one-fifth the range of stress change as the cables in a normal stay bridge; and, third, a greater overall safety results from the substantial girder cross-section which includes the concrete walls above the box.

These advantages in structural efficiency go together with the substantial construction advantage of reducing all the cantilever scaffoldings to one standard form going from a 2.5-meter depth at midspan to a 5-meter depth at support. However, the construction of the concrete walls was expensive and could hardly have been justified without the rigorous standardization in cantilever scaffolding.

Finally, the aesthetic questions were, as usual for Menn, of primary concern. The real origin of the profile did not come from ideas on efficiency and economy, but rather from Menn's simple observation that "the extreme relationship between the extraordinarily powerful pillars and the very narrow bridge girder led to an unusual design *(Ausbildung)* for the superstructure."[28] Here the German word *Ausbildung* connotes the building up of a form during the overall conceptual stage, in contrast to the weak and vague connotations of the English word "design." Thus, Menn's major motivation was aesthetic; the ordinary cantilever form, while technically feasible, would have led to a visually weak horizontal profile compared to the powerful vertical elements required. This aesthetic sensitivity led Menn to explore the problem more deeply and to seek a solution that would then be as efficient and economical as possible.

Having decided to make the horizontal profile visually stronger, Menn began by carrying the pillar up over the girder to make a pylon reaching about 10 meters above the roadway and serving as a support for cable stays. These stays then permitted the maximum cantilever depth to be only 5 meters. Because of the curved approach, the stays had to be encased in concrete walls to follow the roadway. Technically, such walls were not needed on the main span, but one only has to try and imagine the visual consequences of leaving the light cables exposed on that 174-meter span to realize the aesthetic improvement achieved by encasing them everywhere. Full encasement, however, additionally has strong technical advantages. Thus, even in the best design, it is

FIGURE 13.6

The Ganter Bridge on the Simplon Road, above Brig, Switzerland, 1980, by Christian Menn. Replacing Felsenau as Switzerland's longest-spanning bridge, the Ganter main span is 174 meters and the highest column 150 meters. Menn designed a new form in which prestressed cables are embedded in triangular concrete walls above the roadway.

impossible to isolate any one decision with visual consequences as purely aesthetic or purely technical. In the best designs, the aesthetic is the primary motivation which must never violate the technical.

Finally, the section for the narrow two-lane bridge is a single hollow box with no cantilever slabs. Already at Felsenau, Menn had used a prestressed deck slab 25 centimeters thick to span laterally the 10 meters between web walls. Thus, technically, the cantilevers were unnecessary, even though they do provide a counterbalancing moment for dead load. For construction economy, the single box without cantilevers is simple and therefore less expensive, although the walls and pylon are costly.

Aesthetically, the cross-sectional view was the most difficult to predict. The form evolved from an overall perspective which emphasized profile and which shows in the completed stage an impressive combination of articulation and lightness. As one drives over the bridge, it appears heavy because of the scale of the high walls compared to that of the narrow roadway. In addition, the pylons themselves appear transversely to be somewhat heavy, especially the horizontal girder as compared to the relative thinness of the verticals. This problem of two scales—one in profile and one in section—is reminiscent of the Salginatobel Bridge of Robert Maillart. In Maillart's most famous work, the view from the deck is dominated by heavy parapet walls, and the strongly foreshortened views from either approach emphasize a power and even massiveness of the three-hinged, hollow box form which is fundamentally different from the lightness and articulation of its well-known profile.

The Ganter structure has replaced the Felsenau as Switzerland's longest spanning bridge. Based on square meters of roadway surface, the bridge was much more costly than the Felsenau because of its greater spans, the higher columns, and the far more difficult foundation conditions, particularly on the south bank. There is some evidence, however, that it was a relatively inexpensive solution. First, its final cost of 23,500,000 Swiss francs is less than half the cost estimate for the alternative solution originally proposed as a tunnel. Second, during the bidding stage, another designer prepared a competing design which the general contractor, Zublin & Cie., priced along with Menn's design. Zublin found Menn's design to be at least two million francs cheaper and thus only submitted a formal bid on it.

In addition to performance as a measure of efficiency and competition as a measure of economy, the aesthetics of the Ganter Bridge have already stirred substantial interest. In his 1982 book, *Bridges,* the distinguished German structural engineer, Fritz Leonhardt, shows more photographs of the Ganter Bridge than of any other one; and while he is not uncritical of its design, he concludes that "it arouses well-deserved admiration for its innovative and daring structure."[29] The form arose primarily from aesthetic ideas. Once again, these ideas came solely from an engineer's imagination. On Menn's designs there are no architects or other aesthetic consultants involved in any way. As such, the Ganter Bridge stands in that long tradition of modern bridges beginning with Telford's iron arches, a tradition of structures designed to combine technical and aesthetic ideas. At their best, such structures become works of art. The Felsenau and Ganter bridges are two cases in point.

Democracy and Design

Today the classic stature of the Brooklyn Bridge and the Eiffel Tower are beyond dispute, but the Hancock Tower and Ganter Bridge present new problems, new controversies. These late-twentieth-century works symbolize new questions raised at a time when technology itself seems to stand for despoiling both the city and the country. Listen to the critics: "Chicago is building an ugly steel-braced colossus . . . which promises to disrupt not only the appearance but the urban ecology of the downtown area";[30] "Hancock's tapering one hundred stories serve primarily as support for these big-dollar TV masts. They have become its true abstract image. . . ."[31] A passage from Condit exemplifies the sentiments behind these attacks: "Money and technology underlay these potent works of modern structural art. . . . The rage to demolish and build anew reached a kind of frenzy, and no one seemed to have the time . . . to mourn the passing of Mies van der Rohe. Through his own thirty-one-year career in Chicago and through the work of his many students, he left a mark on the metropolitan area so profound

261

that one could find a parallel only in imperial Rome, or Florence under the Medici, or Paris in the heyday of the monarchy."[32]

Here is precisely the point. For the critics the Hancock is mere technology, the result of a purely utilitarian urge, whereas works of the designer from the Bauhaus are likened to things that arose in the past in societies that were not democratic. What the critics sensed about the Hancock Tower was just what earlier critics from the established art world sensed about the Eiffel Tower: it is not architecture in any traditional sense. But the Hancock goes beyond the Eiffel Tower in that it symbolizes directly a new city life—a life that escapes the image of control. Thus, one critic laments "as a symbol of Chicago the tower is superbly expressive. But shouldn't the tallest landmarks in a metropolis be part of a larger plan? In a typically, tragically American way, John Hancock Center is not."[33] The tower is not only a symbol of Chicago, it is an expression of the personality of Fazlur Khan asserting itself against all the cannons of fashion and against what Khan called *"a priori* architectual facade." As we have already noted, Khan described his struggle to convince his associates not to truncate the X-braces and thus destroy the structural and visual unity of the tower. Here is the artist fighting for his individual vision of a "more meaningful and valuable world." In avoiding waste and creating new images of handsome form, Kahn asserted the freedom given to those designers who accept the disciplines of efficiency and economy and who enjoy playing with forms. This freedom will always frighten those whose values do not include the avoidance of waste and who can only see technology as dehumanizing. In a 1967 letter to the editor following a complimentary review of the tower, a Fine Arts student complained that the tower symbolizes a massive dehumanization of the city: "Man becomes merely a number on a grid in a civilization that is becoming too impersonal denying man's individuality."[34] This is ideology unrelated to facts. People clamor to live in the Hancock and they are often artists and people of distinct individuality, hardly dehumanized robots.

FIGURE 13.7
The John Hancock Center, Chicago, 1970, by Skidmore, Owings and Merrill, with Fazlur Khan as structural designer. Here the engineer designed the form and thus created a work of structural art.

THE NEW AGE OF STEEL AND CONCRETE

The John Hancock Center (figure 13.7) symbolizes Chicago and its "all adaptation to use." It is a building that could not have appeared in Boston or New York or Washington. It defies master plans and art juries. It expresses private investment and technology, and not the power of government or aristocracy as did the buildings of imperial Rome, Renaissance Florence, or monarchical Paris. Hancock is one side of the democratic idea of design. The Ganter Bridge is the other side; it expresses the government planning of public works essential to democratic societies.

The Ganter Bridge, like the Brooklyn Bridge, represents a climax; each is the last in a series of bridges that characterize an era. For Roebling's bridge, the era was an iron age without automobiles; it was a time when private bridge companies or railroads undertook major structures without much public control. No later big New York bridge would ever be built under such political ambiguities as the Brooklyn Bridge faced. Moreover, the bridge ended the relative isolation of Brooklyn, which within the next decade became another borough of New York rather than the third largest American city. Visually the great towers overpowered Manhattan buildings in a way no later bridge supports would do; and the great span with its elevated walkway brought Roebling's ideas on engineering as art into the metropolis. He literally humanized the technological environment in a way that rich building decoration could not.

For Menn's Ganter Bridge, the era was one of concrete and the motor car. In this sense, the bridge stands for the government-led construction, in Western Europe and the United States, of highway networks that, after a quarter century of frenzied building, were almost fully shaped. In the two decades between the the late 1950s and 1980, Switzerland alone built over 2,700 new bridges, probably the greatest number per inhabitant of any country at any time in history. What Roebling did visually to the East River and lower Manhattan, Menn has done to the Ganter Valley. The landscape is radically altered by the intervention of a major work on a grand scale. The principal tower is 75 percent higher than either Brooklyn Bridge tower, and the three main spans, while considerably shorter than at Brooklyn, have a similar general form. At Brooklyn, the combination of vertical suspenders and diagonal stays creates a profile with triangular openings at the towers, a dense triangular webbing fanning out from the tower tops to the deck, and a flat slender midspan region. All of these features appear in the Ganter Bridge where the webbing is, however, solid concrete, and the triangular openings are flatter in scale with the smaller projection of the towers above the deck.

Although Menn surely did not have Brooklyn Bridge in mind, his design has certain deep affinities to Roebling's, especially in reflecting a sense that the setting called for a visually striking form. For Roebling, it was the tower design that was paramount, mainly as seen while crossing or from the shore; in Menn's case, it was the profile design that stimulated his imagination and that is the primary visual experience of the bridge. Both bridges are celebrations of civilization; they have forms that come from human desires and imaginations. The Ganter Valley is now dominated by the bridge whereas an earlier bridge (built in 1800 by Napoleon) had inconspicuously carried the old road over the mountain stream. Menn's bridge does not detract from the villages or the mountain forests; rather, it adds something new. Because of the bridge, the valley has become not just a backdrop for the ancient Simplon Road but a place to visit in its own right.

The Ganter Bridge expresses the ideal that out of competition can come new forms of elegance. Engineers trained in the context of design competitions have in view the alternative possibilities more clearly than do other engineers. Design is, after all, a sequence of comparative choices, and design competitions force engineers to contrast their work with that of others. Securing a design commission is thereby less the result of political friendship and more directly tied to a comparative judgment of design quality.

Above all, the Ganter Bridge is a personal design in the direct tradition of Telford, Roebling, Eiffel, and Maillart—each of whom created his personal style—and its deepest meaning lies in its expression of an artistic personality.

THE IDEA OF
STRUCTURE AS ART

Design and Art

Having traced the growth of this new tradition of structural art, we must now at the end look back and find those common themes that might add up to a theory about this art form. The Hancock Tower and the Ganter Bridge are expressions of their designers' personalities, but they also express something about their societies and about the entire tradition of structural art.

In chapter 6 we introduced the idea that function follows form, which means that the designer is free to set form rather than be bound by some automatic application of scientific laws. It is a common fallacy to believe that by following some laws (gravity, material properties, and so forth) strictly, the engineer will achieve the most artistic result. I have tried to show that none of the best designers believed in such an idea; they all recognized that they had the freedom of personal choice and that conscious aesthetic choice was essential to proper design. At the same time, they sought always to understand better both nature's laws and the properties of their materials. They were well trained in detailed mathematical analysis but as they gained more experience with full-scale works, they used such analysis less and less. Thus, they were disciplined but not controlled by nature's laws.

The first fundamental idea of structural art, the discipline of efficiency, is a desire for minimum materials, which results in less weight, less cost, and less visual mass. But as we discovered also in chapter 6, these three results are not merely the consequences of efficiency, because sometimes less material means greater labor cost and, in addition, extreme thinness can never be achieved everywhere in a major structure. Efficiency sometimes requires that some parts of a structure be relatively massive, such as the horizontal parapet in a deck-stiffened arch or the overall tapered form of the Hancock Tower or the triangular walls of the Ganter Bridge. There is no structural art without an expression of thinness, but that ideal does not stand alone: it must always be balanced by safety, and this too has consequences for cost and appearance. Efficiency means, for structural art, the delicate balance between thinness and safety, for which there can never be any automatic optimum. Safety has always been a compromise between economy and politics. Public officials must shape and interpret laws that help to guide decisions between the extremes of cheap structures that may be impermanent and wasteful ones whose high cost may preclude the building of other public works. Freyssinet dramatized this dilemma early in his career by building three thin bridges for the price of one massive structure.

This brings us to the second fundamental idea of structural art, the discipline of economy, the desire for construction simplicity, ease of maintenance, and a final integrated form. In chapter 6, we noted that because of the uncertainty of costs there was no theoretical possibility of deciding on least cost prior to contractors' bidding. Again, this fact allows the designer a great freedom, but costs nevertheless enforce a strict discipline that can only be gained by extensive experience. For his bridges Maillart first built the thin arch slabs on light scaffolding, and then integrally cast the walls and deck once the arch had hardened. Without that integration, the arch would have been far heavier, requiring a much heavier scaffolding, and thereby increasing the construction cost. The columns of the Hancock Tower are integrated by the diagonals so that they each carry about the same load. They are thus each made the same size, simplifying construction and reducing cost. Isler's shells, being of one smooth ribless surface, can be formed cheaply by wood planks and easily cut fiber boards; and Candela's hyperbolic paraboloids achieve construction simplicity with their straight line generators. Both systems of thin shells reflect highly integrated ideas, which, moreover, powerfully express the ideal of thinness. Such designs depend upon their designers' first-hand experience in the field. One can easily draw up on paper a reasonable structural form that simply cannot be built competitively in the desired location. Nervi clearly stated a reservation about building in societies other than his own. There is no such thing as an international style of structural art; its integrity depends upon its integration into local building practice.

The very act of integrating a form during construction depends upon the experience of local builders, not to mention any peculiarities of the climate and site. The designer must feel that he is in active partnership with the builder if he is not actually the builder himself. This feeling of partnership is more than a practical necessity: it is a central basis for the new art form. The designer in his office can sketch beautiful diagrams, make elegant calculations, and build handsome models, but all such professional work is wasted if it does not lead to a structure that can be built economically and well. This partnership extends to the public because the completed design must be needed, fit the need, and be within the means of the public. The designer works, therefore, not just for private profit but also for public welfare. As a student of the laws of nature, the engineer is society's expert; but as an observer of the patterns in society, he is its servant.[1]

The designer must also feel a partnership with the general public. This feeling was expressed by John Roebling when he justified the central elevated walkway as a park for the people of the city. The belief in service to the community carries with it the idea that the works of structural art are truly public: their designs are made public, their calculations are open to review, and their construction is done in full view of the community. Most central is the attitude toward cost. Works of structural art are never justified by some ideology of beauty disconnected from expenses. The designers, being servants of the community, take on the obligation of economy—but not mere cheapness—as their ethic. The designer must think of the overall concept, including its future maintenance and the relationship between construction method and the integrity of the completed object. Menn designed the connection between the mid-span cantilever at Felsenau to be rigidly connected (not usually done before 1970)—a slight extra cost—to avoid the slight bump in the road caused by deflections and hence to reduce later maintenance costs. One has only to look from below at the numerous highway overpasses made of unconnected steel beams resting on heavy concrete piers to see leakage from the roadway, ugly staining, and rapid deterioration. This disintegration, while giving a cheapness of initial cost, leads to greater costs later on for maintenance, and to an ugliness that all structural artists, as Candela put it, seek to avert.

This aversion to ugliness leads directly to the third fundamental idea of structural art, the search for engineering elegance. This idea includes, along with the visual expression of efficiency and economy through thinness and integration, the expression of contrast. In the major structures we have described, the final forms, being works of man, contrast sharply with the natural environment. When built within a city, the work normally contrasts just as sharply with its already constructed surroundings. This is not an arbitrary or willful personal expression by a designer seeking notoriety but only a consequence of disciplined play. Probably the most famous example of this city contrast involves two structural works themselves: the radically different Sears and Hancock towers. Khan did not want prominently displayed another Hancock in Chicago so for the Sears he sought another form, which is no less rational, but visually is entirely distinct.[2] Although he never hesitated to modify a form slightly for a new site, in Chicago side by side, so to speak, Khan sought contrast. The idea of contrast with the natural environment is exemplified by the Ganter and Salgina bridges, which make no concessions whatsoever to the beauty of their stream valleys. Although the contrast with nature could hardly be more emphatic, yet in a deeper sense there is also harmony expressed. This harmony has to do with the harsh climate, to which concrete is relatively impervious, and with the foundations, whose three-hinged arches or slender piers allow the bridges to remain free of dangerous stresses caused by the mountain movements. But there is no question of covering the concrete with stone to harmonize with the rocky banks. Nor, to return to the Hancock Tower, is there any question of making a facade to fit with surrounding facades. Yet the tower does have a deep affinity to Chicago as a pioneering city, far less under the sway of European taste, and far more willing to experiment with new forms, than its east coast rivals. Thus we find three pairs of criteria for structural art: thinness and safety, integration and cost, and contrast and affinity.

Those three pairs of criteria—thinness and safety, integration and cost, contrast and affinity—suggest a way to clarify the idea of a work of structural art. What we designate as thinness are the elements of a structure, not the overall form. For example, the Forth Bridge expresses a massive form (especially in the foreshortened view) that is composed of thin pieces (notably when seen in profile). More accurately, thinness expresses the desire to save materials, which themselves make up the elements; and yet each element must be safe or there can be no structure at all.

Just as materials make up elements so elements make up the overall form. When those elements fit together well there is an integration; when they do not, the structure appears to be the product of several different minds or of a designer unsure of his elements. Maillart's Chiasso structure contains numerous pieces of concrete, each of which can be seen as a separate element, but the primary visual impact is of an overall parabolic shape. In contrast, the Britannia Bridge has tubular beams and stone columns that appear unrelated; whereas the stone towers and metal spans of the Brooklyn Bridge are integrated by the cables, stays, and suspenders.

Integration can, however, lead to construction complexity. Whereas safety often depends upon all elements working together, the structure cannot easily be built all at once. Yet light steel frameworks remain highly unstable until fully braced in their final form. Even more problematic is cast-in-place concrete, which is useless until after it has been in place for some time. The problem of integration is perhaps most critical for concrete shells, which depend upon a practically complete integration for their safety. If the cooperation of elements is essential in the bridges of Maillart and Menn and in the towers of Khan, it is the primary fact in the shells of Nervi, Candela, and Isler.

Finally, the overall form is always set in some environment, and hence its contrast and affinity refer now to form in context. Thus we proceed from materials to elements by thinness, from elements to form by integration, and from form to environment by contrast. The objects of structural art that succeed best in expressing thinness, integration, and contrast are just those designs that we have emphasized in this book.

Designers and Artists

We have seen that the art form of structure lies in discipline and play, and that its status is confirmed by the public as well as by the critic. These ideas would fit architecture and sculpture as well as structure. We have seen, also, that objects of structural art are known by their thinness, integration, and contrast. These criteria do not directly fit architecture and sculpture; here the similarity lies primarily in that general formulation often used to characterize all art: "art uses a minimum of concrete material to express a maximum of meaning."[3] What remains is to say something in general about the artists themselves. The comparison with architects and sculptors does not, at first glance, seem compelling, largely because of that exalted image of the artist carried over to us from nineteenth-century romanticism, itself in part a reaction to the Industrial Revolution.

To understand the engineer as artist we must shed the nineteenth-century romantic image of the genius, expressing himself in beret and cape. Rather, as the Swiss theologian Karl Barth said with respect to eighteenth-century music, "art was in those days still most definitely the product of technical ability. Art was proficiency. It was this proficiency which made Bach famous . . . [and] which made the young Mozart the wonder of Europe." This technical talent was, of course, not mere technique; works of Bach and Mozart are not studied and performed in the late twentieth century as exercises but as surpassingly beautiful compositions. Yet, as Barth continues, this was "art as a skill, as proficiency in manipulation of the most exacting rules [along with] invention in the expression not so much of what the composer himself found personally stimulating, but rather of general laws."[4] These artists, in short, were highly disciplined and, as Barth observed, "the man who can do that, who knows the law involved in doing it . . . is a *maestro*. Bach did not consider himself a genius, nor did his contemporaries, as is well known, treat him as one."[5]

Barth's comments apply today to engineers as artists. Maillart was a master of concrete; no one understood the craft of building with it better than he. He knew its rules and followed nature's general laws. Yet no one referred to him as a genius; he certainly never used such a word himself. Barth continues, "it was only on the basis of this crafts-man's mastery of the art of transforming the world of sounds into music that the game of making music could be played. But on this basis . . . it could be played with assurance and in accordance with the laws of necessity." In this description of eighteenth-century music, disci-pline and play appear as well as the defining attributes of an artist. The beauty of the music "consisted in the freedom founded upon subjection to the law."[6] Within this discipline of structural art, founded upon studies in the laws of nature, we can identify general characteristics that for good reasons do seem common to the greatest figures in our story.

First of all, structural artists are normally trained in engineering schools. Of the twenty-two designers who figure prominently here, fourteen were so trained; the exceptions include all four of British de-signers, two others who were trained as architects (Gaudí and Candela), and two who were self-taught (Eads and Hennebique). Second, these men always worked in collaboration with owners, other engineers, ar-chitects, and builders. Unlike painters and sculptors but like architects, structural artists cannot make their works alone. Often they cannot even design them without substantial pressure from others for compro-mise, as finding acceptance for new ideas is always a struggle. Khan's posthumous article on the Hancock Tower is a clear statement of these difficulties. When a new design does get built, it is all the more an ob-ject of wonder that it could happen at all.

A third characteristic of structural artists, in addition to training and collaboration, is one of public service. A person who can submit to rigorous training in mathematics, science, and engineering must have that inborn aptitude; but what makes such a person a structural artist rather than a scientist or research engineer is a motivation to see structures built. This motivation often takes time to realize. Whereas great scientists frequently do their best work as young researchers, the great structural engineers all did their best work in mid- and late career. Telford designed his first modern iron arch when he was fifty-three, and Menai was completed when he was sixty-nine. Eiffel's Garabit came at age fifty-two and the tower at fifty-seven, Roebling designed the Brooklyn Bridge at age sixty-one, Maillart his Salginatobel at age fifty-six, Freyssinet's Plougastel appeared after he was over fifty, and Ammann's first completed design, the George Washington, opened when its designer was fifty-two. Menn, Isler, and Candela have done their best works after they were forty, and Nervi built nothing on his own until he was forty-one. They all practiced design in the dual sense of both working always to improve at their art and focusing always on the practical matters of efficiency and economy.

These men all worked in design and construction for long periods before creating their best works; they needed considerable experience and time to develop their ideas. All showed talent early but their art matured slowly. They all recognized early that building works of engineering elegance was a difficult profession and that often the most beautiful objects brought them the least money. There had to be another attraction. Maillart liked the idea of giving the tiny community of Schuders a beautiful bridge (Salginatobel) even if his commission hardly paid for the drawings and calculations; and Roebling pursued manufacturing so that he could build bridges. Both engineers believed themselves to be serving more than just their own private interests. All of these designers imagined structures that would have a wide appeal in both the senses of economy and elegance. People, as a community, found the works appealing because they did not overburden the public treasury; and people, as visitors, were attracted by the new forms and striking images. Sometimes these people were famous artists themselves such as Delaunay, Stella, Hart Crane, or critics such as Giedion; sometimes they were simply what we like to call the general public, complete amateurs, who were nevertheless struck by something new, awesome, and uniquely beautiful. These people made the Eiffel Tower and the Brooklyn Bridge cultural landmarks long before Delaunay and Stella began to put them on canvas. The explanation is simple: such works have wide appeal because they seem to be natural, simple, and yet often skeletal and fragile. People respond because the forms are contemporary, of their own era; the forms could not have appeared before and one does not need a trained eye to realize this.

But to serve the public best, these structural artists had to be playful—not denying discipline but expressing surprise and joy. No one did that better than Maillart, but all structural artists surprised their contemporaries with shapes that will always be linked to their creators. Telford's trussed arches, Eiffel's crescents, Roebling's diagonals, Maillart's lens-shaped arches, Ammann's single-braced towers, Menn's thin polygonal arches, Nervi's ribbing, Isler's sheets of waved concrete, Candela's hyperbolic paraboloids, and Khan's skeletal walls are all signals of personal style; they stand for discipline and have universal appeal but, above all, they enliven the community by insisting that structure is play.

To be playful with structure is not to be willful. We first came upon the idea of play with Isler, but it has really been implicit in the work of all structural artists. They studied long and hard to learn the rules (of nature); they tried continually to play fair (with society); and in creating order they surprised others with the beauty of their works. At the heart of technology, they found their own individuality; they created personal styles without denying any of the rigor of engineering.

Notes
Index

NOTES

Chapter 1

1. Raymond J. Sontag, *A Broken World: 1919–1939* (New York: Harper & Row, 1971), p. 214.

2. Walter Gropius, *The Scope of Total Architecture* (New York: Collier, 1962), p. 20.

3. *Ibid.*, p. 65

4. Walter Gropius, *The New Architecture and the Bauhaus* (Cambridge, Mass.: MIT Press, 1965), p. 81. For a discussion of the extent to which the Bauhaus failed to understand modern technology, see Reyner Banham, *Theory and Design in the First Machine Age* (London: The Architectural Press, 1960), especially pp. 320–30.

5. Vannevar Bush, *Science, The Endless Frontier: A Report to the President* (Washington, D.C., 1945), pp. 13–14; cited in Edwin Layton, "American Ideologies of Science and Engineering," *Technology and Culture* 17 (1976):689.

6. *Technology and Culture* 17 (1976): 621–742.

7. The words "technology" and "engineering" are used here as equivalent terms. Modern dictionary definitions make these two indistinguishable. *Technology* has its roots in the Greek *techne* meaning skill or art, and in Greek *tekton* meant carpenter, builder, or architect (chief + builder). *Engineer* comes from the Latin for contriver, one of talent, from which we also derive the word "genius." Engineering schools are often called schools of technology without implying any difference in courses of study at all.

8. Chalmers W. Sherwin and Raymond S. Isenson, "Project Hindsight," *Science* 156 (1967): 1571–77. This is discussed in Edwin Layton, "Mirror-Image Twins: The Communities of Science and Technology in 19th Century America," *Technology and Culture* 12 (1971): 562–80.

9. Michael Mulkay, "Knowledge and Utility: Implications for the Sociology of Knowledge," *Social Studies of Sciences* (London: SAGE, 1979), 9: 63–80.

10. The idea that reliance upon general theories could contribute to defective designs has been vigorously debated by many leading designers. See David P. Billington, "History and Esthetics in Suspension Bridges," *Journal of the Structural Division, American Society of Civil Engineers* 103 (1977):1655–72. In vol. 104 of the *Journal,* see discussions by Herbert Rothman, pp. 246–49; George Schoepfer, pp. 378–79; Peter G. Buckland, pp. 379–80; Hasan I. A. Hegab, p. 619; Harold Samelson, pp. 732–33; Edward Cohen and Frank T. Stahl, pp. 1027–30; Blair Birdsall, pp. 1030–35; John Paul Hartman, pp. 1174–76; in vol. 105, see David P. Billington, pp. 671–87.

11. Jacques Ellul, *The Technological Society,* translated from the 1954 French edition by J. Wilkenson (New York: Vintage, 1964).

12. Vitruvius, *The Ten Books of Architecture,* trans. M. H. Morgan (1914; reprint, New York: Dover Publications, 1960), p. 282. Vitruvius divides his work into structures and machines, "I have thought it not out of place, Emperor, since I have treated of buildings in the earlier books, to set forth and teach in this, which forms the final conclusion of my treatise, the principles which govern machines."

13. The virtue of describing technology in terms of objects and systems is that the culture itself makes such distinctions. In American society we have objects which are relatively fixed (the Constitution) and objects which are relatively changeable (laws). Similarly, we have networks of federal, state, and local traditions, each balanced by its processes of legislation. In the humanities these distinctions also serve to divide the arts into those which are relatively permanent (painting, sculpture, architecture, and literature) and those which are relatively transient (dance, musical performance, and drama). Of course, the static arts do gradually wear away if not maintained or translated into modern languages, and the arts of movement can now be caught in recordings and motion pictures; but we still sense the fundamental differences and even emphasize them by putting the highest value upon the original compositions and the live performances.

14. Perhaps Henri de Saint-Simon was the first to think of the Industrial Revolution as providing images for a new society. See James H. Billington, *Fire in the Minds of Men* (New York: Basic Books, 1980), pp. 214–15.

15. Le Corbusier, *Towards a New Architecture,* trans. F. Etchells (London: The Architectural Press, 1927), pp. 17–18.

16. Montgomery Schuyler, "The Bridge as a Monument," *Harper's Weekly* 27, (May 1883): 326; reprinted in *American Architecture and Other Writings,* ed. William H. Jordy and Ralph Coe. (New York: Atheneum, 1964), p. 164.

17. In a like manner, architects need to satisfy all these criteria but the social one is primary; they design forms to control spaces for direct human use. This type of utility, in the best architecture, is linked to respect for economy as well. Architectural designers have always been conscious of the symbolic criterion for their works, although the separation of appearance from such ideals as minimum materials or minimum cost has turned some of the best known modern works into symbols of waste and arrogance. Satisfying the scientific criterion is also essential to good architecture. For example, the Sydney Opera House roof was designed without any reference to structure, and its cost increased flagrantly as a result. For sculpture the primary criterion is symbolic but again the other two are essential. The works must find some social acceptance and they must have strength and permanence.

18. It is because of this natural impenetrability of stone that the Gothic cathedrals appear to be such overpowering flights. They are almost modern in their fragility and lightness, and they do in fact symbolize a society that was in some surprising ways similar to our modern world. See David P. Billington and Robert Mark, "The Cathedral and the Bridge," *Journal of Technology and Culture* 25 (forthcoming, January 1984).

Chapter 2

1. Thomas S. Ashton, *Iron and Steel in the Industrial Revolution,* 3rd. ed. (Manchester: Manchester University Press, 1963). My own discussion is based largely upon Ashton's chapters 2 and 3. See also Albert E. Musson and Eric Robinson, *Science and Technology in the Industrial Revolution* (Toronto: University of Toronto Press, 1969), pp. 429–30: "Iron, however, was to become the basic material of the Industrial Revolution. There was, as Professor Ashton and others have shown, a close relationship between the Midland iron industry and the manufacture of the steam engine—the supreme achievement of early mechanical engineering. . . . Following the Darbys' revolutionary achievements in iron-founding, cast iron came into widespread use for machine parts."

2. Neil Cossons and Barrie Trinder, *The Iron Bridge* (Bradford-on-Avon: Moonraker Press, 1979).

3. Thomas Telford, *Life of Thomas Telford, Civil Engineer* (London: James and Luke G. Hansard and Sons, 1838), p. 34. Edited by John Rickman and published after Telford's death.

4. Roland A. Paxton, "The Influence of Thomas Telford (1757–1834) on the Use of Improved Constructional Materials in Civil Engineering Practice" (M.S. Thesis, University of Edinburgh, 1975).

5. Thomas Telford, *Fifth Report of the Commissioners for Roads and Bridges in the Highlands of Scotland* (Report of 3 Jan. 1811, House of Commons 8 April 1811), p. 46. Quoted in Paxton, "Influence of Thomas Telford," p. 185. Paxton lists sixteen cast-iron bridges designed by Telford between 1810 and 1829.

6. Ted Ruddock, *Arch Bridges and Their Builders 1735–1835* (Cambridge: Cambridge University Press, 1979); see especially chapters 12 and 13.

7. Paxton, "Influence of Thomas Telford," p. 56.

8. Telford, *Life;* see especially pp. 5–19 and 40–41.

9. Ruddock, *Arch Bridges,* pp. 155–59. See also A. W. Skempton, "Telford and the Design for a New London Bridge," *Thomas Telford: Engineer,* ed. Alastair Penfold (London: Thomas Telford Ltd., 1980), pp. 62–83.

10. John H. Stephens, *Towers, Bridges and Other Structures* (New York: Sterling Publishing Co., 1976), p. 30. There were many suspension bridges built also in the United States and France between 1800 and 1830, but the most celebrated works were those in Britain. See, for example, Emory L. Kemp, "James Finley and the Modern Suspension Bridge," *Long-Span Suspension Bridges: History and Performance* Preprint 3590 (New York: American Society of Civil Engineers, 1979), and Tom Peters, "G-H Dufour and the Development of the Wire Cable Suspension Bridge," *The Development of Long-Span Bridge Building* (Zürich: Eidgenössische Technische Hochschule Zürich, 1979), pp. 173–88. A summary of British designs of this period appears in Emory L. Kemp, "Samuel Brown: Britain's Pioneer Suspension Bridge Builder," *History of Technology,* ed. A. Rupert Hall and Norman Smith (London: Mansell, 1977), pp. 1–37. For Telford's 1811 arch-design proposal over the Menai, see Telford, *Life,* pp. 566–68.

11. Telford, *Life,* pp. 217–29.

12. Paxton, *Influence of Thomas Telford,* pp. 148–56.

13. Othmar H. Ammann, "Present Status of Designs of Suspension Bridges with Respect to Dynamic Wind Action," *Boston Society of Civil Engineers* 40 (1953): 253.

14. Emory L. Kemp, "Thomas Paine and his 'Pontifical Matters,' " *Transactions of The Newcomen Society* 49 (1977–78): 21–40. The 1796 Sunderland Bridge over the River Wear was designed by Rowland Burdon and Thomas Wilson. John Rennie's 1819 Old Southwark Bridge exceeded that span by 4 feet.

15. Ashton, *Iron and Steel,* p. 141.

16. Thomas Telford, "Bridge," *New Edinburgh Encyclopedia,* second American edition, vol. IV (New York: Whiting and Watson, 1814), pp. 470–532 (the Telford article was written in 1812; see Ruddock, *Arch Bridges,* p. 231); "Sixth Report of Commissioners for Highland Roads and Bridges," *Commons Reports* 1812–13 (110) vol. 1, pp. 23–55 (Telford's report on the Bonar appears on pages 37–38 and on Craigellachie on page 36).

17. In several of his late bridges—for example, the 170-foot-span 1824 design for Tewkesbury and 150-foot-span 1829 design at Galton—Telford made the lozenges vertical rather than radial. He thus modified designs as he proceeded, and these last two represent a more correct solution technically than the earlier ones. Although Telford's belief in sloping spandrels is not technically correct, it does not lead to dangers in flat arches; rather it is somewhat overly complex.

18. Ruddock summarizes Telford's architectural views: "where the sensation of beauty is held to depend on recognition of the fitness of an object for its purpose. The dominant purpose in Telford's view of architecture seems to be the support of weight" (*Arch Bridges,* p. 190).

19. George Kubler, *The Shape of Time* (New Haven: Yale University Press, 1962), pp. 15–16.

20. Donald Crawford, *Kant's Aesthetic Theory* (Madison: University of Wisconsin Press, 1974), p. 163; Eva Schaper, *Studies in Kant's Aesthetics* (Edinburgh: Edinburgh University Press, 1979), p. 121.

21. Telford showed how much this revolution could rejuvenate even the design of masonry works and he intimated how this would affect architecture; see note 18.

Notes

22. Ruddock, *Arch Bridges,* p. 157.
23. Ibid., pp. 196–200.
24. Alexander Nimmo, "Theory of Bridges," *New Edinburgh Encyclopedia,* second American edition, vol. IV (New York: Whiting and Watson, 1814), p. 480.
25. Ibid., p. 504.
26. Ibid., p. 483
27. The precise behavior of structures cannot be defined mathematically because of their inherent complexity, a fact arising from the needs of society, as measured by economy. For example, the connection of iron or steel pieces by riveting or welding occasions local stresses that depend upon unpredictable social forces—local labor practices—as well as on the laws of nature.
28. Davies Gilbert, "On the Mathematical Theory of Suspension Bridges, with Tables for Facilitating their Construction," *Philosophical Transactions of the Royal Society* (1826): 202–18. The design modifications are clearly described by Paxton, *Influence of Thomas Telford,* pp. 142–43. See also Roland Paxton, "Menai Bridge 1818–26: Evolution of Design," *Thomas Telford: Engineer* (London, 1980), pp. 84–116 (shortened and revised from a paper in *Transactions of the Newcomen Society* 49 (1979): 27–110.
29. John R. Hume, "Telford's Highland Bridges," *Thomas Telford: Engineer,* ed. Alastair Penfold (London: Thomas Telford Ltd., 1980), pp. 151–181.

Chapter 3

1. Asa Briggs, *Iron Bridge to Crystal Palace* (London: Thames and Hudson, 1979), p. 76.
2. *Report of the Commissioners Appointed to Inquire into the Application of Iron to Railway Structures* (London: HMSO, 1849).
3. William Fairbairn, *An Account of the Construction of the Britannia and Conway Tubular Bridges* (London: John Weale, 1849), pp. 48–50. See also Samuel Smiles, *The Life of George Stephenson and of his Son Robert Stephenson* (London: J. Murray, 1868), pp. 474–75. The towers were useful but not essential to the construction procedure of lifting the prefabricated tube into place; see J. C. Jeaffreson and William Pole, *The Life of Robert Stephenson, F.R.S.,* 2nd ed., vol. 2 (London: Longmans, Green, Reader & Dyer, 1866), p. 107.
4. Joseph Gies, *Bridges and Men* (New York: Grosset & Dunlop, 1963), pp. 123–24. Gies quotes Samuel Smiles on the "genius of the English Nation." See Smiles, *Stephenson,* p. 488.
5. Nathan Rosenberg and Walter G. Vincenti, *The Britannia Bridge: The Generation and Diffusion of Technological Knowledge* (Cambridge, Mass.: MIT Press, 1978), p. 71.
6. L. T. C. Rolt, *Isambard Kingdom Brunel* (Hammondsworth, England: Penguin Books, 1970), p. 35.
7. Roland A. Paxton, "The Influence of Thomas Telford (1757–1834) on the Use of Improved Constructional Materials in Civil Engineering Practice" (M.S. Thesis, University of Edinburgh, 1975), p. 158.
8. O. S. Nock, "Railways," in *The Works of Isambard Kingdom Brunel,* ed. Alfred Pugsley (London: Institute of Civil Engineers, 1976), pp. 69–88; and J. B. Caldwell, "The Three Great Ships," in Pugsley, *Works,* pp. 137–62.
9. Bernard Dumpleton and Muriel Miller, *Brunel's Three Ships* (Melksham, England: Colin Venton, 1974). One of Brunel's ships, *The Great Britain,* has been partially restored as a museum.
10. Rolt, *Brunel,* pp. 411, 421.
11. Eiffel's structural career was prematurely destroyed by his venture into the Panama Canal locks; Robert Maillart's career was nearly ended twenty years before his death by his involvement with huge foreign enterprises having nothing to do with his development of structural form; and the famous French engineer Eugène Freyssinet went bankrupt and almost ended his career in a disastrous business effort having little to do with structural design.
12. Isambard Kingdom Brunel, *Journal,* April 1836; quoted by Rolt, *Brunel,* p. 416.

13. Of course, such a tension exists for all artists because, apart from the very few who become popular in their lifetime, all face the problem of making a living while being free to create new works.

14. Washington A. Roebling, *Early History of Saxonburg* (Saxonburg, Pa.: Butler County Historical Society, 1924), p. 15.

15. Daniel H. Calhoun, *The American Civil Engineer* (Cambridge, Mass.: MIT Press, 1960).

16. Smiles, *Stephenson,* p. 445.

17. For the Britannia quantities see Fairbairn, *Tubular Bridges,* p. 185, and for the Saltash see Hubert Shirley-Smith, "Royal Albert Bridge, Saltash," in Pugsley, *Works,* p. 165.

18. Shirley-Smith, "Saltash," p. 178. Since the Saltash is 2,200 feet long and single track, the cost per foot of length would be £102 per foot whereas the Britannia, being 1,524 feet and double track, cost about £198 per foot of single-lane track. Brunel's bridge cost £225,000 and Stephenson's £602,000.

19. Both designers developed their forms out of earlier types, but in each case the period of study was short and the major work of each cannot be said to represent a mature structure form in the same sense of Telford's Bonar bridge. Telford's form could hardly be improved upon today if cast iron were used; indeed, no one since 1810 has improved markedly upon his designs. In wrought iron, however, there were to be major improvements after the 1859 deaths of Brunel and Stephenson. For a detailed discussion of Brunel's bridge forms leading up to Saltash see his son's book, Isambard Brunel, *The Life of Isambard Kingdom Brunel, Civil Engineer* (London: Longmans, Green & Co., 1870), pp. 171–230 (reprinted 1971, with an introduction by L. T. C. Rolt). For Stephenson's earlier works, see Jeaffreson and Pole, *Life,* pp. 30–72, 113–27.

20. Rolt, *Brunel,* p. 342.

Chapter 4

1. Joseph Harriss, *The Tallest Tower: Eiffel and the Belle Epoque* (Boston: Houghton Mifflin, 1975), p. 10.

2. Ibid., pp. 20–22. The French version appears in Charles Braibant, *Histoire de la Tour Eiffel* (Paris: Plon, 1964), pp 84–85.

3. Harriss, *Tallest Tower,* pp. 24–25.

4. Ibid., p. 25.

5. Ibid.

6. Jean Prévost, *Eiffel* (Paris: Rieder, 1929).

7. Braibant, *Histoire,* p. 249, gives a list of Eiffel's works between 1867 and 1885.

8. Harriss, *Tallest Tower,* pp. 52–53.

9. G. Eiffel, *Mémoire sur les épreuves des arcs métalliques de la Gallerie des Machines du Palais de L'Exposition Universelle de 1867,* Paris, 1867.

10. C. Hobbhouse, *1851 and the Crystal Palace* (New York: E. P. Dutton, 1937), p. 51.

11. Gustave Eiffel, *Les grandes constructions métalliques* (Paris: Association française pour l'avancement des sciences, 1888), pp. 10–11. The other quotations in this section are also from these pages.

12. Italo Insolera, "I grandi viadotti di Eiffel nel Massif Central," *Zodiac* 13 (1964): 61–111. See also Noel Neumann, "Le Centenaire des premiers viaducs d'Effel," *La vie du rail,* Paris, No. 1211 (28 Sept. 1969): 10–14, 39–41.

13. Joseph Gies, *Bridges and Men* (New York: Grosset & Dunlap, 1963), pp. 133–46.

14. Théophile Seyrig, "Le pont sur le Douro," *Memoires des travaux de la Societe des Ingénieurs Civils,* Sept.–Oct. 1878, pp. 743–816.

15. Élie Deydier, *Le Viaduc de Garabit* (Paris: Éditions Gerbert, 1960).

16. Gustave Eiffel, *Notice sur le Viaduc de Garabit* (Paris: P. Dupont, 1888).

17. Théophile Seyrig, *Pont sur le Douro,* p. 755.

18. A word on the overused terms "best" and "greatest." We mean here, specifically, that a work is better than another when it is at the same time more efficient, more economical, and more handsome. More efficient means stronger with less material, more economical means useful for less cost, and more handsome implies of lighter appearance, of a more integrated overall form, and of more visually sophisticated two- and three-dimensional aspects. These last judgments on appearance are necessarily less well defined. We shall, nevertheless, begin to see during the century following Garabit the visual elements common to all of the best works of structural art.

Chapter 5

1. Alan Trachtenberg, *Brooklyn Bridge: Fact and Symbol* (New York: Oxford University Press, 1965). See also David McCullough, *The Great Bridge* (New York: Simon and Schuster, 1972), pp. 21–102.

2. John A. Roebling, "Memoir of the Niagara Falls Suspension and Niagara Falls International Bridge," *Papers and Practical Illustrations of Public Works of Recent Construction both British and American* (London: J. Weale, 1856), p. 2.

3. The Britannia Bridge cost £602,000 for maximum spans of 460 feet and a total length of 1,524 feet (for two tracks). The Niagara Bridge span is 1.8 times 460 feet, or 821 feet, and its total length of about 1,300 feet must be increased (say to about 1,524 feet) to account for the lower carriage deck. Thus if one takes the ratio of the increased cost due to increased span length of $(1.8)^2 = 3.2$ then a single-track Britannia Bridge 1,524-feet long would cost £301,000 $\times$ 3.2 = £960,000, or very close to Roebling's estimate.

4. Roebling, "Memoir," p. 21.

5. What Roebling meant is that its relative deflection is similar to that of the tubular bridges. He noted that Conway tube sunk 3 inches under a 300-ton load placed at midspan whereas the far longer Niagara span sunk about 10 inches under a similar load. The deflection ratio depends upon the cube of the span, hence Niagara to be as stiff as Conway should have deflected $(821/400)^3 = 8.6$ times as much, or 25 inches. Roebling, "Memoir," p. 6 seems to imply that the stiffness is in the ratio of the span squared and believes the two bridges to be comparably stiff. His measurements seem to imply that his bridge is considerably stiffer against static loads.

6. Washington A. Roebling, "Prefatory Note" to *Long and Short Span Railway Bridges,* by John A. Roebling (New York: D. Van Nostrand, 1869). This book was published shortly after the author's death.

7. Roebling, "Memoir," p. 7.

8. Ibid., p. 4.

9. Letter from John A. Roebling at the Niagara Bridge site to Charles Swan in Trenton, May 20, 1854. The Wheeling Bridge had collapsed on May 17th.

10. John A. Roebling, "Report and Plan for a Wire Suspension Bridge Proposed to Be Erected over the Ohio River at Cincinnati," *Order of Reference of the Supreme Court of the United States,* Saratoga Springs, 1851, pp. 457–94. Roebling's report is dated Sept. 1, 1846.

11. The Wheeling Bridge was in 1871 rebuilt in consultation with Washington Roebling, so that today its diagonal stay span looks like a Roebling design; see Clifford M. Lewis, "The Wheeling Suspension Bridge," *West Virginia History* 33 (1972):203–33. The Lewiston–Queenston Bridge over the Niagara was designed by Edward Serrell, completed in 1851, and destroyed in 1864.

12. *Report of John A. Roebling, Civil Engineer, to the President and Board of Directors of the Covington and Cincinnati Bridge Company* (Cincinnati, April 1, 1867) 140 pages. Pages 11–92 are Roebling's report. This report was published in slightly abridged form in the British journal, *Engineering,* July 12, July 26, and Aug. 9, 1867, pp. 23, 75, and 98 respectively. This shortened form included Roebling's discussions of aesthetics and of his feelings for medieval archi-

tecture, but it excluded his more general comments on contemporary culture and the social meaning of technology. In the following citations, where no mention is made of *Engineering*, that referenced quotation was left out in the published version. To get Roebling's full meaning for his bridge, it is therefore essential to see the original report.

13. Ibid., pp. 23–24.

14. Ibid., pp. 23–26, and *Engineering*, p. 23.

15. Ibid., pp. 27–28, and *Engineering*, p. 23.

16. It is true that the Gothic arches that Roebling designed for each of the Brooklyn Bridge towers were not forms dictated by either efficiency or economy. Roebling made numerous visual studies for the towers; but all were disciplined by the need for stiff, massive structures with high, narrow openings for people and traffic to pass through. The arch was a reasonable form for the portals, although the particular Gothic shape is surely nostalgic. At Cincinnati he had used a Roman-type circular arch for the somewhat wider single portal. It was not until reinforced concrete matured in the early twentieth century that designers began to develop new arch forms that were not visually imitative of pre-Industrial Revolution shapes.

17. Roebling, *Report*, p. 52, and *Engineering*, p. 75.

18. Ibid., p. 64.

19. Ibid., p. 64.

20. Ibid., p. 64.

21. Ibid., p. 65, and *Engineering*, p. 98.

Chapter 6

1. Carlton J. H. Hayes, *A Generation of Materialism: 1871–1900* (New York: Harper & Row, 1941), p. 329. The last chapter is entitled "The Climax of the Enlightenment."

2. Thomas P. Hughes, "Introduction," in S. Smiles, *Lives of the Engineers* (Cambridge, Mass.: MIT Press, 1966), p. 11. It was not until well into the twentieth century that most British engineers were trained in engineering schools.

3. This paradox seems to violate Newton's law that reactions always equal actions. Here, to avoid jargon, we use the word reactions loosely. In engineering terms there are three sorts of reactions in a cantilever tower considered as a planar structure: the horizontal load equilibrated by the horizontal reactions anywhere in the tower; the vertical load equilibrated by vertical reactions; and the moment of the load resisted by the moment reaction within the tower. For horizontal wind there is no vertical load; but the moment of the load produces two equal and opposite vertical reactions (tension on the windward side and compression on the leeward) whose size is reduced by spreading. The reaction to the moment is the product of one of the vertical reactions and the distance between the two of them; thus the moment reaction stays constant even though the vertical reactions change.

4. Merritt R. Smith, *The Harpers Ferry Armory* (Ithaca: Cornell University Press, 1977).

5. Both the Eiffel Tower and the Brooklyn Bridge substantially exceeded their designer's cost estimates. Partly this was caused by labor strikes in the case of the tower and political corruption in the case of the bridge.

6. Joseph Harriss, *The Tallest Tower: Eiffel and The Belle Epoque* (Boston: 1975), pp. 14, 61.

7. Hans Straub, *A History of Civil Engineering* (Cambridge, Mass.: MIT Press, 1952). Straub states that for the Eiffel Tower, "Its designer and constructor [was] the Swiss engineer M. Koechlin, who was in charge of the Design Department of the Eiffel Company" (p. 184).

8. Gustave Eiffel, *La Tour Eiffel en 1900* (Paris: Masson et Cie, 1902), p. 4.

9. Théophile Seyrig, "Le Pont Luiz I," *Societé des Ingénieurs Civils de France (Mémoires)* 1ᶜ(1886):54–55.

10. Eiffel, *La Tour Eiffel*, pp. 4–6.

11. Examples of this are Frank Lloyd Wright's works with Louis Sullivan and Van Dyke's work with Rubens.

12. It is possible that with further and detailed research, someone could show that Koechlin did produce, after 1889, works that would allow a case to be made for his artistic nature.

13. Of course, the wind does add stress to the stone, but that stress is so small and so temporary that the slight overstress it causes does not need to be considered by designers. In some modern codes this fact is expressed by saying that the usual allowable stresses (calculated for the gravity loads) can be increased by as much as 33 percent when wind load stresses are included.

Chapter 7

1. Ralph Adams Cram, "Introduction," in Henry Adams, *Mont-Saint-Michel and Chartres* (Garden City, New York: Doubleday Anchor, 1959), p. x.

2. Henry Adams, *The Education of Henry Adams* (New York: Modern Library, 1931), pp. 342–43.

3. Ibid., p. 380.

4. Robert Mark, *Experiments in Gothic Structure* (Cambridge, Mass.: MIT Press, 1982).

5. Carl Condit, *The Chicago School of Architecture: A History of Commercial and Public Buildings in the Chicago Area, 1875–1925* (Chicago: University of Chicago Press, 1964), p. 79.

6. Ibid., p. 91

7. Robert Branner, *Gothic Architecture* (New York: George Braziller, 1965), p. 25.

8. Ibid., p. 12.

9. Ibid., p. 11. See also Erwin Panofsky, *Gothic Architecture and Scholasticism* (New York: World Publishing Co., 1957): "The entire social system was rapidly changing toward an urban professionalism" (p. 24).

10. Branner, *Gothic Architecture*, p. 16.

11. Erwin Panofsky, "Abbot Suger of St. Denis," in *Meaning in the Visual Arts* (Garden City, N.Y.: Doubleday Anchor, 1955). "Suger . . . inaugurated in the theretofore relatively barren Ile-de-France . . . what we call Gothic" (p. 144).

12. Giorgio Vasari, *The Lives of the Painters, Sculptors, and Architects,* vol. 1 (New York: Everyman's Library, 1963), p. 12.

13. Letter from Peter Brooks in Boston to John Root in Chicago, March 25, 1881, quoted in Condit, *Chicago School,* p. 52.

14. Condit, *Chicago School,* pp. 28–31.

15. Peter B. Wight, "On the Present Condition of Architectural Art in Western States," *American Art Review* 1 (1880): 138.

16. Condit, *Chicago School,* p. 83.

17. Donald Hoffmann, *The Architecture of John Wellborn Root* (Baltimore: Johns Hopkins University Press, 1973), pp. 1–5.

18. Ibid., p. 8.

19. Harriet Monroe, *John Wellborn Root* (Boston: Houghton Mifflin, 1896).

20. Hoffmann, *Architecture of Root,* pp. 212–18, quotes Root at some length to show how he articulated these specific functions—"the dimensions, the entrances and circulatory pattern, the details due to the overriding concerns of light and ventilation, the flexibility of partitioning, the public amenities, the structure, and the fireproofing." Root explains all in a careful and reasoned way.

21. Hugh Morrison, *Louis Sullivan: Prophet of Modern Architecture* (New York: W. W. Norton & Co., 1935), pp. 144–45.

22. Condit, *Chicago School,* p. 128.

23. Hoffmann, *Architecture of Root,* p. 163.

Chapter 8

1. Calvin M. Woodward, *A History of the St. Louis Bridge* (St. Louis: G. I. Jones, 1881), chapter 2. In 1840 St. Louis had 16,500 people to Chicago's 4,500, and by 1860 the two cities boomed to 161,000 and 109,000 respectively. For the competition between the two cities, see Wyatt W. Belcher, *The Economic Rivalry Between St. Louis and Chicago, 1850–1880* (Ph.D. diss. Columbia University, 1947).

2. *Annual Report of the Chief of Engineers,* 1878, vol. II, 1024.

3. John A. Kouwenhoven, "The Designing of the Eads Bridge," *Technology and Culture* 23 (1982): 535–68. This is the most authoritative account of the designing of the bridge. It adds substantially to Woodward's book.

4. Woodward, *St. Louis Bridge,* p. 16.

5. *Proceedings and Report of the Board of Civil Engineers,* St. Louis, 1867, p. 78.

6. Ibid., p. 77.

7. Woodward, *St. Louis Bridge,* p. 50.

8. R. Moore, J. P. Davis, and J. A. Ockerson, "Memoir of Henry Flad," *Transactions of the American Society of Civil Engineers* [ASCE] 42 (1899): 561–66; Charles Pfeifer, "The Theory of Ribbed Arches," *Van Nostrand's Engineering Magazine* 14 (1876): 481.

9. Kouwenhoven, "Eads Bridge," pp. 567–68.

10. Eads did write a long paper on arch bridge design later, but it showed more what he had learned from his completed work than what would have been an improved design. See James B. Eads, "Upright Arched Bridges," *Transactions of the American Society of Civil Engineers* 3 (1874): 195–215. Eads's response to discussion is in vol. 3 (1874), pp. 319–34, vol. 4 (1875), pp. 174–76, 177–84.

11. L. U. Reavis, *Saint Louis the Future Great City of the World,* St. Louis, 1871, pp. 111–22.

12. Woodward, *St. Louis Bridge,* p. 50.

13. Rolt Hammond, *The Forth Bridge and Its Builders* (London: Eyre & Spottiswoode, 1964), pp. 79–82.

14. Benjamin Baker, "Long-Span Railway Bridges," *Engineering* 3 (1867): 250, 265, 298–99, 338–39, 426–27, 441, 471, 571–72, 587–88, 611, 658.

15. J. A. L. Waddell, *Bridge Engineering,* vol. 1 (New York: John Wiley & Sons, 1916), p. 607.

16. John H. Stephens, *Towers, Bridges, and Other Structures* (New York: Sterling Publishing Co., 1976), p. 36.

17. Joseph Husband, "The Aesthetic Treatment of Bridge Structures," *Minutes of the Proceedings, The Institute of Civil Engineers* 145 (1901): 139–73.

18. Benjamin Baker, "Discussion," of Husband, "Bridge Structures," *Minutes of the Proceedings, The Institute of Civil Engineers* 145 (1901): 206–209.

19. Othmar H. Ammann, "The Hell Gate Arch Bridge and Approaches of the New York Connecting Railroad over the East River in New York City," *Transactions of the American Society of Civil Engineers* 82 (1918): 863.

20. F. H. Frankland and F. E. Schmitt, "Memoir of Gustav Lindenthal," *Transactions of the American Society of Civil Engineers* 105 (1940): 1790–94. See also *Civil Engineering,* 5 (1935): 594.

21. Gustav Lindenthal, "Rebuilding of the Monongahela Bridge, at Pittsburgh, Pa.," *Transactions of the American Society of Civil Engineers,* 12 (1883): 353–92. The award was the Thomas Fitch Rowland Prize, the second oldest given by the society. Lindenthal was its first recipient. Ammann's article on the Hell Gate Bridge won this award in 1919, as did Lindenthal's 1922 paper (note 23).

22. Frankland and Schmitt, "Lindenthal," p. 1792.

23. Gustav Lindenthal, "The Continuous Truss Bridge over the Ohio River at Sciotoville, Ohio, of the Chesapeake and Ohio Northern Railway," *Transactions of the American Society of Civil Engineers* 85 (1922): 910–75.

24. R. Krohn, "Discussion," *Transactions of the American Society of Civil Engineers* 71 (1911): 258–59. See also *Zeitschrift, Verein Deutches Ingenieurs,* 1897, p. 192.

Notes

25. Ammann, "Hell Gate," p. 871.

26. Ibid., plate 28 facing p. 890. Plate 28 gives the total force in the bottom chord at the support of 28,652 kips (1 kip = 1,000 pounds), while the top chord has only 1,607 kips or 5.6 percent of the bottom-chord force. The short top-chord member that goes into the stone tower has zero force. For the Bayonne Bridge the top chord with 1,721 kips has only 6.6 percent of the force in the bottom chord (26,065 kips). See drawing no. 2, BP-3 *Kill Van Kull Bridge* (Port of New York Authority, October 1, 1928).

27. Carl Condit, *American Building Art: Twentieth Century* (New York: Oxford University Press, 1961), p. 121.

28. Lindenthal, "Truss Bridge," p. 912. He does not explicitly discuss the aesthetics of the Britannia Bridge but does see it as an exemplary work. The towers do not bother him as they did Baker.

29. Wilhelm Ritter, "Statische Berechnung der Versteifungsfachwerke der Hängebrücken," *Schweizerische Bauzeitung* 1 (1883): 6–7, 14, 19–21, 23–25, 31–33, 36–38.

30. Wilhelm Ritter, "Ueber den Werth der Belastungs proben eisernen Brücken," *Schweizerische Bauzeitung* 20 (1892): 14–18.

31. Fritz Stüssi, *Othmar H. Ammann: Sein Beitrag zur Entwicklung des Brückenbaus* (Basel: Birkhauser Verlag, 1974), pp. 36–38, 85.

32. Wilhelm Ritter, *Der Brückenbau in den Vereinigten Staaten Amerikas* (Zurich: Albert Raustein, 1895).

33. Othmar H. Ammann, "The Problem of Bridging the Hudson River at New York with Particular Reference to the Proposed Bridge between Fort Washington Point and Fort Lee," *Proceedings of the Connecticut Society of Civil Engineers* (1924): 5–26.

34. Lewis Mumford, *The Brown Decades* (1931; reprint New York: Dover, 1955), p. 104.

35. Othmar H. Ammann, "The George Washington Bridge: General Conception and Development of Design," *Transactions of the American Society of Civil Engineers* 97 (1933): 39.

36. Ibid., p. 47.

37. Carl Condit, *American Building* (Chicago: University of Chicago Press, 1968), pp. 235–36.

38. Ammann, "George Washington Bridge," p. 33.

39. Ibid., p. 38.

40. Raymond Sontag, *A Broken World: 1919–1939* (New York: Harper & Row, 1971), pp. 179–91.

41. Elting E. Morison, *From Know-How to Nowhere* (New York: Basic Books, 1974), pp. 115–46.

42. Josef Melan, *Theory of Arches and Suspension Bridges*, trans. David B. Steinman (New York: McGraw-Hill, 1913). For Moisseiff's use of the deflection theory in the design of the Manhattan Bridge, see Leon Moisseiff, "Discussion," *Transactions of the American Society of Civil Engineers* 100: 1205–9.

43. Othmar H. Ammann, "George Washington Bridge," pp. 41–42.

44. Othmar H. Ammann, Theodore von Kármán, and Glenn B. Woodruff, "The Failure of the Tacoma Narrows Bridge," Report to the Administrator of the Federal Works Agency, Washington, D.C., March 28, 1941, p. 69. The ratio of deck depth to span length is only roughly a measure of deck stiffness; see chapter 1, note 10.

45. John A. Roebling, "Report and Plan for a Wire Suspension Bridge," *Order of Preference of the Supreme Court of the United States*, Saratoga Springs, N.Y., 1851, p. 479.

46. Edward Cohen and Frank L. Stahl, "Discussion," *Journal of the Structural Division, American Society of Civil Engineers*, 104 (1978): 1027–30.

47. For a comparison of these bridges see Lindenthal's discussion of a paper by O. H. Ammann, "Plans and Research—Kill van Kull Bridge," *Proceedings of the ASCE, Structural Division*, (1930): 513.

48. Ammann, "Kill van Kull Bridge," p. 490. In the context of this quotation Ammann clearly meant to say "with height *increasing* from the center." Earlier, on p. 489, he had rejected Eiffel's crescent shape just because "of its greater height at the center as compared with its ends."

49. Ibid., p. 489.

50. Ibid., p. 490. See also Othmar H. Ammann, "Address Delivered at the Dedication," *Bayonne Bridge*, New York Port Authority (New York: 1931), p. 24.

51. David B. Steinman, "Fifty Years of Progress in Bridge Engineering," *American Institute of Steel Construction* (New York, 1929), p. 50.

52. Othmar H. Ammann, "The Hudson River Bridge at New York between Fort Washington and Fort Lee," *Proceedings of the Connecticut Society of Civil Engineers* (1928): 47–74.

53. David B. Steinman, "Stress Measurements on the Hell Gate Arch Bridge," *Transactions of the American Society of Civil Engineers* 82 (1918): 1040–76. See especially Ammann's critical discussion, pp. 1106–8 and Steinman's reply, pp. 1131–32.

54. See Blair Birdsall, "Discussion," *Journal of the Structural Division, American Society of Civil Engineers* 104 (1978): 1030–35.

55. Steinman claimed to have developed means of stabilizing these bridges as early as 1938 when his Thousand Island designs began to oscillate badly. See Holton P. Robinson, "Building the Deer Isle-Sedgwick Bridge," *Civil Engineering* 9 (1939): 6.

56. David B. Steinman, "Rope-Strand Cables Used in New Bridge at Portland, Oregon," *Engineering News Record* 104 (1930): 272–77.

57. Steinman's St. Johns span used only $3.75 million of the $4.25 million appropriated while Ammann's immense George Washington Bridge, completed at the same time, used only $55 million of the $60 million appropriated.

Chapter 9

1. Fritz von Emperger, "Die Anfänge und die Anfänger," *Beton und Eisen* 2 (1903): 12–15.

2. François Hennebique, "Troisième Congrès du Béton de Ciment Armé: opening address," *Le béton armé* (March and April, 1899) 1 (10): 1–4; (11): 1–5.

3. David A. Molitor, "Three-Hinged Masonry Arches; Long Spans Especially Considered," *Transactions of the American Society of Civil Engineers* 40 (1898): 31–76.

4. D. Meisenhelder, "50 Jahre Beton-und Eisenbetonbau," *Festschrift: Aus Anlass des Fünfzig-Jahren Bestehens der Wayss und Freytag A.G. 1875–1925* (Stuttgart: Konrad Wittwer, 1925), pp. 259–260.

5. W. Noble Twelvetrees, "François Hennebique: A Biographical Memoir," *Ferro-Concrete* 13 (1921): 119–144. For the growth of Hennebique's business see F. Hennebique, *Relevé* (Paris) for the years 1892–1902.

6. The Châtellerault bridge is made of a thin barrel-arch slab, stiffened with ribs, and connected by vertical struts to a horizontal deck. The Liège bridge is a sculpted monolithic continuous beam of solid cross-section; the girder is slightly arched and the heavy moment at the mainspan haunches is balanced by thick back spans and anchor piles. The Risorgimento Bridge in Rome is a hollow box of 100 meters span. It is very difficult to see a common idea in these three works.

7. *Elenco dei lavori esequiti in calcestruzzo armato sistema Hennebique* (Turin: Società Porcheddu Ing. G.A., 1910).

8. Emil Mörsch, *Concrete–Steel Construction*, trans. E. P. Goodrich (New York: McGraw-Hill, 1910).

9. Probably the first American text to detail the Hennebique work was Charles F. Marsh, *Reinforced Concrete* (New York: Van Nostrand, 1904). In texts after Hennebique's death there is little mention of his work except in brief historical introductions.

10. Wilhelm Oechsli, *Geschichte der Gründung des Eidgenössische Polytechnikums mit einer Übersicht seiner Entwicklung 1855–1905* (Frauenfeld, 1905), pp. 35–121.

11. Wilhelm Ritter, "Karl Culmann," *Allgemeine Deutsche Biographie*, vol. 47 (1903; reprint, Berlin: Duncker and Humblot, 1971), pp. 571–574.

12. David P. Billington, "Wilhelm Ritter: Teacher of Maillart and Ammann," *Journal of the Structural Division, American Society of Civil Engineers*, 106 (1980): 1103–16.

13. Wilhelm Ritter, "Statische Berechnung der Versteifungsfachwerke der Hängebrücken," *Schweizerische Bauzeitung* 1 (1883): 6–7, 14, 19–21, 23–25, 31–33, 36–38.

Notes

14. Wilhelm Ritter, "Die Bauweise Hennebique," *Schweizerische Bauzeitung* 33 (1899): 41–43, 49–52, 59–61.

15. A. Geiser, Wilhelm Ritter, and F. Schüle, "Expertenbericht betreffend den Gebäude-Einsturz in der Aeschenvorstadt Basel," Zurich, Nov. 1901.

16. *Schweizerische Bauzeitung* 40 (Nov. 22, 1902): 244.

17. A. Favre, "Einiges über den 'Beton Armé,' nach dem System Hennebique," *Schweizerische Bauzeitung* 25 (1895): 31–32.

18. Wilhelm Ritter, "Ueber den Werth der Belastungs proben eisernen Brücken," *Schweizerische Bauzeitung* 20 (1892): 14–18.

19. For a more complete discussion of Maillart's works, see David P. Billington, *Robert Maillart's Bridges: The Art of Engineering* (Princeton: Princeton University Press, 1979). All details about Maillart's works not separately referenced here can be found in this work.

20. None of Maillart's works are known to have failed. Of the three lost bridges, two were taken down while still in full service—one after seventy-five years, the other after more than forty. The third bridge, at Tavanasa, was destroyed by an avalanche. Seven bridges have had substantial rehabilitation, most others have needed only standard maintenance. For the gasholders, see R. Wuczkowski, "Flüssigkeits-behälter," *Handbuch für Eisenbetonbau*, vol. 3, ed. F. von Emperger (Berlin: Verlag von W. Ernst & Sohn, 1907), pp. 407–14. The gasholders did require some waterproofing but served for nearly three-quarters of a century before being partly removed to serve as parts of new buildings. The Cement Hall was demolished after the fair for which it was designed.

21. Of course, Wayss, Hennebique, and others also recognized new possibilities in concrete and designed new forms, but they tended to reflect masonry in arches and wood or steel in framed buildings.

22. Wilhelm Ritter, "Bericht über die Belastungsprobe der neuen Inn-Brücke bei Zuoz," Zurich, 1901.

23. For the Hennebique response to questions of cracking at Châtellerault, see *Le béton armé* 7 (1904): 283. For the Hennebique discussion of Zuoz, see *Le béton armé* 5 (1903): 167–69. This latter is a biting attack on the idea of putting hinges into concrete arch bridges.

24. Billington, *Robert Maillart's Bridges*, chapter 9.

25. Robert Mark, James K. Chiu, and John F. Abel, "Stress Analysis of Historic Structures: Maillart's Warehouse at Chiasso," *Technology and Culture* 15 (1974): 49–63.

26. Mirko Roš, "Ergebnisse der Belastungsversuche an der Schweizerischen Landesausstellung Zürich 1939," *Bericht 99, Eisenbeton-Bauwerken in der Schweiz*, zweite Ergänzung (Zurich: Verein schweizerischen Zement-, Kalk-, und Gips-Fabrikanten, 1940), pp. 21–60.

27. "The Phillips Pavilion at the 1958 Brussels World's Fair" includes I: Y. Xenakis, "The Architectural Design of Le Corbusier and Xenakis"; II: C. G. J. Vreedenburgh, "The Hyperbolic-Paraboloidal Shell and its Mechanical Properties"; III: A. L. Bouma and F. K. Ligtenberg, "Model Tests for Proving the Construction of the Pavilion"; H. C. Duyster, "Construction of the Pavilion in Prestressed Concrete." In *Philips Technical Review* 20 (1958): 1–36.

28. Probably the best known proclamation came from Sigfried Giedion, *Space, Time and Architecture*, 5th ed. (Cambridge, Mass.: Harvard University Press, 1967). See especially the introduction, "Architecture in the 1960s: Hopes and Fears," where on page xli he states that "shell construction appears ever more strongly to be the starting point for the solution of the vaulting problem for our period." Giedion's own starting point had been Maillart but unfortunately he became more excited about the nonstructural forms of Le Corbusier.

Chapter 10

1. Sigfried Giedion, *Space, Time and Architecture*, 4th ed. (Cambridge, Mass.: Harvard University Press, 1962), pp. 463–73.

2. Ibid., p. xxxvi.

3. Ibid., p. 471.

4. Eugene S. Ferguson, "The American-ness of American Technology," *Technology and Culture* 20 (1979): 3–24.

5. The history of this development is given in more detail in David P. Billington, *Thin-Shell Concrete Structures*, 2nd. ed. (New York: McGraw-Hill, 1982), chapter 1.

6. Franz Dischinger, "Schalen und Rippenkuppeln," in *Handbuch für Eisenbetonbau*, 3rd ed., ed. Fritz von Emperger (Berlin: 1928), 12: 151–371.

7. The loads themselves also had to be defined mathematically, even if, as with wind, such definitions were very far from reality.

8. Hubert Rüsch, "Ulrich Finsterwalder zu seinem fünfzigsten Dienstjubilaum, Sein Lebensweg als Mensch und Ingenieur," *Festchrift Ulrich Finsterwalder, 50 Jahr für Dywidag* (Karlsruhe: Dyckerhoff and Widmann, 1973), pp. 9–18.

9. Ulrich Finsterwalder, "Die Querversteiften Zylindrischen Schalengewölbe mit kreissegmentförmigem Querschnitt," *Ingenieur Archiv* 6 (1933): 43–65. The work was submitted for a prize competition to the Prussian Academy of Construction on Jan. 15, 1930, where it won second prize.

10. Franz Dischinger, "Schalen und Rippenkuppeln," p. 326.

11. Ada L. Huxtable, *Pier Luigi Nervi* (New York: George Braziller, 1960), p. 119.

12. Pier Luigi Nervi, *Scienza o arte del costruire? [Is Building an Art or a Science?]* (Rome: Edizioni della Bussolo, 1945).

13. Pier Luigi Nervi, *Structures* (New York: McGraw-Hill, 1956), p. 13.

14. Ibid., p. 15.

15. Nervi has written about the Roman vaults and their expressive qualities as compared to Greek building. See Pier Luigi Nervi, *Aesthetics and Technology in Building*, trans. Robert Einaudi (Cambridge, Mass.: Harvard University Press, 1965), pp. 1–10. For Nervi, even more powerful than the Roman and Renaissance works are the Gothic structures "with the equilibrium of forces created by the interplay of thrust and counterthrust of slender ribs built with very good materials" (p. 5).

16. Nervi, *Aesthetics and Technology*, p. 24.

17. Ibid., pp. 23–24.

18. Ibid., p. 23.

19. Ibid., pp. 25–28.

20. Ibid., pp. 98–100.

21. Ibid., p. 99.

22. Ibid., pp. 100–102.

23. Ibid., pp. 102–103.

24. Ibid., pp. 104–105.

25. George R. Collins, "Antonio Gaudí and the Uses of Technology in Modern Architecture," *Civil Engineering: History, Heritage and the Humanities* (Princeton: Department of Civil Engineering, Princeton University, 1971) 1: 69.

26. Ibid., p. 70.

27. Ibid., p. 61. See also George R. Collins, "The Transfer of Thin Masonry Vaulting from Spain to America," *Journal of the Society of Architectural Historians* 27, no. 3 (October 1968). For a full study of Gaudí see Cesar Martinell, *Gaudí: His Life, His Theories, His Work*, trans. Judith Rohrer and ed. George Collins (Cambridge, Mass.: MIT Press, 1975). Martinell (1888–1973) knew Gaudí personally. This laminated tile vaulting was brought to America in the last half of the nineteenth century by Rafael Gustavino who built the vaulting for many famous buildings including St. John the Divine in New York, the Girard Trust Company in Philadelphia, the new dome on the University of Virginia rotunda, and the Princeton University Chapel.

28. George R. Collins, *Antonio Gaudí* (New York: George Braziller, 1960), p. 23.

29. The conoid has, along the two long sides of the rectangular plan building, a wave form which flattens out to a straight line along the longitudinal axis of the building where it is fully supported by an I-beam.

30. Eduardo Torroja, *The Structures of Eduardo Torroja: An Autobiography of Engineering Accomplishment* (New York: F. W. Dodge, 1958), p. 7.

31. Ibid., p. 40.

32. Ibid., pp. 23–28.

33. Eduardo Torroja, *Elasticidad*, 4th ed. (Madrid: Editorial Dossat, 1967).

34. Colin Faber, *Candela, The Shell Builder* (New York: Reinhold, 1963), p. 11.

Notes

35. Felix Candela, "New Architecture," *Maillart Papers,* ed. David P. Billington, Robert Mark, and John F. Abel (Princeton, New Jersey: Publ. Department of Civil Engineering, Princeton University, 1973), pp. 119–26.
36. Faber, *Candela, The Shell Builder,* p. 14.
37. *Ibid.,* p. 80.
38. Candela has always emphasized that his success has depended upon his being his own builder and upon his learning from his own difficulties. His emphasis on very simplified analysis must always therefore be recognized as going together with this building practice. Unfortunately, his striking forms and his downgrading of complex analysis has, it seems, sometimes misled designers without Candela's experience to think that the design of hyperbolic paraboloids was a simple matter.
39. Candela could not return to Spain for political reasons, and he could not build much in the United States, for example, because of high labor costs and more restrictive building codes.
40. Felix Candela, "Structural Applications of Hyperbolic Paraboloidal Shells," *Journal of the American Concrete Institute* 26 (1955): 397–415, for example.
41. Just as Maillart had on occasion inverted his floor system to serve as the design for a column base and foundation slab, so Candela inverted his hyperbolic paraboloids to form a column foundation on specially prepared soil shaped below.
42. Faber, *Candela,* pp. 194–99.
43. Anton Tedesko, "How Have Concrete Shell Structures Performed? An Engineer Looks Back at Years of Experience with Shells," *Bulletin of the International Association for Shell and Spatial Structures* [IASS] (1980).
44. Faber, *Candela,* p. 184. See also Robert Mark, *Experiments in Gothic Structure* (Cambridge, Mass.: MIT Press, 1981), p. 13.

Chapter 11

1. Eugène Freyssinet, "Préface," in J. Barets, *Le béton précontraint* (Paris: Eyrolles, 1950), p. 7.
2. Of course, a lighter beam is often also less expensive but not necessarily so. In addition, lighter beams frequently lead to less costly foundations. On the other hand, less steel does not mean a measurably lighter structure since the steel is usually about 1 percent of the volume of the concrete and hence a saving of 80 percent of a material three times the density of concrete means only a 2.4 percent saving in overall weight.
3. Eugène Freyssinet, "New Ideas and Methods," *A Half-Century of French Prestressing Technology,* special English edition of *Travaux* 50 (April–May 1966): 607–22; article originally published 1933. Here Freyssinet writes about the properties of concrete in a way that is difficult for a structural engineer to follow and which is unnecessary to a full understanding of prestressing.
4. Eugène Freyssinet, "A General Introduction to the Idea of Prestressing," *A Half-Century of French Prestressing Technology,* special English edition of *Travaux* 50 (1966): 25.
5. These two writings were translated into English and published in *A Half-Century of French Prestressing Technology* as "Eugène Freyssinet by Himself," pp 3–18, and "A General Introduction," pp. 19–49.
6. Freyssinet, "Freyssinet by Himself," *A Half-Century of French Prestressing Technology,* p. 18.
7. Eugène Freyssinet, "Souvenirs," in *Cent Ans de Béton Armé* (Paris: Editions Science et Industrie, 1949), p. 52.
8. Freyssinet, "Freyssinet by Himself," p. 8.

9. A table of reinforced concrete bridges collected from all over the world, published in 1908, listed the 1904 Isar River Bridge at Grünewald by Wayss and Freytag as the longest span—70 meters (230 feet)—then completed. See *Handbuch für Eisenbetonbau,* ed. Fritz von Emperger (Berlin: Wilhelm Ernst & Sohn, 1908)3: 217.

10. Freyssinet, "A General Introduction," *A Half-Century of French Prestressing Techno-logy,* p. 19.

11. Freyssinet, "Freyssinet by Himself," *A Half-Century of French Prestressing Technology,* p. 9.

12. Freyssinet and Maillart were the only engineers elected in 1937 as honorary correspond-ing members of the Royal Institute of British Architects along with eminent architects including Le Corbusier. See G. Collins, "The Discovery of Maillart as Artist," *Maillart Papers* (Princeton: Department of Civil Engineering, Princeton University, 1973), p. 38. Freyssinet was discovered before Maillart and written about in the 1920s. Le Corbusier used Freyssinet's work to illustrate his most widely read work, *Towards a New Architecture* (London: The Architectural Press, 1927).

13. Freyssinet, "Souvenirs," p. 56.

14. Eugène Freyssinet, "Naissance du béton précontraint et vues d'avenir," *Travaux* 38 (June 1954); 467, 474D.

15. Eugène Freyssinet, "Les hangars à dirigeables de l'aeroport d'Orly," *Génie civil* 83 (Sept. 22 and 29, Oct. 6, 1923), pp. 265–73; 291–97; 313–19.

16. Sigfried Giedion, "Lumière et construction: Réflexions à propos des ateliers de chemins de fer de Freyssinet," *Cahiers d'Art* 4 (1929): 275–82.

17. Freyssinet, "Freyssinet by Himself," p. 10.

18. Robert Maillart, Letter to his daughter, Marie-Claire, May 5, 1931.

19. Felix Candela, "New Architecture," *Maillart Papers* (Princeton: Dept. of Civil Engi-neering, Princeton University, 1973), p. 125.

20. José A. Fernández Ordóñez, *Eugène Freyssinet* (Barcelona: 2c Ediciones, 1978).

21. Eugène Freyssinet, "Les Ponts en béton armé de très grande portée," *L'Architecture Vivante* 11 (Spring 1931): 12–16, with twenty-six pages of photos.

22. Fernández Ordóñez, *Freyssinet,* pp. 210, 253, 271.

Chapter 12

1. For a lively discussion of this postwar period, see Raymond J. Sontag, *A Broken World: 1919–1939* (New York: Harper & Row, 1971), chapter 7.

2. This contrast is described in detail in David P. Billington, "Unknown Contributions of Robert Maillart to Thin Shell Concrete Structures," *71 Jahresbericht* (Zurich: Verein Schweiz-erischer Zement-, Kalk-, und Gips-Fabrikanten, 1981), pp. 64–72.

3. Fritz von Emperger, ed., *Handbuch für Eisenbetonbau* (Berlin: Verlag von W. Ernst & Sohn, 1907). For Maillart's analysis and design, see vol. 3, pp. 407–414. For subsequent writings see vol 4, 2nd ed, 1910, pp. 329, 483–490; 3rd ed., vol 5, 1923, pp. 279–281; and in the 4th ed., vol 9, 1934, there is no mention of Maillart's gasholders at all.

4. Citations in the *Index to ASCE* (American Society of Civil Engineers) *Publications,* shows the following trend for articles on thin shells:

1930–49: 3
1950–59: 37
1960–69: 124
1970–79: 176

While it is difficult to document the decline in built shells, leading authorities widely commented on this perceived phenomena in conferences held in Madrid in 1969 and New York in 1970.

5. Anton Tedesko, "Shells 1970—History and Outlook," *Concrete Thin Shells* (ACI Publication SP-28), American Concrete Institute, Detroit, 1971, p. 7.

6. John F. Abel, "Interactive Computer Graphics for Applied Mechanics," *Proceedings of the Ninth U.S. National Congress of Applied Mechanics* (New York: American Society of Mechanical Engineers, 1982), pp. 3–27.

7. Felix Candela, "New Architecture," *Maillart Papers* (Princeton, New Jersey: Department of Civil Engineering, Princeton University, 1973), pp. 119–21. Candela begins this essay by stating that "I have not too much to do with this subject" and goes on to talk about how Maillart stimulated him and how similar he feels to Maillart in his own work. See also Felix Candela, "Mein Weg und was ich Maillart verdanke," *Archithèse* 6 (1973): 18–29.

8. Candela, New Architecture, *Maillart Papers*, pp. 121–23.

9. Ibid., pp. 123–25.

10. Ibid., p. 125.

11. Peter Blake, *Le Corbusier: Architecture and Form* (Hammondsworth, England: Penguin, 1966), p. 11.

12. Candela, "New Architecture," *Maillart Papers*, pp. 125–26.

13. Although Torroja had published many technical works in Spanish, his aesthetic ideas were not well known outside of Spain before the publication in English of *The Structures of Eduardo Torroja: An Autobiography of Engineering Accomplishment* (New York: F. W. Dodge, 1958). For a brief summary of Lardy's life, see Fritz Stüssi, "Pierre Lardy," *Schweizerische Bauzeitung* (December 13, 1958): 762–63.

14. Personal communication, given to me by Isler on April 29, 1983.

15. Heinz Isler, "Discussion in Session IIIB," *Second Congress of the Fédération Internationale de la Précontrainte* (Amsterdam, 1955), pp. 736–42.

16. The title of the congress, "Colloquium on Nontraditional Construction Processes of Shell Structures," seemed to express the viewpoint that the future of shells lay in new ideas rather than in looking backward at what had been done. None of the papers came from West Germany nor did any refer directly to Dyckerhoff and Widmann's works. Nothing of Candela's was presented even though he had gained substantial fame by 1959; he was still not welcomed in Spain.

17. Heinz Isler, "New Shapes for Shells," *Bulletin of the International Association for Shell Structures*, no. 8 (1960), paper C-3.

18. Johan Huizinga, *Homo Ludens: A Study of the Play Element in Culture* (Boston: Beacon Press, 1955) foreword.

19. Ibid., pp. 8–10.

20. O. N. Arup and C. J. Kunz, "Sydney Opera House," *Civil Engineering* 41 (December 1971): 50–54. The article states that the building "is not really of this age and in concept is more appropriate to the product of autocratic rule of a former era." (p. 50) The original cost estimate was $7.8 million in 1957, and by completion in 1973, nine years late, it had cost $142 million, although the parking garage had been eliminated and the main concert hall scaled down. See *Engineering News Record*, April 5, 1973, p. 13.

21. Huizinga, *Homo Ludens*, p. 211.

22. It would be too much to argue that Isler and other structural artists do not try to make a living, to run a business, to sell themselves, and to compete sharply for design commissions. But their selling point is always structures of minimum materials and costs as well as of great beauty.

Chapter 13

1. Johan Huizinga, *Homo Ludens: A Study of the Play Element in Culture* (Boston: Beacon Press, 1955), p. 11.

2. Ibid., p. 172.

3. "Construction's Man of the Year: Fazlur R. Khan," *Engineering News Record*, 183 (February 10, 1972): 20–25.

4. Ibid., p. 23.

5. "Design Stretches Concrete's Potential," *Engineering News Record*, 192 (April 23, 1981): 10–11.

6. Hal S. Iyengar, *Composite of Mixed Steel–Concrete Construction for Buildings* (New York: American Society of Civil Engineers, 1977). Iyengar was an assistant of Khan's at the Skidmore firm.

7. Fazlur R. Khan, "A Philosophical Comparison between Maillart's Bridges and Some Recent Concrete Buildings," *Background Papers*, 2nd National Conference on Civil Engineering: History, Heritage, and the Humanities (Princeton: Department of Civil Engineering, Princeton University, 1972) pp. 1–19. Two buildings use this arch design: Two Shell Plaza in Houston and the Marine Midland Bank in Rochester.

8. There is some question about the origin of the framed-tube idea. Leslie Robertson, structural designer of the World Trade Center, wrote that "in 1962 . . . perhaps for the first time, the concept of the tube was employed in a high-rise building [the design for the World Trade Center completed in 1972]. Later, in 1963, a tubular concept in reinforced concrete was developed for the 43-story DeWitt Chestnut Apartments." "Structural Systems—Theme Report," *Proceedings of the International Conference on Planning and Design of Tall Buildings*, August 21–26, 1972, vol. 1a: *Tall Building Systems and Concepts* (New York: American Society of Civil Engineers, 1972), p. 405.

9. Khan, "Philosophical Comparison," p. 13.

10. "Design Stretches Concrete's Potential," *Engineering News Record* (April 23, 1981): 10–11. See also Lynn S. Beedle and Hal S. Iyengar, "Selected Works of Fazlur R. Khan (1929–1982)," *IABSE Structures*, C-23/82, International Association for Bridge and Structural Engineering (November 1982): 63–83.

11. Fazlur R. Khan, "The Future of Highrise Structures," *Progressive Architecture* (October 1972): 83. The thesis project for the diagonally braced concrete tower was directed by architect Myron Goldsmith, one of Khan's partners and his colleague as an adjunct professor at Illinois Institute of Technology.

12. "The Future of the Super Hi-Rise Buildings," *Modern Steel Construction* 12 (1972): 3–9.

13. Carl Condit, *Chicago: 1930–70* (Chicago: University of Chicago Press, 1974): 102–14.

14. Fazlur R. Khan, "The John Hancock Center," *Civil Engineering* 37 (October 1967): 40.

15. "Fazlur Khan: Avant Garde Designer of High-Rises," *Engineering News Record* 182 (August 26, 1971): 16–18.

16. Fazlur R. Khan, "100-Story John Hancock Center in Chicago—A Case Study of the Design Process," *IABSE Journal*, J-16/82, August 1982, p. 28.

17. Ibid., p. 30.

18. Ibid., p. 28.

19. Ibid., pp. 31–32.

20. Ibid., p. 34.

21. Lewis Mumford, *The Highway and the City* (New York: New American Library, Mentor Books, 1964), chapter 22.

22. Lewis Mumford, *Art and Technics* (New York: Columbia University Press, 1952), pp. 16–22.

23. Lewis Mumford, *Brown Decades* (1931; reprint, New York: Dover, 1955), p. 106.

24. Mumford, *Art and Technics*, pp. 82–83.

25. Ibid., pp. 156–60.

26. Mumford, *The Highway and the City*, p. 256.

27. Christian Menn, "New Bridges," in David P. Billington et al., eds., *The Maillart Papers*, from the Second National Conference on Civil Engineering: History, Heritage, and the Humanities, October 1972 (Princeton, New Jersey: Department of Civil Engineering, Princeton University, 1973), p. 105.

28. Christian Menn and Hans Rigendinger, "Ganterbrücke," *Schweizer Ingenieur und Architekt* 97 (1979): 736; David P. Billington, "Swiss Bridge Design Spans Time and Distance," *Civil Engineering* 51 (November 1981): 42–46.

29. Fritz Leonhardt, *Bridges: Aesthetics and Design* (Stuttgart: Deutsche Verlags-Anstalt, 1982), p. 278. In this beautifully illustrated book, Leonhardt shows hundreds of photographs of modern bridges, including many of Menn's designs.

30. Wolf von Eckardt, "New York's Trade Center: World's Tallest Fiasco," *Harper's* 232 (May 1966): 96.

31. M. W. Newman, "Chicago: City of the Big Tombstones," *Chicago Daily News Panorama* (January 24, 1970): 4.

32. Condit, *Chicago,* pp. 112–13.

33. John M. Dixon, "The Tall One," *Architectural Forum* 133 (July/August 1970): 44.

34. James T. Biehle, "Chicago's New Giant—for Giant's Only?" *Architectural Record* (March 1967): 46. This letter followed an article by James S. Hornbeck, "Chicago's Multi-Use Giant," *Architectural Record* 141 (January 1967): 137–44.

Epilogue

1. For an articulate discussion of the artist as a servant of the community, working in partnership with the general public, see R. G. Collingwood, *The Principles of Art* (1938; reprint New York: Oxford University Press, 1958), pp. 300–24.

2. Khan discussed this question at a lecture in Princeton on February 25, 1982, just a few weeks before his death. To my knowledge, he never put the idea into print, although I believe he would have had he lived.

3. See, for example, Lewis Mumford, *Art and Technics* (New York: Columbia University Press, 1952), p. 20.

4. Karl Barth, *From Rousseau to Ritschl* (London: SCM Press, 1959), pp. 46–51. This reference was brought to my attention by James H. Billington.

5. Ibid., p. 49.

6. Ibid., p. 50. I am not implying here that art is merely highly refined craft. See Collingwood, *The Principles of Art,* pp. 15–41, for a clear refutation of that idea.

INDEX

Aarburg Bridge, 161
Abeles, Paul, 197
Adams, Henry, 101–2
Adler, Dankmar, 108
aesthetics, *see* structural art, aesthetic
  basis of
Agnelli Exhibition Hall, 180, 206
Algeciras Market Hall, 188
Allegheny River Bridge (Lindenthal), 123
American Concrete Institute, 216
American Institute of Steel Construction,
  239
American Society of Civil Engineers, 75,
  116, 123, 125
Amiens Cathedral, 103
Ammann, Othmar, 21, 22, 36–37, 113,
  123, 126, 128, 148, 152, 210, 237, 273,
  274, 285n21, 286n48; aesthetic moti-
  vation of, 130–34, 137, 138–40;
  Bayonne Bridge, 130, *fig. 8.5,* 286n26;
  Bayonne Bridge compared with Hell
  Gate Bridge, 138–40; Bronx Whitestone Bridge, 144, 145, *fig. 8.6;* compared with Steinman, 141–46; early experience of, 130–31; Goethals Bridge,
  130; Outerbridge Crossing, 130; rivalry
  with Steinman, 141–42; Swiss background of, 129–30; Verrazano Narrows
  Bridge, 16, 21, 37, 129, 137, 142;
  George Washington Bridge, 16, 21,
36–37, 130, 131, *fig. 8.4,* 134–39, 143,
  287n57
arch bridges: in cast iron, *fig. 2.1,* 30,
  31–32, *fig. 2.2,* 33–34, 38, 39, 46–47;
  in concrete, 148–49, *fig. 9.1,* 158–59,
  195–97, 202–3, *fig. 11.3,* 291n9; in
  concrete, deck-stiffened, 153, 161–63,
  fig. 9.6, 250; in concrete, three-hinged,
  fig. 9.2, 156–59, *fig. 9.4, fig. 9.5;* in
  steel, 114–17, *fig. 8.1;* in steel, two-
  hinged, 126–28, 138–40, *fig. 8.5;* in
  wrought iron, two-hinged, 69, 70, *fig.
  4.4,* 95
architecture, *see* structural art, as contrasted to architecture
art and business, tension between, 52–53,
  210; *see also* structural art, and business
Arup, Ove, 223–24
Assuan (Aswan) Dam, 118, 121
Astrodome, 17

Bacardi Rum Factory, 192–93
Bach, J.S., 51–52, 212, 271
Bad Ragaz Br., 250
Baker, Benjamin, 112–13, 118–22; aes-
  thetic ideas of, 119–21, 128; Assuan
  Dam, 118, 121; evaluation of Britannia